Autodesk® Revit® 2021
for Project Managers

Learning Guide
Imperial Units - 1st Edition

Authorized Publisher

ASCENT - Center for Technical Knowledge®
Autodesk® Revit® 2021
for Project Managers
Imperial Units - 1st Edition

Prepared and produced by:

ASCENT Center for Technical Knowledge
630 Peter Jefferson Parkway, Suite 175
Charlottesville, VA 22911

866-527-2368
www.ASCENTed.com

Lead Contributor: Cherisse Biddulph

ASCENT - Center for Technical Knowledge (a division of Rand Worldwide Inc.) is a leading developer of professional learning materials and knowledge products for engineering software applications. ASCENT specializes in designing targeted content that facilitates application-based learning with hands-on software experience. For over 25 years, ASCENT has helped users become more productive through tailored custom learning solutions.

We welcome any comments you may have regarding this guide, or any of our products. To contact us please email: feedback@ASCENTed.com.

AS-REV2101-PMR1IM-SG   //   IS-REV2101-PMR1IM-SG

Contents

Preface

The Autodesk® Revit® software is a powerful Building Information Modeling (BIM) program that works the way architects and engineers think. The software streamlines the design process with a central 3D model. Changes made in one view update across all views and on the printable sheets. This guide is designed to give you an overview of the Autodesk Revit (Architecture, MEP, and Structure) functionality, especially as it pertains to project managers.

Topics Covered

- Understanding the purpose of Building Information Modeling (BIM) and how it is applied in the Autodesk Revit software.
- Navigating the Autodesk Revit workspace and interface.
- Working with the basic modifying and modeling tools.
- Troubleshooting elements in projects.
- Viewing models using plans, elevations, sections, and 3D views.
- Putting together construction documents by adding views to sheets that can then be printed.
- Exporting files to CAD formats and DXF (the Autodesk® Design Review software).
- Working with schedules.
- Linking and importing CAD files and Autodesk Revit models into projects.
- Using worksets in a collaborative environment.
- (Optional) Creating details.

Prerequisites

- Access to the 2021.0 version of the software, to ensure compatibility with this guide. Future software updates that are released by Autodesk may include changes that are not reflected in this guide. The practices and files included with this guide might not be compatible with prior versions (e.g., 2020).

Note on Software Setup

This guide assumes a standard installation of the software using the default preferences during installation. Lectures and practices use the standard software templates and default options for the Content Libraries.

Students and Educators Can Access Free Autodesk Software and Resources

Autodesk challenges you to get started with free educational licenses for professional software and creativity apps used by millions of architects, engineers, designers, and hobbyists today. Bring Autodesk software into your classroom, studio, or workshop to learn, teach, and explore real-world design challenges the way professionals do.

Get started today - register at the Autodesk Education Community and download one of the many Autodesk software applications available.

Visit www.autodesk.com/education/home/

Note: Free products are subject to the terms and conditions of the end-user license and services agreement that accompanies the software. The software is for personal use for education purposes and is not intended for classroom or lab use.

Lead Contributor: Cherisse Biddulph

Cherisse is an Autodesk Certified Professional for Revit as well as an Autodesk Certified Instructor. She brings 15 years of industry, teaching and technical support experience to her role as a Learning Content Developer with ASCENT. With a passion for design and architecture, she received her Associate of Applied Science in Drafting and Design and worked in the industry assisting several firms with CAD Manager needs and getting others up to speed on the latest software. In 2004 she joined IMAGINiT as an Application Engineer (AE), where she developed custom training and provided support for customers. She transitioned from her work as an AE to the IMAGINIT Solution Center as a Senior Technical Support Specialist where she became proficient in AutoCAD, BIM 360, Navisworks, and Revit. Today, Cherisse continues to expand her knowledge in the ever-evolving AEC industry and the software used to support it.

Cherisse Biddulph has been the Lead Contributor for *Autodesk Revit for Project Managers* since 2019.

In This Guide

The following highlights the key features of this guide.

Feature	Description
Practice Files	The Practice Files page includes a link to the practice files and instructions on how to download and install them. The practice files are required to complete the practices in this guide.
Chapters	A chapter consists of the following - Learning Objectives, Instructional Content, Practices, Chapter Review Questions, and Command Summary. • **Learning Objectives** define the skills you can acquire by learning the content provided in the chapter. • **Instructional Content**, which begins right after Learning Objectives, refers to the descriptive and procedural information related to various topics. Each main topic introduces a product feature, discusses various aspects of that feature, and provides step-by-step procedures on how to use that feature. Where relevant, examples, figures, helpful hints, and notes are provided. • **Practice** for a topic follows the instructional content. Practices enable you to use the software to perform a hands-on review of a topic. It is required that you download the practice files (using the link found on the Practice Files page) prior to starting the first practice. • **Chapter Review Questions**, located close to the end of a chapter, enable you to test your knowledge of the key concepts discussed in the chapter. • **Command Summary** concludes a chapter. It contains a list of the software commands that are used throughout the chapter and provides information on where the command can be found in the software.
Appendices	Appendices provide additional information to the main course content. It could be in the form of instructional content, practices, tables, projects, or skills assessment.

Practice Files

To download the practice files for this guide, use the following steps:

1. Type the URL *exactly as shown below* into the address bar of your Internet browser, to access the Course File Download page.

   Note: If you are using the ebook, you do not have to type the URL. Instead, you can access the page simply by clicking the URL below.

   ## https://www.ascented.com/getfile/id/urostriatum

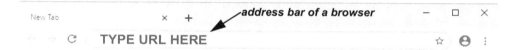

2. On the Course File Download page, click the **DOWNLOAD NOW** button, as shown below, to download the .ZIP file that contains the practice files.

3. Once the download is complete, unzip the file and extract its contents.

   The recommended practice files folder location is:
   C:\Autodesk Revit 2021 for Project Managers Practice Files

   Note: It is recommended that you do not change the location of the practice files folder. Doing so may cause errors when completing the practices.

Stay Informed!

To receive information about upcoming events, promotional offers, and complimentary webcasts, visit:

www.ASCENTed.com/updates

Introduction to BIM and Autodesk Revit

Building Information Modeling (BIM) and the Autodesk® Revit® software work hand in hand to help you create smart, 3D models that are useful at all stages in the building process. Understanding the software interface and terminology enhances your ability to create powerful models and move around in the various views of the model.

Learning Objectives in This Chapter

- Describe the concept and workflow of Building Information Modeling in relation to the Autodesk Revit software.
- Navigate the graphic user interface, including the ribbon (where most of the tools are found), the Properties palette (where you make modifications to element information), and the Project Browser (where you can open various views of the model).
- Open existing projects and start new projects using templates.
- Use viewing commands to move around the model in 2D and 3D views.

1.1 BIM and Autodesk Revit

Building Information Modeling (BIM) is an approach to the entire building life cycle, including design, construction, and facilities management. The BIM process supports the ability to coordinate, update, and share design data with team members across disciplines.

The Autodesk Revit software is a true BIM product. It enables you to create complete 3D building models (as shown on the left in Figure 1–1) that provide considerable information reported through construction documents, and enables you to share these models with other programs for more extensive analysis.

Figure 1–1

The Autodesk Revit software is considered a Parametric Building Modeler:

- *Parametric:* A relationship is established between building elements: when one element changes, other related elements change as well. For example, if you add an element in a plan view, it also displays in all of the other views.

- *Building:* The software is designed for working with buildings and the surrounding landscape, as opposed to gears or highways.

- *Modeler:* A project is built in a single file based on the 3D building model, as shown on the left in Figure 1–1. All views, such as plans (as shown on the right in Figure 1–1), elevations, sections, details, construction documents, and reports are generated based on the model.

- It is important that everyone who is collaborating on a project works in the same version and build of the software.

Workflow and BIM

BIM has changed the process of how a building is planned, budgeted, designed, constructed, and (in some cases) operated and maintained.

In the traditional design process, construction documents are created independently, typically including plans, sections, elevations, details, and notes. Sometimes, a separate 3D model is created in addition to these documents. Changes made in one document, such as the addition of a light fixture in a plan, have to be coordinated with the rest of the documents and schedules in the set, as shown in Figure 1–2.

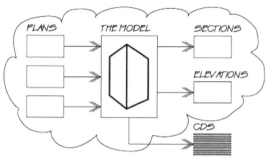

Figure 1–2

In BIM, the design process revolves around the model, as shown in Figure 1–3. Plans, elevations, and sections are simply 2D versions of the 3D model, while schedules are a report of the information stored in the model. Changes made in one view automatically update in all views and related schedules. Even Construction Documents update automatically with callout tags in sync with the sheet numbers. This is called bidirectional associativity.By creating complete models and associated views of those models, the Autodesk Revit software takes much of the tediousness out of producing a building design.

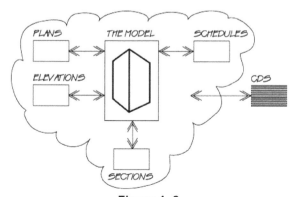

Figure 1–3

Revit Terms

When working in the Autodesk Revit software, it is important to know the typical terms used to describe items. Views and reports display information about the elements that form a project. There are three types of elements: Model, Datum, and View-specific, as shown in Figure 1–4 and described below:

Figure 1–4

Views	Enable you to display and manipulate the model. For example, you can view and work in floor plans, ceiling plans, elevations, sections, schedules, and 3D views. You can change a design from any view. All views are stored in the project.
Reports	Reports, including schedules, gather information from the building model element that can be presented in the construction documents or used for analysis.
Model Elements	Include all parts of a building such as walls, floors, roofs, ceilings, doors, windows, plumbing fixtures, lighting fixtures, mechanical equipment, columns, beams, furniture, plants and many more. • Host elements support other categories of elements. • Hosted elements must be attached to a host element. • Standalone elements do not require hosts.
Datum Elements	Define the project context such as the levels for the floors and other vertical distances, column grids, and reference planes.
View-specific Elements	Only display in the view in which they are placed. The view scale controls their size. These include annotation elements such as dimensions, text, tags, and symbols as well as detail elements such as detail lines, filled regions, and 2D detail components.

• Autodesk Revit elements are "smart": the software recognizes them as walls, columns, plants, ducts, or lighting fixtures. This means that the information stored in their properties automatically updates in schedules, which ensures that views and reports are coordinated across an entire project, and are generated from a single model.

Revit and Construction Documents

In the traditional workflow, the most time-consuming part of the project is the construction documents. With BIM, the base views of those documents (i.e., plans, elevations, sections, and schedules) are produced automatically and update as the model is updated, saving hours of work. The views are then placed on sheets that form the construction document set.

For example, a floor plan is duplicated. Then, in the new view, all but the required categories of elements are hidden or set to halftone and annotations are added. The plan is then placed on a sheet, as shown in Figure 1–5.

Figure 1–5

• Work can continue on a view and is automatically updated on the sheet.

• Annotating views in the preliminary design phase is often not required. You might be able to wait until you are further along in the project.

1.2 Overview of the Interface

The Autodesk Revit interface is designed for intuitive and efficient access to commands and views. It includes the ribbon, Quick Access Toolbar, Navigation Bar, and Status Bar, which are common to most of the Autodesk® software. It also includes tools that are specific to the Autodesk Revit software, including the Properties Palette, Project Browser, and View Control Bar. Revit includes access to tools for architectural, mechanical, electrical, plumbing, and structural design but can be altered by utilizing the Customized Workspace. Setting up a Customized Workspace tailors your Revit environment to your specific discipline. A breakdown of the Revit interface is shown in Figure 1–6.

Figure 1–6

1. Quick Access Toolbar	6. Properties Palette
2. Status Bar	7. Project Browser
3. File tab	8. View Tabs
4. Ribbon	9. Navigation Bar
5. Options Bar	10. View Control Bar

For more information on how to use BIM 360 inside Revit, refer to the ASCENT guide Autodesk BIM 360: Fundamentals.

The Home Screen

When you first open the Autodesk Revit software, the **Home** screen displays, showing recently used projects and families, as well as links to BIM 360 files, as shown in Figure 1–7.

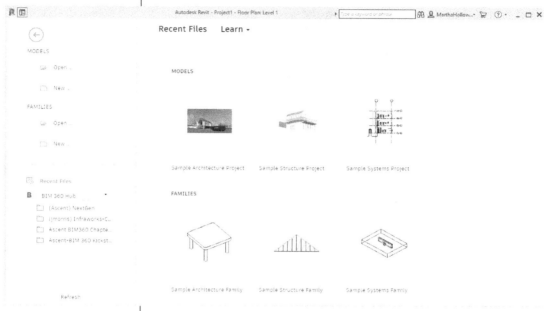

Figure 1–7

- Click on the picture to open a recent project. Hover over the name of the file, to display additional information.

- In the Quick Access Toolbar, click 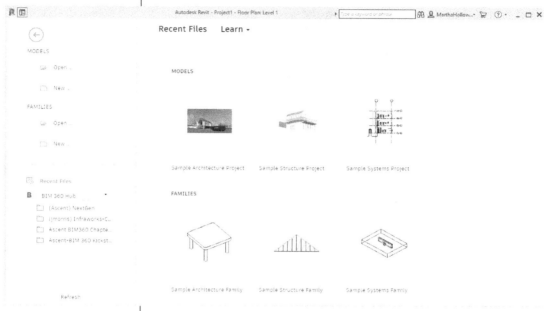 (Home) to return to the screen.

- In the Home screen, click (Back) to return to the active model.

- Press **\<Ctrl\>+\<D\>** to toggle between the Home screen and active model.

1. Quick Access Toolbar

The Quick Access Toolbar (shown in Figure 1–8) includes commonly used commands, such as **Home, Open**, **Save**, **Undo**, **Redo,** and **Print**. It also includes frequently used annotation tools, including Measuring tools, **Aligned Dimension**, **Tag by Category**, and **Text**. Viewing tools, including several different 3D Views and **Sections**, are also easily accessed here.

Figure 1–8

> ### Hint: Customizing the Quick Access Toolbar
>
> Right-click on the Quick Access Toolbar to change the docked location of the toolbar to be above or below the ribbon, or to add, relocate, or remove tools on the toolbar. You can also right-click on a tool in the ribbon and select **Add to Quick Access Toolbar**, as shown in Figure 1–9.
>
>
>
> Figure 1–9

The top toolbar also hosts the InfoCenter (as shown in Figure 1–10) which includes the Autodesk sign-in, access to the Autodesk App Store, and Help options. A search field, as shown in Figure 1–11, is also available to find help on the web

Figure 1–10

Type a keyword or phrase

—— *Click here to expand or collapse the search field*

Figure 1–11

2. Status Bar

The Status Bar provides information about the current process, such as the next step for a command, as shown in Figure 1–12.

Figure 1–12

Other options in the Status Bar are related to Worksets and Design Options (advanced tools) as well as selection methods and filters.

Hint: Shortcut Menus

Shortcut menus help you to work smoothly and efficiently by enabling you to quickly access required commands. These menus provide access to basic viewing commands, recently used commands, and the available Browsers, as shown in Figure 1–13. Additional options vary depending on the element or command that you are using.

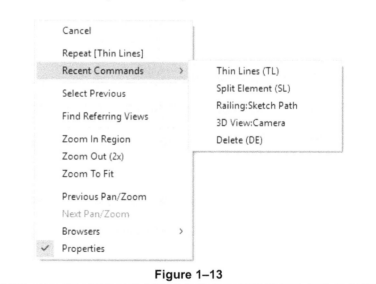

Figure 1–13

3.File Tab

The *File* tab of the ribbon provides access to file commands, settings, and documents, as shown in Figure 1–14. Hover the cursor over a command to display a list of additional tools.

For more information on how to use Cloud Model inside Revit, refer to the ASCENT guide Autodesk BIM 360: Fundamentals.

If you click the primary icon, rather than the arrow, it starts the default command.

Figure 1–14

- To display a list of recently used documents, click

  (Recent Documents). The documents can be reordered as shown in Figure 1–15.

Click (Pin) next to a document name to keep it available.

Figure 1–15

- To display a list of open documents and views, click (Open Documents). The list displays the documents and views that are open, as shown in Figure 1–16.

You can use the Open Documents list to change between views.

Open Documents

> Project1 - Elevation: East
>
> Project1 - Floor Plan: Level 1
>
> BHM-Office-Grids-10 - Reflected Ceiling Plan: First Floor
>
> BHM-Office-Grids-10 - Floor Plan: First Floor
>
> BHM-Office-Grids-10 - Elevation: North

Figure 1–16

- Click (Close) to close the current project.

- At the bottom of the menu, click **Options** to open the Options dialog box or click **Exit Revit** to exit the software.

4. Ribbon

The ribbon contains tools in a series of tabs and panels as shown in Figure 1–17. Selecting a tab displays a group of related panels. The panels contain a variety of tools, grouped by task.

Figure 1–17

When you start a command that creates new elements or you select an element, the ribbon displays the *Modify | contextual* tab. This contains general editing commands and command specific tools, as shown in Figure 1–18.

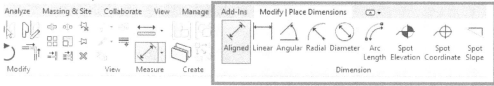

Contextual tab

Figure 1–18

- When you hover over a tool on the ribbon, tooltips display the tool's name and a short description. If you continue hovering over the tool, a graphic displays (and sometimes a video), as shown in Figure 1–19.

Figure 1–19

- Many commands have shortcut keys. For example, type **AL** for **Align** or **MV** for **Move**. They are listed next to the name of the command in the tooltips. Do not press <Enter> when typing shortcuts.

- To arrange the order in which the ribbon tabs are displayed, select the tab, hold <Ctrl>, and drag it to a new location. The location is remembered when you restart the software.

- Any panel can be dragged by its title into the view window to become a floating panel. Click the **Return Panels to Ribbon** button (as shown in Figure 1–20) to reposition the panel in the ribbon.

Figure 1–20

Hint: You are always in a command when using the Autodesk Revit software.

When you are finished working with a tool, you typically default back to the **Modify** command. To end a command, use one of the following methods:

- In any tab on the ribbon, click (Modify).
- Press <Esc> once or twice to revert to **Modify**.
- Right-click and select **Cancel...** once or twice.
- Start another command.

5. Options Bar

The Options Bar displays options that are related to the selected command or element. For example, when the **Rotate** command is active it displays options for rotating the selected elements, as shown at the top in Figure 1–21. When the **Place Dimensions** command is active it displays dimension related options, as shown at the bottom in Figure 1–21.

Modify | Multi-Select   ☐ Disjoin ☐ Copy Angle: 45| Center of rotation: [Place] [Default]

Options Bar for Rotate Command

Modify | Place Dimensions   Wall centerline ▼ Pick: Individual Reference ▼ [Options]

Options Bar for Dimension Command

Figure 1–21

6. Properties Palette

The Properties palette contains several parts, as shown in Figure 1–22. The Type Selector can be found at the top, which enables you to choose the size or style of the element you are adding or modifying. The options available on the palette enable you to make changes to information (parameters). There are two types of properties:

- **Instance Properties** are set for the individual element(s) you are creating or modifying.

- **Type Properties** control options for all elements of the same type. If you modify these parameter values, all elements of the selected type change.

The Properties palette is usually kept open while working on a project to easily permit changes at any time. If it does not display, in the Modify tab>Properties panel, click ⬚ (Properties) or type PP.

Some parameters are only available when you are editing an element. They are grayed out when unavailable.

Figure 1–22

- Options for the current view display if the **Modify** command is active, but you have not selected an element.

- If a command or element is selected, the options for the associated element display.

- You can save the changes by either moving the cursor off of the palette, or by pressing <Enter>, or by clicking **Apply**.

- When you start a command or select an element, you can set the element type in the Type Selector, as shown in Figure 1–23.

You can limit what shows in the drop-down list by typing in the search box.

Figure 1–23

- When multiple elements are selected, you can filter the type of elements that display using the drop-down list, as shown in Figure 1–24.

The Properties palette can be placed on a second monitor, or floated, resized, and docked on top of the Project Browser or other dockable palettes, as shown in Figure 1–25. Click the tab to display its associated panel.

Figure 1–24

Figure 1–25

7. Project Browser

The Project Browser lists all views of the model in which you can work (as shown in Figure 1–26) and any additional views that you create, such as floor plans, ceiling plans, 3D views, elevations, sections, etc. It also includes schedules, legends, sheets (for plotting), lists of families by category, groups, and Autodesk Revit Links.

The Project Browser displays the name of the active project.

Figure 1–26

- To open a view, double-click on the view name or right-click and select **Open**.

- To rename a view, slowly click twice on the view name and the text highlights as shown in Figure 1–27. You can also right-click on a view name and select **Rename...** or press <F2>.

Figure 1–27

To display the views associated with a view type, click

⊞ (Expand) next to the section name. To hide the views in the

section, click ⊟ (Collapse). You can also expand and collapse
sets using the shortcut menu, as shown in Figure 1–28.

Figure 1–28

- If you no longer require a view, you can delete it. Right-click
  on its name in the Project Browser and select **Delete**.

- The Project Browser can be customized by changing the
  Browser Organization or its location within the application.
  The Project Browser can be floated, resized, or docked on
  top of the Properties palette.

How To: Search the Project Browser

1. In the Project Browser, right-click on a view and select
   Search....
2. In the Search in Project Browser dialog box, type the words
   that you want to find (as shown in Figure 1–29), and
   click **Next**.

3. In the Project Browser, the first instance of that search displays, as shown in Figure 1–30.

Figure 1–29   Figure 1–30

4. Continue using **Next** and **Previous** to move through the list.
5. Click **Close** when you are done.

8. View Tabs

Each view of a project opens in its own tab and can be pulled out of the application window and moved to another monitor. Each view displays a Navigation Bar (for quick access to viewing tools) and the View Control Bar, as shown in Figure 1–31. You can drag tabs to other monitors.

In 3D views you can also use the ViewCube to rotate the view.

Figure 1–31

- Click on the tab to switch between views. You can also:
  - Press <Ctrl>+<Tab>.
  - Select the view in the Project Browser.
  - In the Quick Access Toolbar or *View* tab>Windows panel, expand (Switch Windows) and select the view from the list.
  - Expand the drop-down list at the far end of the tabs, as shown in Figure 1–32.

Figure 1–32

- To close a tab, press the **X** that displays when you hover over the tab or the name in the list, as shown in Figure 1–32.

- To close all open views except the current view, in the Quick Access Toolbar or *View* tab>Windows panel, click (Close Inactive Views). If you have multiple projects open, one view of each project remains open. If you have dragged a view to another monitor, that view will need to be manually closed by clicking the **X** in the upper right corner.

- You can switch between tabbed and tiled views from the *View* tab>Windows panel by clicking (Tab Views) or (Tile Views).

- Drag the edge of tiled views to resize them. The other views resize to match.

9. Navigation Bar

The Navigation Bar enables you to access the 2D and Full Navigation (3D views) Wheel to navigate the view, as well as the Zoom in Region viewing commands, as shown in Figure 1–33.

Figure 1–33

10. View Control Bar

The View Control Bar (shown in Figure 1–34) displays at the bottom of each view window. It controls aspects of that view, such as the scale and detail level. It also includes tools that display parts of the view and hide or isolate elements in the view.

1/8" = 1'-0"

Figure 1–34

• The number of options in the View Control Bar change when you are in a 3D view, as shown in Figure 1–35.

1/8" = 1'-0"

Figure 1–35

1/8" = 1'-0"	**View Scale**	Set the scale of individual views.
	Detail Level	Set the detail level of a view.
	Visual Style	Various graphic style representations.
	Sun Path On/Off	Controls the visibility of the sun's path.
	Shadows On/Off	Controls elements' shadow visibility in a view.
	Show/Hide Rendering Dialog	Available in 3D only. Shows or hides the rendering dialog box.
	Crop View	Define the crop boundaries for a view.
	Show/Hide Crop Region	Display the crop region in a view.
	Unlocked/Locked 3D Views	Lock a 3D view's orientation.
	Temporary Hide/Isolate	Temporarily isolate/hide by category or element.
	Reveal Hidden Elements	View hidden elements or unhide them in the active view.
	Worksharing Display	Available when worksharing is enabled. Controls display settings.
	Temporary View Properties	Enable, apply or restore view properties and display recent templates and apply them.
	Show or Hide the Analytical Model	Only used for Structural and MEP to display the analytical information.
	Highlight Displacement Sets	Also known as exploded views.
	Reveal Constraints	Temporarily view the dimension and alignment constraints in the active view.
	Preview Visibility	Available in the Family Editor only. Controls the visibility of the preview.

1.3 Starting Projects

File operations to open existing files, create new files from a template, and save files in the Autodesk Revit software are found in the *File* tab, as shown in Figure 1–36.

Figure 1–36

There are three main file formats:

- **Project files (.rvt):** These are where you do the majority of your work in the building model by adding elements, creating views, annotating views, and setting up printable sheets. They are initially based on template files.

- **Family files (.rfa):** These are separate components that can be inserted in a project. They include elements that can stand alone (e.g., a table or piece of mechanical equipment) or are items that are hosted in other elements (e.g., a door in a wall or a lighting fixture in a ceiling). Title block and Annotation Symbol files are special types of family files.

- **Template files (.rte and .rft):** These are the base files for any new project or family. Project templates hold standard information and settings for creating new project files. The software includes several templates for various types of projects. You can also create custom templates. Family templates include base information for creating families. Template files are usually saved as a new file.

Opening Projects

To open an existing project, in the Quick Access Toolbar or *File* tab, click (Open), or press <Ctrl>+<O>. The Open dialog box opens, and you can navigate to the required folder and select a project file. An example of the Open dialog box is shown in Figure 1–37.

Figure 1–37

- The software release version of the currently selected project displays below the preview. Do not open a drawing that should remain in an earlier version, as you cannot save back to previous versions.

   Note: It is important that everyone working on a project uses the same software version (e.g., 2021) and is on the same updated version (e.g., 2021.1). While your software may be able to open files created in its earlier versions, it will not be able to open files created in versions newer than the one you are using currently. For example, if you are working in Revit 2020, you cannot open a model created in Revit 2021.

- When you open a file created in an earlier version, the Model Upgrade dialog box (shown in Figure 1–38) indicates the release of a file and the release to which it will be upgraded. If needed, you can cancel the upgrade before it completes.

Figure 1–38

Hint: Opening Workset-Related Files

Worksets are used when the project becomes large enough for multiple people to work on it at the same time. At this point, a central file with multiple worksets (such as element interiors, building shell, and site) that are used by the project team members is created.

When you open a workset-related file it creates a new local file on your computer as shown in Figure 1–39. Do not work in the main central file.

Figure 1–39

- When you click on a central model showing in the Home screen, a local copy of the file is created.

- For more information on establishing and using Worksets, refer to the ASCENT guide *Autodesk Revit: Collaboration Tools*.

Starting New Projects

New projects are based on a template file. The template file includes preset levels, views, and some families, such as wall styles and text styles. Check with your BIM Manager about which template you need to use for your projects. Your company might have more than one based on the types of building that you are designing.

How To: Start a New Project

1. In the *File* tab, expand 🗋 (New) and click 🗋 (Project) (as shown in Figure 1–40), or press <Ctrl>+<N>.

Figure 1–40

2. In the New Project dialog box (shown in Figure 1–41), select the template that you want to use and click **OK**.

The list of Template files is set in the Options dialog box in the File Locations pane. It might vary depending on the installed product and company standards.

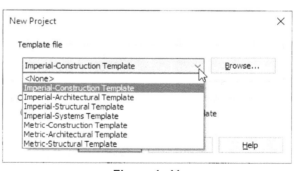

Figure 1–41

- You can select from a list of templates if they have been set up by your BIM Manager.

- You can add 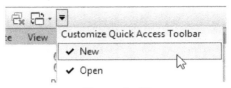 (New) to the Quick Access Toolbar. At the end of the Quick Access Toolbar, click ▼ (Customize Quick Access Toolbar) and select **New**, as shown in Figure 1–42.

Figure 1–42

Saving Projects

It is important to save your projects frequently. In the Quick Access Toolbar or *File* tab click 💾 (Save), or press <Ctrl>+<S> to save your project. If the project has not yet been saved, the Save As dialog box opens, where you can specify a file location and name.

- To save an existing project with a new name, in the *File* tab, expand 📑 (Save As) and click 🗔 (Project).

- If you have not saved in a certain amount of time, the software will notify you with the Project Not Saved Recently alert box, as shown in Figure 1–43. Select **Save the project**. If you want to set reminder intervals or not save at this time, select the other options.

Figure 1–43

- You can set the *Save Reminder interval* to **15** or **30 minutes**, **1**, **2**, or **4 hours**, or to have **No reminders** display. In the *File* tab, click **Options** to open the Options dialog box. In the left pane, select **General** and set the interval as shown in Figure 1–44.

Figure 1–44

Saving Backup Copies

By default, the software saves a backup copy of a project file when you save the project. Backup copies are numbered incrementally (e.g., **My Project.0001.rvt**, **My Project.0002.rvt**, etc.) and are saved in the same folder as the original file. In the Save As dialog box, click **Options...** to control how many backup copies are saved. The default number is three backups. If you exceed this number, the software deletes the oldest backup file.

Hint: Saving Workset-Related Projects

If you use worksets in your project, you need to save the project locally and to the central file. It is recommended to save the local file frequently, just like any other file, and save to the central file every hour or so by synchronizing with the central file.

To synchronize your changes with the main file, in the Quick Access Toolbar expand ⬚ (Synchronize and Modify Settings) and click ⬚ (Synchronize Now). After you save to the central file, save the file locally again.

At the end of the day, or when you are finished with the current session, in the Quick Access Toolbar, expand ⬚ (Synchronize and Modify Settings) and click ⬚ (Synchronize and Modify Settings) to relinquish the files you have been working on to the central file.

• The maximum number of backups for workset-enabled files is set to 20 by default.

1.4 Viewing Commands

Viewing commands are crucial to working efficiently in most drawing and modeling programs and the Autodesk Revit software is no exception. Once in a view, you can use the Zoom controls to navigate in it. You can zoom in and out and pan in any view. There are also special tools for viewing in 3D.

Zooming and Panning

Using the Mouse to Zoom and Pan

Use the mouse wheel (shown in Figure 1–45) as the main method of moving around the models.

Mouse Wheel

Figure 1–45

- Scroll the wheel on the mouse up to zoom in and down to zoom out.
- Hold the wheel and move the mouse to pan.
- Double-click on the wheel to zoom to the extents of the view.
- In a 3D view, hold <Shift> and the mouse wheel and move the mouse to rotate around the model.
- When you save a model and exit the software, the pan and zoom location of each view is remembered. This is especially important for complex models.

Zoom Controls

A number of additional zoom methods enable you to control the screen display. **Zoom** and **Pan** can be performed at any time while using other commands.

- You can access the **Zoom** commands in the Navigation Bar in the upper right corner of the view (as shown in Figure 1–46). You can also access them from most shortcut menus and by typing the shortcut commands.

 (2D Wheel) provides cursor-specific access to Zoom and Pan.

Figure 1–46

Zoom Commands

	Zoom In Region (ZR)	Zooms into a region that you define. Drag the cursor or select two points to define the rectangular area you want to zoom into. This is the default command.
	Zoom Out(2x) (ZO)	Zooms out to half the current magnification around the center of the elements.
	Zoom To Fit (ZF or ZE)	Zooms out so that the entire contents of the project only display on the screen in the current view.
	Zoom All To Fit (ZA)	Zooms out so that the entire contents of the project display on the screen in all open views.
	Zoom Sheet Size (ZS)	Zooms in or out in relation to the sheet size.
N/A	**Previous Pan/Zoom (ZP)**	Steps back one **Zoom** command.
N/A	**Next Pan/Zoom**	Steps forward one **Zoom** command if you have done a **Previous Pan/Zoom**.

Viewing in 3D

Even if you started a project entirely in plan views, you can quickly create 3D views of the model, as shown in Figure 1–47. There are two types of 3D views: isometric views created by the **Default 3D View** command and perspective views created by the **Camera** command.

Figure 1–47

Working in 3D views helps you visualize the project and position some of the elements correctly. You can create and modify elements in both isometric and perspective 3D views, just as you can in plan views.

*   Once you have created a 3D view, you can save it and easily return to it.

How To: Create and Save a 3D Isometric View

1. In the Quick Access Toolbar or *View* tab>Create panel, click
    (Default 3D View). The default 3D Southeast isometric view opens, as shown in Figure 1–48.

You can spin the view to a different angle using the mouse wheel or the middle button of a three-button mouse. Hold <Shift> as you press the wheel or middle button and drag the cursor.

Figure 1–48

2. Modify the view to display the building from other directions.

3. In the Project Browser, double-click slowly or right-click on the {3D} view and select **Rename...**.
4. The name is placed in a text box with the original name highlighted, as shown in Figure 1–49. Type a new name in the Rename View dialog box, as shown in Figure 1–50.

Figure 1–49   Figure 1–50

All types of views can be renamed.

• When changes to the default 3D view are saved and you start another default 3D view, it displays the Southeast isometric view once again. If you modified the default 3D view but did not save it to a new name, the **Default 3D View** command opens the view in the last orientation you specified.

How To: Create a Perspective View

1. Switch to a Floor Plan view.
2. In the Quick Access Toolbar or *View* tab>Create panel, expand 🏠 (Default 3D View) and click ▣ (Camera).
3. Place the camera on the view.
4. Point the camera in the direction in which you want it to shoot by placing the target on the view, as shown in Figure 1–51.

Figure 1–51

Use the round controls to modify the display size of the view and press <Shift> + the mouse wheel to change the view.

A new view is displayed, as shown in Figure 1–52.

Figure 1–52

5. In the Properties palette scroll down and adjust the *Eye Elevation* and *Target Elevation* as needed.

• If the view becomes distorted, reset the target so that it is centered in the boundary of the view (called the crop region).

In the *Modify | Cameras* tab>Camera panel, click (Reset Target).

• You can further modify a view by adding shadows, as shown in Figure 1–53. In the View Control Bar, toggle (Shadows Off) and (Shadows On). Shadows display in any model view, not just in the 3D views. To set up the sun location, expand (Sun Path Off) and select **Sun Settings...** Select (Sun Path On) to see the visual location of the sun.

Figure 1–53

Hint: Using the ViewCube

The ViewCube provides visual clues as to where you are in a 3D view. It helps you move around the model with quick access to specific views (such as top, front, and right), as well as corner and directional views, as shown in Figure 1–54.

ViewCube

Figure 1–54

Move the cursor over any face of the ViewCube to highlight it. Once a face is highlighted, you can select it to reorient the model. You can also click and drag on the ViewCube to rotate the box, which rotates the model.

- (Home) displays when you roll the cursor over the ViewCube. Click it to return to the view defined as **Home**. To change the Home view, set the view as you want it, right-click on the ViewCube, and select **Set Current View as Home**.

- The ViewCube is available in isometric and perspective views.

- You can switch between Perspective and Isometric mode by right-clicking on the View Cube and selecting **Perspective** or **Orthographic**.

Visual Styles

Any view can have a visual style applied. The **Visual Style** options found in the View Control Bar (as shown in Figure 1–55), specify the shading of the building model. These options apply to plan, elevation, section, and 3D views.

Figure 1–55

*   (Wireframe) displays the lines and edges that make up elements, but hides the surfaces. This can be useful when you are dealing with complex intersections.

*   (Hidden Line) displays the lines, edges, and surfaces of the elements, but it does not display any colors. This is the most common visual style to use while working on a design.

*   (Shaded) and (Consistent Colors) give you a sense of the materials, including transparent glass. An example that uses Consistent Colors is shown in Figure 1–56.

Figure 1–56

- (Realistic) displays what is shown when you render the view, including RPC (Rich Photorealistic Content) components and artificial lights. It takes a lot of computer power to execute this visual style. Therefore, it is better to use the other visual styles most of the time as you are working.

Hint: Rendering

Rendering is a powerful tool which enables you to display a photorealistic view of the model you are working on, such as the example shown in Figure 1–57. This can be used to help clients and designers understand a building's design in better detail.

Figure 1–57

- In the View Control Bar, click ⟳ (Show Rendering Dialog) to set up the options. **Show Rendering Dialog** is only available in 3D views.

Practice 1a

Review an Architectural Project

Practice Objectives

- Navigate the graphic user interface.
- Manipulate 2D and 3D views by zooming and panning.
- Create 3D Isometric and Perspective views.
- Set the Visual Style of a view.

In this practice, you will open a project file and view each of the various areas in the interface. You will investigate elements, commands, and their options. You will also open views through the Project Browser and view the model in 3D, as shown in Figure 1–58.

Figure 1–58

- This is a version of the main project you will work on throughout this guide.

Task 1 - Explore the interface.

1. In the *File* tab, expand 📂 (Open) and click 🗔 (Project).

2. In the Open dialog box, navigate to the practice files folder and select **Modern-Hotel-Final.rvt**.

3. Click **Open**. The 3D view of the modern hotel building opens in the view window.

If the Project Browser and Properties palette are docked over each other, use the Project Browser tab at the bottom to display it.

4. In the Project Browser, expand the *Floor Plans* node. Double-click on **Floor 1** to open it. This view is referred to as **Floor Plans: Floor 1**.

5. Take time to review the floor plan to get acquainted with it.

6. Review the various parts of the screen.

7. In the view, hover the cursor over one of the doors. A tooltip displays describing the element, as shown in Figure 1–59.

Figure 1–59

8. Hover the cursor over another element to display its description.

9. Select a door. The ribbon changes to the *Modify | Doors* tab.

10. Click in an empty space in the view to release the selection.

11. Hold <Ctrl> and select several elements of different types. The ribbon changes to the *Modify | Multi-Select* tab.

12. Press <Esc> to clear the selection.

13. In the *Architecture* tab>Build panel, click ⬚ (Wall). The ribbon changes to the *Modify | Place Wall* tab and at the end of the ribbon, the Draw panel is displayed. It contains tools that enable you to create walls. The rest of the ribbon displays the same tools that are found on the *Modify* tab.

14. In the Select panel, click ⬚ (Modify) to return to the main ribbon.

15. In the *Architecture* tab>Build panel, click ⬚ (Door). The ribbon changes to the *Modify | Place Door* tab and displays the options and tools you can use to create doors.

16. In the Select panel, click ⬚ (Modify) to return to the main ribbon.

Task 2 - Look at views.

You might need to widen the Project Browser to display the full names of the views.

1. In the Project Browser, verify that the *Floor Plans* node is open. Double-click on the **Floor 1 - Furniture Plan** view.

2. The basic floor plan displays with the furniture, but without the annotations that were displayed in the **Floor 1** view.

3. Open the **Floor1 - Life Safety Plan** view by couble-clicking on it.

4. The walls and furniture display, but the furniture is grayed out and red lines describing important life safety information display.

5. At the top of the views, click each tab to switch between the open views.

6. In the *View* tab>Windows panel, click ⬚ (Tile Views) or type **WT**. All of the open views are tiled. Type **ZA** (for Zoom All) to zoom out to the extents of each view, as shown in Figure 1–60.

Figure 1–60

7. Click inside the 3D view to make it active.

8. In the *View* tab>Windows panel, click ▢ (Tab Views) or type **TW**. The views return to the tabs and the 3D view is first in the group.

*This view is referred to as **Elevations (Building Elevation): East** view.*

9. In the Project Browser, scroll down and expand *Elevations (Building Elevation)*. Double-click on the **East** elevation to open the view.

10. Expand *Sections (Building Section)* and double-click on the **East-West Section** to open it.

11. At the bottom of the view window, in the View Control Bar, click ▱ (Visual Style) and select **Shaded**. The elements in the view are now easier to read.

12. In the Project Browser, scroll down to the *Sheets (all)* node and expand the node.

13. View several of the sheets. Some have views already applied, (e.g., **A2.3 - 2nd-8th Floor Plan (Typical)** as shown in Figure 1–61).

Figure 1–61

14. Which sheet displays the view that you just set to **Shaded**?

Task 3 - Practice viewing tools.

1. At the far right of the view tabs, expand Switch Windows and select **Floor 1**, as shown in Figure 1–62.

Figure 1–62

2. In the Navigation Bar, click and select **Zoom In Region** or type **ZR**. Zoom in on the stairs.

3. Pan to another part of the building by holding and dragging the middle mouse button or wheel. Alternatively, you can use the 2D Wheel in the Navigation Bar.

4. Double-click on the mouse wheel to zoom out to fit the extents of the view.

5. In the Quick Access Toolbar, click (Default 3D View) to open the default 3D view, as shown in Figure 1–63.

Figure 1–63

6. Hold <Shift> and use the middle mouse button or wheel to rotate the model in the 3D view.

7. In the View Control Bar, change the *Visual Style* to ▱ (Shaded). Then try ▱ (Consistent Colors). Which one works best when you view the back of the building?

8. Use the ViewCube to find a view that you want to use.

9. In the Project Browser, expand *3D Views* and right-click on the {3D} view and select **Rename...**. and type in a new name for the view.

10. Review the other 3D views that have already been created.

11. Press <Ctrl>+<Tab> to cycle through the open views.

12. In the Quick Access Toolbar, expand ⛶ (Switch Windows) and select the **Modern-Hotel-Final.rvt - Floor Plan: Floor 1** view.

13. In the Quick Access Toolbar, click ⬚ (Close Inactive Views). This closes all of the other windows except the one in which you are working.

14. In the Quick Access Toolbar, expand ⬡ (Default 3D View) and click ⬚ (Camera), as shown in Figure 1–64.

Figure 1–64

15. Click the first point near the Lobby room name and click the second point (target) outside the building, as shown in Figure 1–65.

1st point   *2nd point*

Figure 1–65

16. The furniture and planters display even though they did not display in the floor plan view.

17. In the View Control Bar, set the *Visual Style* to ⬡ (Realistic).

18. In the Project Browser, right-click on the new camera view and select **Rename...**. Type **Lobby Seating Area**.

19. In the Quick Access Toolbar, click 💾 (Save) to save the project.

20. In the *File* tab, click ⬚ (Close). This closes the entire project.

Practice 1b | Review an MEP Project

Practice Objectives

- Navigate the graphic user interface.
- Manipulate 2D and 3D views by zooming and panning.
- Create 3D Isometric and Perspective views.
- Set the Visual Style of a view.

In this practice, you will open a project file, as shown in Figure 1–66, and display each of the various parts of the Autodesk Revit interface. You will open views through the Project Browser and switch between different views. You will also select elements and display the information about them in the Properties palette. Finally, you will create and save 3D views.

Figure 1–66

Task 1 - Open an Autodesk Revit MEP project and review it.

1. In the *File* tab, expand (Open) and click (Project).

2. In the Open dialog box, navigate to the practice files folder and select **Review-School-MEP.rvt**, then click **Open**.

3. The project opens in the **3D Plumbing** view.

4. In the Project Browser, expand Mechanical>HVAC>Floor Plans, as shown in Figure 1–67.

Figure 1–67

5. Double-click on **01 Mechanical Plan** to open up the floor plan view, as shown in Figure 1–68.

Figure 1–68

6. Use the middle mouse (scroll) wheel to zoom and pan around the view.

7. Double-click on the middle mouse (scroll) wheel or type **ZF** (Zoom to Fit) to return to the full view.

8. Expand Plumbing>Plumbing>Floor Plans and double-click on the **01 Plumbing Plan** view to open it.

9. Expand Coordination>MEP>Floor Plans and double-click on **01 Space Planning** to open this view.

10. All of the previous views are still open and can be see in the tabs, as shown in Figure 1–69.

Figure 1–69

11. In the *View* tab>Windows panel, click ⊟ (Tile Views) or type **WT** to display all of the open views on the screen at the same time.

12. Type **ZA** (Zoom All to Fit) to have the model display completely within each view window, as shown in Figure 1–70.

Figure 1–70

13. Click in the open **01 Mechanical Plan** view to make it active.

14. In the *View* tab>Windows panel, click ⬜ (Tab View) or type **TW**.

15. In the Quick Access Toolbar, click 🔲 (Close Inactive Windows). Only the current active view is open.

Task 2 - Display the element properties.

1. In the **01 Mechanical Plan** view, hover over a duct without selecting it first. The duct highlights and a tooltip displays as shown in Figure 1–71. Information about the element also displays in the Status Bar but not in Properties.

Figure 1–71

2. Click on the duct to select it. The selection color and tabs on the ribbon at the top of the screen change. Properties now displays information about this piece of ductwork, as shown in Figure 1–72.

Figure 1–72

3. Hold <Ctrl> and in the view, select another, similar Duct element, as shown in Figure 1–73. Properties now displays that two ducts (Ducts(2)) are selected with the same information.

Figure 1–73

4. Hold <Ctrl> and select an air terminal. Properties now displays Common (3) in the Filter drop-down list, because the three selected elements are not of the same type. Therefore they do not share the same type of properties.

5. In Properties, expand the Filter drop-down list and select **Air Terminals**, as shown in Figure 1–74.

Figure 1–74

6. Only the Air Terminal properties are displayed, but the selection set has not changed. In the view they are all still selected.

7. End the command using one of the following methods:
   - In *Modify | Multi-Select* tab>Select panel, click (Modify).
   - Press <Esc> twice.
   - Click in the view window (without selecting an element).
   - Right-click in the view window and select **Cancel**.

Task 3 - Create 3D views.

1. In the Quick Access Toolbar, click 🏠 (Default 3D View).

2. A 3D Isometric view displays, as shown in Figure 1–75.

Figure 1–75

3. Press and hold <Shift> and press the middle mouse (scroll) button to orbit the view.

4. In the View Control Bar, select several different Visual Styles to see how they impact the view, as shown in Figure 1–76.

Figure 1–76

5. Select a view and visual style that you like. In the Project Browser, expand Coordination>All>**3D Views**, double-click on **{3D}** and name the view **3D Exterior** and click **OK**.

Task 4 - Create a camera view.

---

1. Switch back to the **01 Mechanical Plan** view.

2. In the Quick Access Toolbar, expand 🏠 (Default 3D View) and click ◉ (Camera).

3. Place the camera and select a point for the target similar to that shown in Figure 1–77.

Figure 1–77

4. The new view displays. Use the controls on the outline of the view to resize the view.

5. Click inside the 3D view and use <Shift>+ mouse wheel to rotate around until you get a good view of the ductwork.

6. Set the Visual Style, as required.

7. In the Project Browser, expand Mechanical>???>3D Views and select the new **3D View 1**, as shown in Figure 1–78.

The new view displays in the ??? category because it has not been assigned a Sub-Discipline.

Figure 1–78

8. In Properties, in the *Graphics* area, expand *Sub-Discipline* and select **HVAC**, as shown in Figure 1–79.

9. Click **Apply**. The view moves to the correct sub-discipline group, as shown in Figure 1–80. Rename the view as required.

Figure 1–79   Figure 1–80

10. Save the project.
11. In the *File* tab, click [icon] (Close).

Practice 1c

Review a Structural Project

Practice Objectives

- Navigate the graphic user interface.
- Manipulate 2D and 3D views by zooming and panning.
- Create 3D Isometric and Perspective views.
- Set the Visual Style of a view.

In this practice, you will open a project file and view each of the various areas in the interface. You will investigate elements, commands, and their options. You will also open views through the Project Browser and view the model in 3D, as shown in Figure 1–81.

Figure 1–81

Task 1 - Explore the interface.

1. In the *File* tab, expand (Open) and click (Project).

2. In the Open dialog box, navigate to the practice files folder and select **Syracuse-Suites.rvt**.

3. Click **Open**. The 3D view of the building opens in the view window.

If the Project Browser and Properties palette are docked over each other, use the Project Browser tab at the bottom to display it.

4. In the Project Browser, double-click on the **Structural Plans: 00 GROUND FLOOR** view. It opens a plan with the *Visual Style* set to **Wireframe** so that the footings and foundation walls display, although there is a slab over them.

5. In the View Control toolbar, change the *Visual Style* to **Hidden Line**. The lines that are hidden in the view display as dashed, as shown in Figure 1–82.

Figure 1–82

6. In the Project Browser, double-click on the **Structural Plans: T.O. FOOTING** view. The strip footings and spread footings display as continuous lines because they are not obscured by a slab, as shown in Figure 1–83.

Figure 1–83

7. Zoom in on one corner of the building. The foundation walls are in-filled with the appropriate concrete hatch, as shown in Figure 1–84.

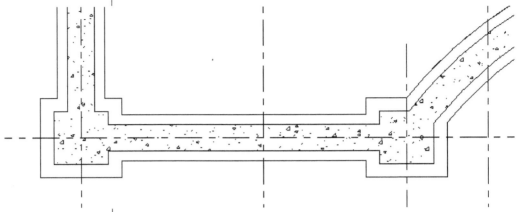

Figure 1–84

8. Double-click the mouse wheel or type **ZE** to zoom to the extents of the view. (**ZA** zooms to the extents of all of the opened view windows.) Find the section marker that extends vertically along the model as shown in Figure 1–85.

Figure 1–85

9. Double-click on the section head to open the **NORTH-SOUTH SECTION** view.

10. In the Project Browser, navigate to the *Sections (Building Section)* category. The **NORTH-SOUTH SECTION** view name is bold. You can navigate through your model by double-clicking on the element in the Project Browser or by using the graphical view elements in the model.

11. In the section view, zoom in on the area in which the callout has been placed, as shown in Figure 1–86. Double-click on the callout-head to open the **TYPICAL EDGE DETAIL** view.

Figure 1–86

12. In the **TYPICAL EDGE DETAIL** view, select the floor, as shown in Figure 1–87.

Figure 1–87

13. This is a full 3D floor element. You can edit it using the standard modify tool and the concrete floor-specific tools found in the *Modify | Floors* contextual tab, as shown in Figure 1–88.

Figure 1–88

14. The Properties palette displays the Instance Parameters for the element, as shown in Figure 1–89.

Any changes made here are applied to the selected element only.

Figure 1–89

15. In Properties, click (Edit Type) to access the Type Parameters in the Type Properties dialog box, as shown in Figure 1–90.

Any changes made to the element here are applied to all its other instances in the project.

Figure 1–90

16. Click **Cancel** to close the Type Properties dialog box.

17. Press <Esc> or click in an empty space in the view to clear the selection.

18. Select one of the bolted connections. This is a detail component (2D element). The *Modify | Detail Items* contextual tab displays the modifying options specific to this element, as shown in Figure 1–91.

Figure 1–91

19. Press <Esc> to clear the selection.

Task 2 - Work with multiple views and 3D views.

1. At the top of the views, click each tab to switch between the open views.
2. In the *View* tab>Windows panel, click ⬒ (Tile Views). All of the open views are tiled. Type **ZA** (for Zoom All) to zoom out to the extents of each view, as shown in Figure 1–92.

Figure 1–92

3. Click inside the 3D view to make it active.

4. In the *View* tab>Windows panel, click ⬜ (Tab Views). The views return to the tabs and the 3D view is first in the group.

5. In the Quick Access Toolbar, click 🗗 (Close Inactive Windows) so that only the current window remains open.

6. Using the mouse wheel, zoom in on the building.

7. Press and hold <Shift> and then press and hold the wheel on the mouse. Move the mouse to dynamically view the 3D model. You can also navigate in 3D using the ViewCube in the upper right corner of the view.

8. Expand the *File* tab and click 🗎 (Close) to exit the project. Do not save changes.

Chapter Review Questions

1. When you create a project in the Autodesk Revit software, do you work in 3D (as shown on the left in Figure 1–93) or 2D (as shown on the right in Figure 1–93)?

3D view ⟶   2D view ⟶

Figure 1–93

   a. You work in 2D in plan views and in 3D in non-plan views.

   b. You work in 3D almost all of the time, even when you are using what looks like a flat view.

   c. You work in 2D or 3D depending on how you toggle the 2D/3D control.

   d. You work in 2D in plan and section views and in 3D in isometric views.

2. What is the purpose of the Project Browser?

   a. It enables you to browse through the building project, similar to a walk through.

   b. It is the interface for managing all of the files that are required to create the complete architectural model of the building.

   c. It manages multiple Autodesk Revit projects as an alternative to using Windows Explorer.

   d. It is used to access and manage the views of the project.

3. Which parts of the interface change when you start a command such as Wall or Doors? (Select all that apply.)

   a. Ribbon

   b. View Control Bar

   c. Options Bar

   d. Properties Palette

4. What is the difference between Type Properties and Properties? (The ribbon location is shown in Figure 1–94.)

Figure 1–94

   a. Properties stores parameters that apply to the selected individual element(s). Type Properties stores parameters that impact every element of the same type in the project.

   b. Properties stores the location parameters of an element. Type Properties stores the size and identity parameters of an element.

   c. Properties only stores parameters of the view. Type Properties stores parameters of model components.

5. When you start a new project, how do you specify the base information in the new file?

   a. Transfer the base information from an existing project.

   b. Select the right template for the task.

   c. The Autodesk Revit software automatically extracts the base information from imported or linked file(s).

6. What is the main difference between a view made using (Default 3D View) and a view made using (Camera)?

   a. Use Default **3D View** for exterior views and **Camera** for interiors.

   b. **Default 3D View** creates a static image and a **Camera** view is live and always updated.

   c. **Default 3D View** is isometric and a **Camera** view is perspective.

   d. **Default 3D View** is used for the overall building and a **Camera** view is used for looking in tight spaces.

Command Summary

Button	Command	Location
General Tools		
	Home	• Quick Access Toolbar
		• **Shortcut:** <Ctrl>+<D>
	Modify	• **Ribbon:** All tabs>Select panel
		• **Shortcut:** MD
	New	•
		• *File* tab
		• **Shortcut:** <Ctrl>+<N>
	Open	• **Quick Access Toolbar**
		• *File* tab
		• **Shortcut:** <Ctrl>+<O>
	Open Documents	• *File* tab
	Properties	• **Ribbon:** *Modify* tab>Properties panel
		• **Shortcut:** PP
	Recent Documents	• *File* tab
	Save	• **Quick Access Toolbar**
		• *File* tab
		• **Shortcut:** <Ctrl>+<S>
	Synchronize and Modify Settings	• **Quick Access Toolbar**
	Synchronize Now	• **Quick Access Toolbar**>expand Synchronize and Modify Settings
	Type Properties	• **Ribbon:** *Modify* tab>Properties panel
		• **Properties palette**
Viewing Tools		
	Camera	• **Quick Access Toolbar**> Expand Default 3D View
		• **Ribbon:** *View* tab>Create panel> expand Default 3D View
	Close Inactive Views	• **Quick Access Toolbar**
		• **Ribbon:** *View* tab> Windows panel
	Default 3D View	• **Quick Access Toolbar**
		• **Ribbon:** *View* tab>Create panel
	Home	• **ViewCube**
N/A	Next Pan/Zoom	• **Navigation Bar**
		• **Shortcut Menu**

N/A	Previous Pan/Zoom	• **Navigation Bar** • **Shortcut Menu** • **Shortcut:** ZP
	Shadows On/Off	• **View Control Bar**
	Show Rendering Dialog/ Render	• **View Control Bar** • **Ribbon:** *View* tab>Graphics panel • **Shortcut:** RR
	Switch Windows	• **Quick Access Toolbar** • **Ribbon:** *View* tab> Windows panel
	Tab Views	• **Ribbon:** *View* tab> Windows panel • **Shortcut: TW**
	Tile Views	• **Ribbon:** *View* tab> Windows panel • **Shortcut: WT**
	Zoom All to Fit	• **Navigation Bar** • **Shortcut:** ZA
	Zoom in Region	• **Navigation Bar** • **Shortcut Menu** • **Shortcut:** ZR
	Zoom Out (2x)	• **Navigation Bar** • **Shortcut Menu** • **Shortcut:** ZO
	Zoom Sheet Size	• **Navigation Bar** • **Shortcut:** ZS
	Zoom to Fit	• **Navigation Bar** • **Shortcut Menu** • **Shortcut:** ZF, ZE

Visual Styles

	Consistent Colors	• **View Control Bar**:
	Hidden Line	• **View Control Bar** • **Shortcut:** HL
	Realistic	• **View Control Bar**
	Shaded	• **View Control Bar** • **Shortcut:** SD
	Wireframe	• **View Control Bar** • **Shortcut:** WF

Reviewing Projects

Basic sketching, selecting, and modifying tools are the foundation of working with all types of elements in the Autodesk® Revit® software. Using these tools with drawing aids helps you to place and modify elements to create accurate building models. You can also troubleshoot a project by reviewing warnings and running interference checks between disciplines.

Learning Objectives in This Chapter

- Sketch linear elements such as walls, beams, and pipes.
- Ease the placement of elements by incorporating drawing aids such as alignment lines, temporary dimensions, and snaps.
- Place Reference Planes as temporary guide lines.
- Use techniques to select and filter groups of elements.
- Modify elements using a contextual tab, Properties, temporary dimensions, and controls.
- Work with errors and warnings in models.
- Run Interference Check to find out if there are problems within a model or between disciplines.

2.1 Using General Sketching Tools

When you start a command, the contextual tab on the ribbon, the Options Bar, and the Properties palette (as shown in Figure 2–1) enable you to set up features for each new element you are placing in the project. As you are working, several features called *drawing aids* display, as shown in Figure 2–1. They help you to create designs quickly and accurately.

Figure 2–1

- In Autodesk Revit, you are most frequently creating 3D model elements rather than 2D sketches. These tools work with both 3D and 2D elements in the software.

Draw Tools

Many linear elements (such as walls, beams, ducts, pipes, and conduits) are modeled using the tools on the contextual tab on the *Draw* panel. Other elements (such as floors, ceilings, roofs, and slabs) have boundaries that are sketched using many of the same tools. Draw tools are also used when you create details or schematic drawings.

The exact tools vary according to the element being modeled.

Two methods are available:

- *Draw* the element using a geometric form
- *Pick* an existing element (such as a line, face, or wall) as the basis for the new element's geometry and position.

How To: Create Linear Elements

1. Start the command you want to use.
2. In the contextual tab>Draw panel (shown in Figure 2–2), select a drawing tool.
3. Select points to define the elements or watch the Status Bar, in the lower left corner, for hints on what to do.

You can change from one Draw tool shape to another in the middle of a command.

Draw

Figure 2–2

4. Finish the command using one of the standard methods:

- Click   (Modify).
- Press <Esc> twice.
- Start another command.

Draw Options

When you are in Drawing mode, several options display in the Options Bar, as shown in Figure 2–3.

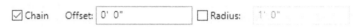

Figure 2–3

Different options display according to the type of element that is selected or the command that is active.

- **Chain:** Controls how many segments are created in one process. If this option is not selected, the **Line** and **Arc** tools only create one segment at a time. If it is selected, you can continue adding segments until you press <Esc> or select the command again.

- **Offset:** Enables you to enter values so you can create linear elements at a specified distance from the selected points or element.

- **Radius:** Enables you to enter values when using a radial tool or to add a radius to the corners of linear elements as you sketch them.

Draw Tools

	Line	Draws a straight line defined by the first and last points. If Chain is enabled, you can continue selecting end points for multiple segments.
	Rectangle	Draws a rectangle defined by two opposing corner points. You can adjust the dimensions after selecting both points.
	Inscribed Polygon	Draws a polygon inscribed in a hypothetical circle with the number of sides specified in the Options Bar.
	Circumscribed Polygon	Draws a polygon circumscribed around a hypothetical circle with the number of sides specified in the Options Bar.
	Circle	Draws a circle defined by a center point and radius.
	Start-End-Radius Arc	Draws a curve defined by a start, end, and radius of the arc. The outside dimension shown is the included angle of the arc. The inside dimension is the radius.
	Center-ends Arc	Draws a curve defined by a center, radius, and included angle. The selected point of the radius also defines the start point of the arc.
	Tangent End Arc	Draws a curve tangent to another element. Select an end point for the first point, but do not select the intersection of two or more elements. Then select a second point based on the included angle of the arc.
	Fillet Arc	Draws a curve defined by two other elements and a radius. Because it is difficult to select the correct radius by clicking, this command automatically moves to edit mode. Select the dimension and then modify the radius of the fillet.
	Spline	Draws a spline curve based on selected points. The curve does not actually touch the points (Sketches, Model and Detail Lines only).
	Ellipse	Draws an ellipse from a primary and secondary axis (Walls, Sketches, Model and Detail Lines only).
	Partial Ellipse	Draws only one side of the ellipse, like an arc. A partial ellipse also has a primary and secondary axis (Sketches, Model and Detail Lines only).

Pick Tools

![Pick Lines icon]	**Pick Lines**	Use this option to select existing linear elements in the project. This is useful when you start the project from an imported 2D drawing.
![Pick Face icon]	**Pick Face**	Use this option to select the face of a 3D massing element (walls and 3D views only).
![Pick Walls icon]	**Pick Walls**	Use this option to select an existing wall in the project to be the basis for a new sketch line (floors, ceilings, etc.).

Drawing Aids

As soon as you start sketching or placing elements, three drawing aids display, as shown in Figure 2–4:

- Alignment lines

- Temporary dimensions

- Snaps

These aids are available with most modeling and many modification commands.

Figure 2–4

Alignment lines display as soon as you select your first point. They help keep lines horizontal, vertical, or at a specified angle. They also line up with the implied intersections of walls and other elements.

- Hold <Shift> to force the alignments to be orthogonal (90 degree angles only).

Temporary dimensions display to help place elements at the correct length, angle and location.

- You can type in a value, or move the cursor until you see the dimension you want, or you can place the element and then modify the value as needed.

- The length and angle increments shown vary depending on how far in or out the view is zoomed.

- For Imperial measurements (feet and inches), the software uses a default of feet. For example, when you type **4** and press <Enter>, it assumes 4'-0". For a distance such as 4'-6", you can type any of the following: **4'-6"**, **4'6**, **4-6**, or **4 6** (the numbers separated by a space). To indicate distances less than one foot, type the inch mark (") after the distance, or enter **0**, a space, and then the distance.

Hint: Temporary Dimensions and Permanent Dimensions

Temporary dimensions disappear as soon as you finish adding elements. If you want to make them permanent, select the dimension symbol ( ), as shown in Figure 2–5.

Figure 2–5

Snaps are key points that help you reference existing elements to exact points when modeling, as shown in Figure 2–6.

Figure 2–6

- When you move the cursor over an element, the snap symbol displays. Each snap location type displays with a different symbol.

Hint: Snap Settings and Overrides

In the *Manage* tab>Settings panel, click (Snaps) to open the Snaps dialog box, which is shown in Figure 2–7. The Snaps dialog box enables you to set which snap points are active, and set the dimension increments displayed for temporary dimensions (both linear and angular).

Snaps	✕

☐ Snaps Off   (SO)

Dimension Snaps

Snaps adjust as views are zoomed.
The largest value that represents less than 2mm on screen is used.

☑ Length dimension snap increments

4' ; 0' 6" ; 0' 1" ; 0' 0 1/4" ;

☑ Angular dimension snap increments

90.00° ; 45.00° ; 15.00° ; 5.00° ; 1.00° ;

Object Snaps

☑ Endpoints   (SE) ☑ Intersections   (SI)

☑ Midpoints   (SM) ☑ Centers   (SC)

☑ Nearest   (SN) ☑ Perpendicular   (SP)

☑ Work Plane Grid   (SW) ☑ Tangents   (ST)

☑ Quadrants   (SQ) ☑ Points   (SX)

Check All	Check None

☑ Snap to Remote Objects   (SR) ☑ Snap to Point Clouds   (PC)

Temporary Overrides

While using an interactive tool, keyboard shortcuts (shown in parentheses) can be used to specify a snap type for a single pick.

Object snaps   Use shortcuts listed above
Close   (SZ)
Turn Override Off   (SS)
Cycle through snaps   (TAB)
Force horizontal and vertical   (SHIFT)

Restore Defaults

OK	Cancel	Help

Figure 2–7

- Keyboard shortcuts for each snap can be used to override the automatic snapping. Temporary overrides only affect a single pick, but can be very helpful when there are snaps nearby other than the one you want to use.

Reference Planes

As you develop designs in the Autodesk Revit software, there are times when you need lines to help you define certain locations. You can sketch reference planes (displayed as dashed green lines) and snap to them whenever you need to line up elements. For the example shown in Figure 2–8, the lighting fixtures in the reflected ceiling plan are placed using reference planes.

Reference planes do not display in 3D views.

- To insert a reference plane, in the *Architecture, Structure,* or *Systems* tab>Work Plane panel, click (Ref Plane) or type **RP**.

Figure 2–8

- Reference planes display in associated views because they are infinite planes, and not just lines.
- You can name Reference planes by clicking on **<Click to name>** and typing in the text box, as shown in Figure 2–9.

Figure 2–9

- If you sketch a reference pane in Sketch Mode (used with floors and similar elements), it does not display once the sketch is finished.
- Reference planes can have different line styles if they have been defined in the project. In Properties, select a style from the Subcategory list.

Hint: Model Line vs. Detail Line

While most of the elements that you create are representations of actual building elements, there are times you may need to add lines to clarify the design intent. These can be either detail lines, as shown in Figure 2–10, or model lines. Detail lines are also useful as references because they are only reflected in the view in which you sketch them.

Figure 2–10

• A model line (*Architecture* or *Structure* tab>Model panel>

  ⌐ (Model Line)) functions as a 3D element and displays in all views.

• A detail line (*Annotate* tab>Detail panel> ⌐ (Detail Line)) is strictly a 2D element that only displays in the view in which it is drawn.

• In the *Modify* contextual tab, as shown in Figure 2–11, select a Line Style and then the Draw tool that you want to use to draw the model or detail line.

Figure 2–11

2.2 Editing Elements

Building design projects typically involve extensive changes to the model. The Autodesk Revit software was designed to make such changes quickly and efficiently. You can change an element using the following methods, as shown in Figure 2–12:

- Type Selector enables you to specify a different type. This is frequently used to change the size and/or style of the elements.

- Properties enables you to modify the information (parameters) associated with the selected elements.

- The contextual tab in the ribbon contains the Modify commands and element-specific tools.

- Temporary dimensions enable you to change the element's dimensions or position.

- Controls enable you to drag, flip, lock, and rotate the element.

- Shape handles enable you to drag elements to modify their height or length.

Figure 2–12

- To delete an element, select it and press <Delete>, right-click and select **Delete**, or in the Modify panel, click ✖ (Delete).

Working with Controls and Shape Handles

When you select an element, various controls and shape handles display depending on the element and view. For example, in plan view you can use controls to drag the ends of a wall and change its orientation. You can also drag the wall ends in a 3D view, and you can also use the arrow shape handles to change the height of the wall, as shown in Figure 2–13.

Figure 2–13

• If you hover the cursor over the control or shape handle, a tool tip displays showing its function.

Hint: Editing Temporary Dimensions

Temporary dimensions automatically link to the closest wall. To change this, drag the *Witness Line* control, as shown in Figure 2–14, to connect to a new reference. You can also click on the control to toggle between justifications in the wall.

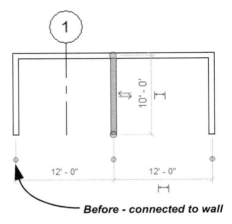

Before - connected to wall

After - connected to grid line

Figure 2–14

- The new location of a temporary dimension for an element is remembered as long as you are in the same session of the software.

Selecting Multiple Elements

- Once you have selected at least one element, hold <Ctrl> and select another item to add it to a selection set.

- To remove an element from a selection set, hold <Shift> and select the element.

- If you click and drag the cursor to *window* around elements, you have two selection options, as shown in Figure 2–15. If you drag from left to right, you only select the elements completely inside the window. If you drag from right to left, you select elements both inside and crossing the window.

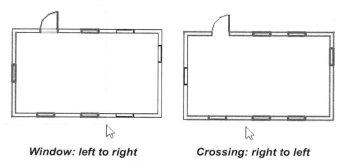

Window: left to right   Crossing: right to left

Figure 2–15

- If several elements are on or near each other, hover your cursor over an edge and press <Tab> to cycle through them before you click. If there are elements that might be linked to each other, such as walls that are connected, pressing <Tab> selects the chain of elements.

- Press <Ctrl>+<Left Arrow> to reselect the previous selection set. You can also right-click in the view window with nothing selected and select **Select Previous**.

- To select all elements of a specific type, right-click on an element and select **Select All Instances>Visible in View** or **In Entire Project**, as shown in Figure 2–16. For example, if you select a column of a specific size and use this command, only the columns of the same size are selected.

Figure 2–16

- You can save selections and use them again.

Hint: Measuring Tools

When modifying a model, it is useful to know the distance between elements. This can be done with temporary dimensions, or more frequently, by using the measuring tools found in the Quick Access Toolbar or on the *Modify* tab> Measure panel, as shown in Figure 2–17.

Figure 2–17

- (Measure Between Two References) - Select two elements and the measurement displays.

- (Measure Along An Element) - Select the edge of a linear element and the total length displays. Use <Tab> to highlight other elements and then click to measure along all of them, as shown in Figure 2–18.

Figure 2–18

- References include any snap point, wall lines, or other parts of elements (such as door center lines).

Filtering Selection Sets

When multiple element categories are selected, the *Multi-Select* contextual tab opens in the ribbon. This gives you access to all of the Modify tools, and the **Filter** command. The **Filter** command enables you to specify the types of elements to select. For example, you might only want to select columns, as shown in Figure 2–19.

Figure 2–19

How To: Filter a Selection Set

1. Select everything in the area.
2. in the *Modify | Multi-Select* tab>Selection panel, or in the Status Bar, click ▽ (Filter). The Filter dialog box opens, as shown in Figure 2–20.

The Filter dialog box displays all types of elements in the original selection.

Figure 2–20

3. Click **Check None** to clear all of the options or **Check All** to select all of the options. You can also select or clear individual categories as needed.
4. Click **OK**. The selection set is now limited to the elements you specified.

- The number of elements selected displays on the right end of the status bar and in the Properties palette.

Hint: Selection Options

You can control how the software selects specific elements in a project by toggling selection options on and off on the Status Bar, as shown in Figure 2–21. Alternatively, in any tab on the ribbon that has the Modify command, expand the Select panel's title and select the option.

Figure 2–21

- **Select links:** When toggled on, you can select linked CAD drawings or Autodesk Revit models. When it is toggled off, you cannot select them when using **Modify** or **Move**.

- **Select underlay elements:** When toggled on, you can select underlay elements. When toggled off, you cannot select them when using **Modify** or **Move**.

- **Select pinned elements:** When toggled on, you can selected pinned elements. When toggled off, you cannot select them when using **Modify** or **Move**.

- **Select elements by face:** When toggled on you can select elements (such as the floors or walls in an elevation) by selecting the interior face or selecting an edge. When toggled off, you can only select elements by selecting an edge.

- **Drag elements on selection:** When toggled on, you can hover over an element, select it, and drag it to a new location. When toggled off, the Crossing or Box select mode starts when you press and drag, even if you are on top of an element. Once elements have been selected they can still be dragged to a new location.

Practice 2a

Sketch and Edit Architectural Elements

Practice Objective

- Use sketch tools and drawing aids.

In this practice, you will use the **Wall** command along with sketching tools and drawing aids, such as temporary dimensions and snaps. You will use the **Modify** command and modify the walls using grips, temporary dimensions, the Type Selector, and Properties. You will add a door and modify it using temporary dimensions and controls. The completed model is shown in Figure 2–22.

Figure 2–22

Task 1 - Use sketching tools and temporary dimensions to model and modify walls.

1. In the *File Tab*, click ☐ (New)> 📑 (Project).

2. In the New Project dialog box, select **Imperial-Architectural Template** in the Template file drop-down list, and click **OK**.

3. In the Quick Access Toolbar, click 💾 (Save). When prompted, name the project **Simple Building.rvt**.

4. In the *Architecture* tab>Build panel, click ⬜ (Wall).

5. In the *Modify | Place Wall* tab>Draw panel, click

    ⬜ (Rectangle) and sketch a rectangle approximately **100' x 70'**. You do not have to be precise because you can change the dimensions later.

6. Note that the dimensions are temporary. Select the vertical dimension text and type **70'-0"**, as shown in Figure 2–23. Press <Enter>.

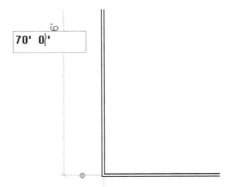

Figure 2–23

7. The dimensions are still displayed as temporary. Click the dimension controls of both the dimensions to make them permanent, as shown in Figure 2–24.

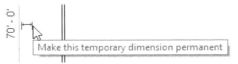

Figure 2–24

8. In the Select panel, click ⬐ (Modify). You can also use one of the other methods to switch to **Modify:**

    -   Type the shortcut **MD**.
    -   Press <Esc> once or twice.

9. Select either vertical wall. The horizontal dimension becomes active (changes to blue). Click the dimension text and type **100'-0"**, as shown in Figure 2–25.

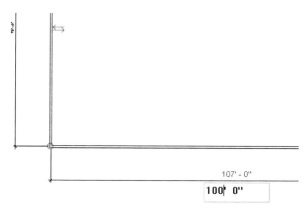

Figure 2–25

10. Click in an empty space in the view to end the selection. You are still in the **Modify** command.

11. In the *Architecture* tab>Build panel, click ⬭ (Wall). In the Draw panel, verify that ⟋ (Line) is selected. Sketch a wall horizontally from midpoint to midpoint of the vertical walls.

12. Draw another horizontal wall **8'-0"** above the middle horizontal wall. You can use temporary dimensions to adjust if needed.

13. Draw a vertical wall exactly **16'-0"** from the left wall, as shown in Figure 2–26.

Figure 2–26

14. In the Draw panel, click ⟳ (Circle) and sketch a **14'-0"** radius circular wall at the midpoint of the lower interior horizontal wall, as shown in Figure 2–27.

Figure 2–27

15. Click ⬈ (Modify) to finish the command.

16. Hover the cursor over one of the outside walls, press <Tab> to highlight the chain of outside walls, and click to select the walls.

17. In the Type Selector, select **Basic Wall: Generic-12"**, as shown in Figure 2–28. The thickness of the outside walls change.

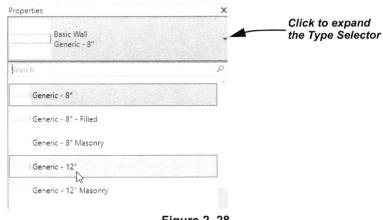

Click to expand the Type Selector

Figure 2–28

18. Click in an empty space in the view to release the selection.

19. Select the vertical interior wall. In the Type Selector, change the wall to one of the small interior partition styles.

20. Click in an empty space in the view to release the selection.

Task 2 - Add and modify a door.

1. Zoom in on the room in the upper left corner.

2. In the *Architecture* tab>Build panel, click (Door).

3. In the *Modify | Place Door* tab>Tag panel, click (Tag on Placement).

4. Place a door anywhere along the wall in the hallway.

5. Click (Modify) to finish the command.

6. Select the door. Use temporary dimensions to move it so that it is **2'-6"** from the right interior vertical wall. If needed, use controls to flip the door so that it swings into the room, as shown in Figure 2–29.

Figure 2–29

7. Type **ZE** to zoom out to the full view.

8. Save the project.

Practice 2b | Select and Edit MEP Elements

Practice Objectives

- Use a variety of selection methods.
- Use temporary dimensions and connectors to modify the location of elements.

In this practice, you will select lighting fixtures and change the type (as shown in Figure 2–30), as well as test a variety of selection methods and filters. You will then use connectors to modify the location of an air terminal and use **Create Similar** to add additional components. You will also modify the height of the air terminals in Properties.

Figure 2–30

Task 1 - Use a variety of selection methods.

1. In the practice files folder, open **Simple-Building-Edit.rvt**. It opens in the **1 - Lighting** view.

2. Select one of the light fixtures. The connectors and controls are displayed.

3. Hold <Ctrl> and select the other fixture. The connectors no longer display, but you can still modify the fixture type.

4. In the Type Selector, change the type to **Plain Recessed Lighting Fixture: 1x4 - 277**. Both fixtures change, as shown in Figure 2–31.

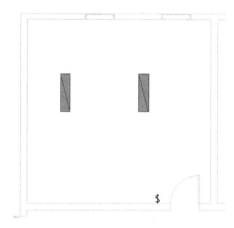

Figure 2–31

5. Click in an empty space to clear the selection.

6. Open the Mechical>HVAC>Floor Plans>**1 - Mech** view.

7. Draw a window selection from left to right around some of the elements so only those completely inside the window are selected, as shown in Figure 2–32.

Figure 2–32

8. Click in an empty space in the view to clear the selection.

9. Draw a crossing window (i.e., from right to left) around the same area, as shown in Figure 2–33. Note that any elements that the window touches are included in the selection, including the linked architectural model.

You can toggle

(Select Links) in the Status Bar to keep the link from being selected.

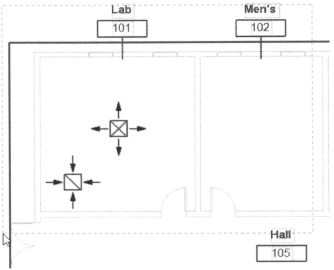

Figure 2–33

10. Hold <Shift> and select the edge of the architectural model. This removes the element from the selection set.

11. In the Status Bar, note the number of items that are selected and click (Filter).

12. In the Filter dialog box, view the categories and clear the check from **Air Terminals**.

13. Click **OK**. Only the room tags are still selected.

14. Press <Esc>. The elements are no longer selected.

15. Select one of the room tags. Right-click and select **Select All Instances>Visible in View**. All of the tags are selected.

16. Click (Modify). The elements are no longer selected.

• Remember these selection methods as you start working in the projects.

Task 2 - Modify elements using controls and properties.

1. Open the Mechical>HVAC>Floor Plans>**1 - Mech** view.

2. Select, click and drag the supply air terminal to a new location using the alignment lines referencing the return air terminal.

3. Right-click on the control and look at the variety of options you can use, as shown in Figure 2–34.

Figure 2–34

4. In the shortcut menu, select **Create Similar**. This starts the **Air Terminal** command using that type. Place two more air terminals in the same room, using alignment lines to place them.

5. Click   (Modify) and select all three of the supply air terminals. Note the information in Properties. The *Offset from Host* is set to **0'-0"** above Level 1.

6. Hold <Ctrl> and select the return air terminal. The *Level* and *Offset from Host* are available to change, although two different types of components are selected.

7. Change the *Offset from Host* to **8'-0"** and click **Apply**. The offset for all of the air terminals is updated, as shown in Figure 2–35.

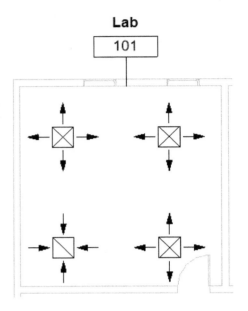

Figure 2–35

8. Click away from any elements to clear the selection.

9. Save and close the project.

Practice 2c

Sketch and Edit Structural Elements

Practice Objective

- Use modify tools and drawing aids.

In this practice, you will use a variety of ways to select elements, use the Filter dialog box to only select one type of element, select only elements of one type in the view, and use the Type Selector to change the type. You will then modify element locations using temporary dimensions as shown in Figure 2–36.

Figure 2–36

Task 1 - Select elements.

1. Open **Select Practice.rvt** from the practice files folder.

2. Create a selection window around the building by selecting a point just outside the upper left corner of the building and, while continuing to hold the left mouse button, drag the mouse toward the lower right corner and click to select the second point, as shown in Figure 2–37.

First select point

Second select point

Figure 2–37

3. All of the elements inside the window are selected and those outside the window are not selected. Press <Esc>.

4. Select the building again, but this time use a crossing window by selecting a point just outside the upper right corner of the building and, while continuing to hold the left mouse button, drag the mouse toward the lower left corner, as shown in Figure 2–38. All of the elements inside and touching the window are selected.

First select point

Second select point

Figure 2–38

5. In the Status Bar, click ▽ (Filter).

6. In the Filter dialog box shown in Figure 2–39, review the selected element categories.

The numbers here and in the next steps might be slightly different depending on your selection set.

Filter		✕
Category:	**Count:**	
☑ Array	1	Check All
☑ Grids	9	
☑ Model Groups	4	Check None
☑ Railings	2	
☑ Ramps	1	
☑ Rectangular Straight Wall Opening	2	
☑ Shaft Openings	2	
☑ Slab Edges	1	
☑ Stairs	1	
☑ Structural Area Reinforcement	1	
☑ Structural Columns	34	
☑ Structural Foundations	33	
☑ Structural Rebar	11	
☑ Walls	15	
Total Selected Items:	117	
	OK Cancel Apply	

Figure 2–39

7. Click **Check None**.

8. Select only the Structural Columns category and click **OK**.

9. The total number of Structural Columns in the selection set displays in the Status Bar as shown in Figure 2–40.

Figure 2–40

10. In Properties, the display indicates that multiple Families are selected.

11. Click in an empty space in the view to clear the selection.

12. Zoom in on the lower left corner of the building and select one Structural Column as shown in Figure 2–41.

Structural Columns : W-Wide Flange-Column : W10X49

Figure 2–41

13. In the Type Selector, the column name and type are displayed as shown in Figure 2–42.

Figure 2–42

14. In the view, right-click, expand **Select All Instances**, and select **Visible in View** as shown in Figure 2–43.

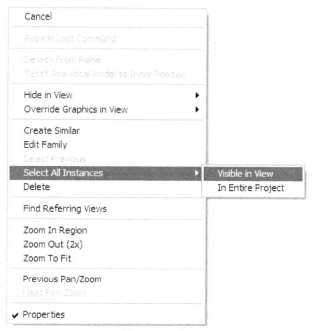

Figure 2–43

15. The total number of this type of column displays in the Status Bar by Filter and in Properties.

16. In the Type Selector, select **W-Wide Flange-Column: W12x40**, as shown in Figure 2–44.

Figure 2–44

17. The view regenerates and the selected columns are updated to the new type. Press <Esc> to release the selection set.

Task 2 - Using temporary dimensions.

1. Zoom out to see the entire building.

2. Select Grid C.

3. If the temporary dimensions are not displayed, in the Options Bar, click **Activate Dimensions**.

4. The temporary dimensions are automatically connected to the closest structural elements.

5. Use the **Move Witness Line** controls on the temporary dimensions and move them to the nearest grid lines as shown in Figure 2–45.

Figure 2–45

6. Click 🗒 (Make this temporary dimension line permanent).

7. Click in an empty space in the view to release the selection. The new dimensions are now part of the view.

8. Select Grid C again.

9. Click **Activate Dimensions**, if needed.

10. Select the lower dimension text and change it to **24'-0"** as shown in Figure 2–46. Press <Enter>.

Figure 2–46

11. The model regenerates and the percentage of completion is displayed in the Status Bar as shown in Figure 2–47. This change is being made to the grid and throughout the model, wherever elements touch the grid.

Figure 2–47

12. Save and close the project.

2.3 Troubleshooting

The Autodesk Revit software provides you with many options for troubleshooting while you are working. Two that are most helpful for project managers are reviewing warnings (such as that shown in Figure 2–48) and Interference Checking if you are working with other disciplines.

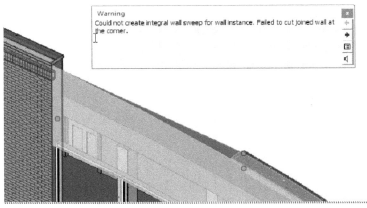

Figure 2–48

Reviewing Warnings

Because the Autodesk Revit software works with smart elements that know how other elements relate to them, you can easily check whether there are any problems with the connections. There are two types of error alerts. Those that you cannot ignore (as shown in Figure 2–49) and those that can be ignored but need to be dealt with at a later time.

Figure 2–49

When errors that cannot be ignored display you must take action. They force you to stop and fix the situation. In some cases you can resolve the error if it gives you an option, in other cases you have to cancel and try again.

Warnings (such as the one shown in Figure 2–50) display when something is wrong, but you can keep on working. In many cases, you can close the dialog box and fix the issue or wait and do it later.

Figure 2–50

- Click ▣ (Expand Warning Dialog) to open the dialog box as shown in Figure 2–51. You can expand each node in the box and select elements to show or delete.

If there are a lot of warnings to review, you can click Export... and save an HTML report to review separately.

Figure 2–51

- Sometimes issues that create warnings are dealt with as you continue working on a project. If numerous warnings have been ignored you might want to check the project and deal with each of the warnings individually.

- When you select an element for which there has been a warning, ⚠ (Show Related Warnings) displays in the Ribbon. It opens a dialog box in which you can review the warning(s) related to the selected element. You can also display a list of all of the warnings in the project by clicking

  ⚠ (Review Warnings) in the *Manage* tab>Inquiry panel.

Interference Checking

Interference Checking can be used when there are potential overlaps between disciplines, such as the structural column and ducts shown in Figure 2–52.

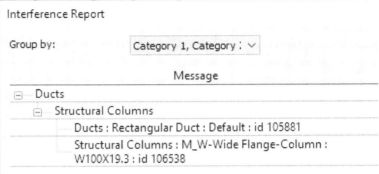

Figure 2–52

- Typical items to check include structural elements against architectural columns, walls, door or window openings, floors and roofs, specialty equipment and floors, and any elements in a linked file with the host file.

- For more complex projects and those that include files from other software, the Navisworks software provides a much more powerful solution than this basic interference checking.

How To: Run an Interference Check

1. In the *Collaborate* tab>Coordinate panel, expand (Interference Check) and click (Run Interference Check).

   - To filter out unneeded elements, select the elements first and then run the interference check.

2. In the Interference Check dialog box, as shown in Figure 2–53, in the *Categories From* drop-down list, select the projects that you want to compare. This can be the same project or any linked projects.

Select only the categories that you need to review. In a large project, selecting all categories can take a very long time to process.

Figure 2–53

3. Select the element types that you want to compare.
4. Click **OK**.
5. If there are interferences, the Interference Report dialog box opens as shown in Figure 2–54.

Figure 2–54

6. To see the elements that are interfering, select an element in the list and click **Show**.
7. If you need to create a report that can be viewed by other users, click **Export...**. This creates an HTML file listing the conflicts.
8. The dialog box can remain open while you make changes or you can click **Close** and then expand (Interference Check) and click (Show Last Report) to see the report again.
9. In the Interference Report dialog box, click **Refresh** to display any changes.
10. Refreshing the report only reviews the elements selected when the report was first run. If you need to select other elements, run a new report.

Chapter Review Questions

1. What is the purpose of an alignment line?

   a. Displays when the new element you are placing or modeling is aligned with the grid system.

   b. Indicates that the new element you are placing or modeling is aligned with an existing element.

   c. Displays when the new element you are placing or modeling is aligned with a selected tracking point.

   d. Indicates that the new element is aligned with true north rather than project north.

2. When you are modeling (not editing) a linear element, how do you edit the temporary dimension shown in Figure 2–55?

Figure 2–55

   a. Select the temporary dimension and enter a new value.

   b. Type a new value and press <Enter>.

   c. Type a new value in the Distance/Length box in the Options Bar and press <Enter>.

3. How do you select all the doors of various sizes, but no other elements in a view?

   a. In the Project Browser, select the *Door* category.

   b. Select one door, right-click and select **Select All Instances>Visible in View**.

   c. Select all of the elements in the view and use ▽ (Filter) to clear the other categories.

   d. Select one door, and click ▣ (Select Multiple) in the ribbon.

Command Summary

Button	Command	Location
Draw Tools		
	Center-ends Arc	• **Ribbon:** *Modify	(various linear elements)* tab>Draw panel
	Circle	• **Ribbon:** *Modify	(various linear elements)* tab>Draw panel
	Circumscribed Polygon	• **Ribbon:** *Modify	(various linear elements)* tab>Draw panel
	Ellipse	• **Ribbon:** *Modify	Place Lines, Place Detail Lines, and various boundary sketches*>Draw panel
	Ellipse Arc	• **Ribbon:** *Modify	Place Lines, Place Detail Lines, and various boundary sketches*>Draw panel
	Fillet Arc	• **Ribbon:** *Modify	(various linear elements)* tab>Draw panel
	Inscribed Polygon	• **Ribbon:** *Modify	(various linear elements)* tab>Draw panel
	Line	• **Ribbon:** *Modify	(various linear elements)* tab>Draw panel
	Pick Faces	• **Ribbon:** *Modify	Place Wall*> Draw panel
	Pick Lines	• **Ribbon:** *Modify	(various linear elements)* tab>Draw panel
	Pick Walls	• **Ribbon:** *Modify	(various boundary sketches)*>Draw panel
	Rectangle	• **Ribbon:** *Modify	(various linear elements)* tab>Draw panel
	Spline	• **Ribbon:** *Modify	Place Lines, Place Detail Lines, and various boundary sketches*>Draw panel
	Start-End-Radius Arc	• **Ribbon:** *Modify	(various linear elements)* tab>Draw panel
	Tangent End Arc	• **Ribbon:** *Modify	(various linear elements)* tab>Draw panel
Select Tools		
	Drag elements on selection	• **Ribbon:** All tabs>Expanded Select panel • **Status Bar**
	Filter	• **Ribbon:** *Modify	Multi-Select* tab> Filter panel • **Status Bar**

	Select Elements By Face	• **Ribbon**: All tabs>Expanded Select panel • **Status Bar**
	Select Links	• **Ribbon**: All tabs>Expanded Select panel • **Status Bar**
	Select Pinned Elements	• **Ribbon**: All tabs>Expanded Select panel • **Status Bar**
	Select Underlay Elements	• **Ribbon**: All tabs>Expanded Select panel • **Status Bar**

Additional Tools

	Aligned Dimension	• **Ribbon**: *Modify* tab>Measure panel • Quick Access Toolbar
	Detail Line	• **Ribbon**: *Annotate* tab>Detail panel • **Shortcut**: DL
	Interference Check	• **Ribbon**: *Collaborate* tab>Coordinate panel
	Model Line	• **Ribbon**: *Architectural* tab>Model panel • **Shortcut**: LI
	Properties	• **Ribbon**: *Modify* tab>Properties panel> Properties • **Shortcut**: PP
	Reference Plane	• **Ribbon**: *Architecture/Structure/ Systems* tab> Work Plane panel
	Review Warnings	• **Ribbon**: *Manage* tab>Inquiry panel> Review Warnings

Working in a Model

Views are the cornerstone of working with Autodesk® Revit® models as they enable you to see the model in both 2D and 3D. As you are working, you can duplicate and change views to display different information based on the same view of the model. Accurate schedules and views (callouts, elevations, and sections) are important tools for reviewing and creating construction documents.

Learning Objectives in This Chapter

- Change the way elements display in different views to show required information and set views for construction documents.
- Duplicate views so that you can modify the display as you are creating the model and for construction documents.
- Create callout views of parts of plans, sections, or elevations for detailing.
- Add building and interior elevations that can be used to demonstrate how a building will be built.
- Create building and wall sections to help you create the model and to include in construction documents.
- Modify schedule content including the instance and type properties of related elements.
- Add schedules to sheets as part of the construction documents.

3.1 Modifying the View Display

Views are powerful tools that enable you to create multiple versions of a model without having to recreate building elements. For example, you can have views that are specifically used for working on the model, while other views are annotated and used for construction documents. Different disciplines can have different views that show only the features they require, as shown in Figure 3–1. Properties of one view can be independent of the properties in other views.

Architectural

Mechanical

Figure 3–1

The view display can be modified in the following locations:

- View Control Bar
- Properties
- Shortcut menu
- Visibility/Graphic Overrides dialog box

View Properties

The most basic properties of a view are accessed using the View Control Bar, shown in Figure 3–2. These include the *Scale*, *Detail Level*, and *Visual Style* options. Additional options include temporary overrides and other advanced settings.

1/8" = 1'-0"

Figure 3–2

- The **Detail Level** controls whether you see schematic elements (Coarse or Medium Detail) or full scale elements (Fine Detail), as shown in Figure 3–3.

Coarse or Medium   *Fine*

Figure 3–3

Other modifications to views are available in Properties, as shown in Figure 3–4. These properties include *Underlays* and *View Range* as well as many others. The *Discipline* and *Sub-Discipline* of a view can also be set here. This is especially important for MEP projects.

The options in Properties vary according to the type of view. A plan view has different properties than a 3D view.

Figure 3–4

Setting an Underlay

Setting an *Underlay* is helpful if you need to display elements on a different level, such as the basement plan shown with an underlay of the first floor plan in Figure 3–5. You can then use the elements to trace over or even copy to the current level of the view.

Underlays are only available in Floor Plan and Ceiling Plan views.

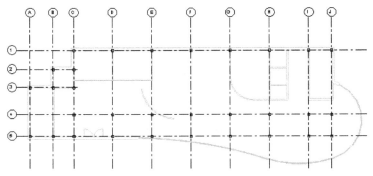

Figure 3–5

In Properties in the *Underlay* area, specify the *Range: Base Level* and the *Range: Top Level*. You can also specify the Underlay Orientation to **Look down** or **Look up**, as shown in Figure 3–6.

Figure 3–6

- To prevent moving elements in the underlay by mistake, in the Select panel, expand the panel title, and clear **Select underlay elements**. You can also toggle this on/off using

  ⟲ (Select Underlay Elements) in the Status Bar.

Setting the View Range

The View Range controls the cut planes that control the visibility of plan views, as shown in the Sample View Range key in Figure 3–7. Elements outside the cut planes do not display unless you include an underlay.

View Range

Sample View Range

Key

1: Primary Range Top
2: Primary Range Cut plane
3: Primary Range Bottom
4: View Depth Level
5: Primary Range
6: View Depth
7: View Range

Figure 3–7

How To: Set the View Range

1. In Properties, in the *Extents* area, beside *View Range*, select **Edit...** or type **VR**.
2. In the View Range dialog box, as shown in Figure 3–8, modify the Levels and Offsets for the *Primary Range* and *View Depth.*
   - Click **<<Show** to display the Sample View Range key.
3. Click **OK**.

Figure 3–8

- If the settings used cannot be represented graphically, a warning displays, stating the inconsistency.

- A Reflected Ceiling Plan (RCP) is created, as if the ceiling is reflected by a mirror on the floor, so that the ceiling is the same orientation as the floor plan. The cutline is placed just below the ceiling to ensure that any windows and doors below do not display.

Setting the Discipline of a View

Disciplines are frequently used with MEP projects.

Many times when you duplicate or create a view it will not be in the expected grouping in the Project Browser. The view properties of *Discipline* and *Sub-Discipline*, as shown in Figure 3–9, control the visibility of some elements and applies grouping in the Project Browser. For example, you can separate the Plumbing Plans from the Fire Plumbing plans, as shown in Figure 3–10.

Figure 3–9

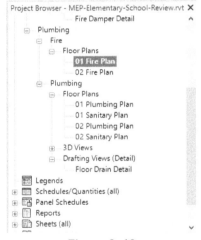

Figure 3–10

- You can add additional sub-disciplines by typing in a new name but the list of disciplines is set by the software.

Hiding and Overriding Graphics

Two common ways to customize a view are to:

- Hide individual elements or categories

- Modify how graphics display for elements or categories (e.g., altering lineweight, color, or pattern)

An element is an individual item such as one wall in a view, while a category includes all instances of a selected element, such as all walls in a view.

In the example shown in Figure 3–11, a Furniture Plan has been created by toggling off the structural grids category, and then graying out all of the walls and columns.

Figure 3–11

How To: Hide Elements or Categories in a View

1. Select the elements or categories you want to hide.
2. Right-click and select **Hide in View>Elements** or **Hide in View>Category**, as shown in Figure 3–12.
3. A quick way to hide entire categories is to select an element(s) and type **VH**.

The elements or categories are hidden in current view only.

Figure 3–12

How To: Override Graphics of Elements or Categories in a View

1. Select the element(s) you want to modify.
2. Right-click and select **Override Graphics in View>By Element** or **By Category**. The View-Specific Element (or Category) Graphics dialog box opens, as shown in Figure 3–13.

The exact options in the dialog box vary depending on the type of elements selected.

Figure 3–13

Select the changes you want to make and click **OK**.

View-Specific Options

- Clearing the **Visible** option is the same as hiding the elements or categories.

- Selecting the **Halftone** option grays out the elements or categories.

- The options for *Projection Lines* and *Cut Lines* include **Weight**, **Color**, and **Pattern**. The options for *Surface Patterns* and *Cut Patterns* include **Visibility**, **Pattern**, and **Color** for the Foreground and Background, as shown in Figure 3–13.

- **Surface Transparency** can be set by moving the slider bar, as shown in Figure 3–14.

Figure 3–14

- The View-Specific Category Graphics dialog box includes **Open the Visibility Graphics dialog...**, which opens the full dialog box of options.

The Visibility/Graphic Overrides Dialog Box

The options in the Visibility/Graphic Overrides dialog box (shown in Figure 3–15) control how every category and sub-category of elements is displayed per view. You can toggle categories on and off, override the *Projection/Surface* and *Cut* information, set categories to **Halftone**, and change the *Detail Level*.

Figure 3–15

To open the Visibility/Graphic Overrides dialog box, type **VV** or **VG**. It is also available in Properties: in the *Graphics* area, beside *Visibility/Graphic Overrides*, click **Edit...**.

- The Visibility/Graphic Overrides are divided into *Model*, *Annotation*, *Analytical Model*, *Imported,* and *Filters* categories.

- Other categories might be available if specific data has been included in the project, including *Design Options*, *Linked Files*, and *Worksets*.

- To limit the number of categories showing in the dialog box select a discipline from the *Filter list,* as shown in Figure 3–16.

Figure 3–16

- To help you select categories, use the **All**, **None**, and **Invert** buttons. The **Expand All** button displays all of the sub-categories.

Hint: Restoring Hidden Elements or Categories

If you have hidden categories, you can display them using the Visibility/Graphic Overrides dialog box. To display hidden elements, however, you must temporarily reveal the elements first.

1. In the View Control Bar, click ♀ (Reveal Hidden Elements). The border and all hidden elements are displayed in magenta, while visible elements in the view are grayed out, as shown in Figure 3–17.

Figure 3–17

2. Select the hidden elements you want to restore, right-click, and select **Unhide in View>Elements** or **Unhide in View>Category**. Alternatively, in the *Modify |* contextual tab>Reveal Hidden Elements panel, click ⌐ (Unhide Element) or ⊞ (Unhide Category).

3. When you are finished, in the View Control Bar, click ⌐ (Close Reveal Hidden Elements) or, in the *Modify |* contextual tab>Reveal Hidden Elements panel, click ⊠ (Toggle Reveal Hidden Elements Mode).

Using View Templates

A powerful way to use views effectively is to set up a view and then save it as a View Template. You can apply view templates to views - individually or through the Properties palette. Setting the View Template using the Properties palette helps to ensure that you do not accidentally modify the view while interacting with it.

How To: Create a View Template from a View

1. Set up a view, as needed.
2. In the Project Browser, right-click on the view and select **Create View Template from View**.
3. In the New View Template dialog box, type in a name and then click **OK**.
4. The new view template is listed in the View Templates dialog box. Make any modifications needed in the View properties section.
5. Click **OK**.

How To: Specify a View Template for a View

1. In the Project Browser, select the view or views to which you want to apply a view template.
2. In Properties, scroll down to the *Identity Data* section and click the button beside *View Template*.
3. In the Apply View Template dialog box, select the view template from the list, as shown in Figure 3–18.

Figure 3–18

4. Click **OK**.

- In the View Control Bar, use (Temporary View Properties) to temporarily apply a view template to a view.

3.2 Duplicating Views

Once you have created a model, you do not have to recreate the elements at different scales or copy them so that they can be used on more than one sheet. Instead, you can duplicate the required views and modify them to suit your needs.

Duplication Types

Duplicate creates a copy of the view that only includes the building elements, as shown in Figure 3–19. Annotation and detailing are not copied into the new view. Building model elements automatically change in all views, but view-specific changes made to the new view are not reflected in the original view.

Original   *Duplicate*

Figure 3–19

Duplicate with Detailing creates a copy of the view and includes all annotation and detail elements (such as tags), as shown in Figure 3–20. Any annotation or view-specific elements created in the new view are not reflected in the original view.

Original   *Duplicate with Detailing*

Figure 3–20

Duplicate as a Dependent creates a copy of the view and links it to the original (parent) view, as shown in the Project Browser in Figure 3–21. View-specific changes made to the overall view, such as changing the *Scale*, are also reflected in the dependent (child) views and vice-versa.

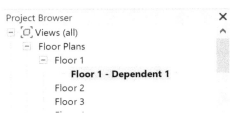

Figure 3–21

• Use dependent views when the building model is so large that you need to split the building onto separate sheets, while ensuring that the views are all same scale.

• If you want to separate a dependent view from the original view, right-click on the dependent view and select **Convert to independent view**.

How To: Create Duplicate Views

1. Open the view you want to duplicate.
2. In the *View* tab>Create panel, expand **Duplicate View** and select the type of duplicate view you want to create, as shown in Figure 3–22.

Most types of views can be duplicated.

Figure 3–22

- Alternatively, you can right-click on a view in the Project Browser and select the type of duplicate that you want to use, as shown in Figure 3–23.

Figure 3–23

- To rename a view, double-click on the view name slowly and the text highlights, as shown in Figure 3–24. You can also right-click on a view name and select **Rename...** or press <F2>.

Figure 3–24

Practice 3a

Duplicate Views in an Architectural Project

Practice Objectives

- Duplicate and rename views.
- Hide elements in views.
- Modify the graphic display of elements in views.

In this practice, you will duplicate views and then modify them by changing the scale, hiding some elements, and changing other elements to halftone to prepare them to be used in construction documents. The finished views of the second floor are shown in Figure 3–25.

Figure 3–25

Task 1 - Duplicate and modify the first floor plan view.

1. Open the project **Modern-Hotel-Display.rvt** from the practice files folder.

2. Close any other projects you may have open.

3. Open the **Floor Plans: Floor 1** view. This view includes a variety of tags.

4. In the Project Browser, right-click on the **Floor Plans: Floor 1** view and select **Duplicate View>Duplicate with Detailing**. This creates a view with all of the tags.

5. In the Project Browser, slowly double-click on the duplicated view name. Rename it **Floor 1 - Reference**. You will use this view later to place callouts and sections.

6. In the Project Browser, right-click on the **Floor Plans: Floor 1** view and select **Duplicate View>Duplicate**. This creates a view without all of the tags, but includes the grids and elevation markers.

7. Rename it to **Floor 1 - Overall**.

8. In the View Control Bar, change the *Scale* to **1/16"=1'-0"**. All of the annotations become larger, as they need to plot correctly at this scale.

9. Type **WT** to tile the 4 open windows and then **ZA** to zoom out to fit all the view in their new windows. Compare the various floor plans as shown in Figure 3–26.

Figure 3–26

10. Save the project.

Task 2 - Duplicate and modify a second floor plan view.

1. Type **TW** to return to the tab views.

2. Click on the X, as shown in Figure 3–27, to close the **Floor 1 - Reference** and **Floor 1 - Overall** views.

Figure 3–27

3. Open the **Floor Plans: Floor 2** view.

4. In the Project Browser, right-click on the same view and select **Duplicate View>Duplicate**. This creates a new view without any annotation.

5. Rename this view to **Typical Guest Room Floor Plan**.

6. Select one of the grids and one of the elevation markers and type **VH** (Hide in View Category).

7. Select one of the railings along the balconies. Right-click and select **Select All Instances>Visible in View**. The railings are selected as shown in Figure 3–28.

Figure 3–28

8. With all the railings selected, right-click again and select **Override Graphics in View>By Element....**

9. In the View Specific Element Graphics dialog box, select **Halftone** and click **OK**.

10. Click in an empty space in the view to release the selection. The railings are now gray and not as prominent.

11. Type **WT** to tile the four windows and then type **ZA** so the model displays fully in the view so that you can see the differences in the views.

12. Save and close the project.

Practice 3b

Duplicate Views in an MEP Project

Practice Objectives

- Duplicate views.
- Apply view filters.
- Modify the view display using the Visibility/Graphic Overrides dialog box.

In this practice, you will duplicate views and modify them using filters and Visibility/Graphic Overrides.

1. In the practice files folder, open **Views-School-MEP.rvt**.

2. In the Project Browser, right-click on the **3D Plumbing** view and select **Duplicate View>Duplicate**.

3. Right-click on the new view name and select **Rename**, or double-click on the new view name, and type **3D HVAC**.

4. In Properties, change the *Discipline* to **Mechanical** and the *Sub-Discipline* to **HVAC**, as shown in Figure 3–29. The view moves to this category in the Project Browser.

Figure 3–29

5. Open the Visibility/Graphic Overrides dialog box and in the *Filters* tab, uncheck anything that is checked and only select **Mechanical - Supply** and **Mechanical - Return**. Click **OK**.

6. Select one of the plumbing fixtures and type **VH** (for Hide category in view). Now only the HVAC systems display as shown in Figure 3–30.

Figure 3–30

7. Save and close the project.

Practice 3c | Duplicate Views in a Structural Project

Practice Objectives

- Duplicate and rename views.
- Change the view template.

In this practice, you will create an analytical view by duplicating a view and then applying an analytical view template that sets the view display, as shown in Figure 3–31.

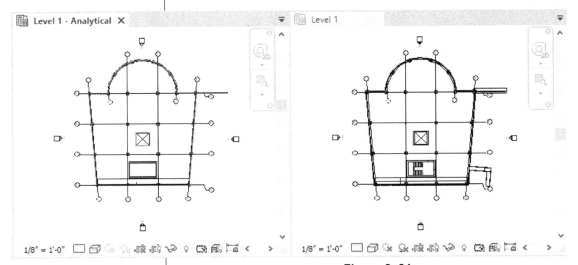

Figure 3–31

Task 1 - Duplicate views and apply a View Template.

1. Open **Views Practice.rvt** from the practice files folder, then open the **Structural Plans: Level 2** and **Structural Plans: Level 2 - Analytical** views to see the difference between the two views.

2. Close both of the **Level 2** views.

3. Right-click on **Level 1** and select **Duplicate View> Duplicate**.

4. In the Project Browser, rename the copy as **Level 1 - Analytical**.

5. Verify that only the two **Level 1** views are open and tile them. (Hint: Type **WT**.)

6. Zoom each view so that you can see the entire building. (Hint: Type **ZA**.)

7. Note that both of the views are the same, as shown in Figure 3–32.

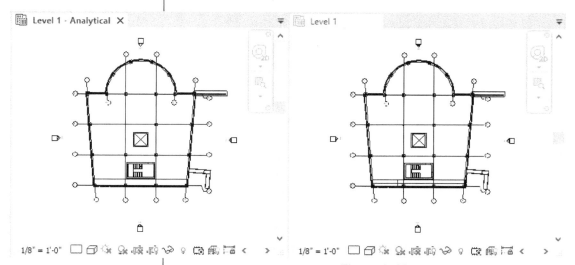

Figure 3–32

8. In the Project Browser, select the new **Level 1 - Analytical** view. Right-click and select **Apply Template Properties...**

9. In the Apply View Template dialog box, in the *Names* area select **Structural Analytical Stick** and click **OK**.

10. Zoom in on the view to see the analytical indicators, as shown in Figure 3–33.

Figure 3–33

11. Close the analytical view and maximize the **Level 1** view window.

12. Save and close the project.

3.3 Adding Callout Views

Callouts are details of plan, elevation, or section views. When you place a callout in a view, as shown in Figure 3–34, it automatically creates a new view clipped to the boundary of the callout, as shown in Figure 3–35. You can create rectangular or sketched callout boundaries.

Callout in a view	Callout view
Figure 3–34	Figure 3–35

- Callout views are saved in the same node in the Project Browser as the original view. For example, the callout view of a floor plan is placed within the Floor Plans node.

- To open the callout view, double-click on its name in the Project Browser or on the callout head (verify that the callout bubble is not selected before you double-click on it).

How To: Create a Rectangular Callout

1. In the *View tab>Create panel,* click ⌀ **(Callout)**.
2. Select points for two opposite corners to define the callout bubble around the area you want to detail.
3. Select the callout bubble and use the shape handles to modify the location of the bubble and any other edges that might need changing.
4. In the Project Browser, you can rename the callout view.

How To: Create a Sketched Callout

1. In the *View tab>Create panel,* expand ⬭ (Callout), and click
   ⬭ (Sketch).
2. Sketch the shape of the callout bubble using the tools in the
   Modify | Edit Profile tab>Draw panel, as shown in
   Figure 3–36.

Figure 3–36

3. Click ✓ (Finish) to complete the boundary.
4. Select the callout bubble and use the shape handles to
   modify the location of the bubble and any other edges that
   might need to be changed.
5. In the Project Browser, rename the callout.

Modifying Callouts

Callouts are cropped versions of the original view. When you
modify them you are changing the Crop Region of the view.

- If you change the size of the callout bubble in the original
  view, it automatically updates the callout view and vice-versa.

- Callouts can be reshaped. Select the callout bubble or crop
  region and, in the *Modify | Floor Plan* tab>Mode panel, click
  ⬭ (Edit Crop) and use the Draw tools to modify the sketch.

- If you want to return a sketched or modified callout or crop
  region to a rectangular configuration, click ⬭ (Reset Crop).

Working with Crop Regions

Plans, sections, elevations, and 3D views can all be modified by changing how much of the model is displayed in a view. One way to do this is to set the Model crop region. If there are dimensions, tags, or text near the crop region, you can also use the Annotation crop region to include these, as shown in Figure 3–37.

Figure 3–37

Zoom out if you do not see the crop region when you set it to be displayed.

- To display the crop region, in the View Control Bar, click ⌕ (Show Crop Region). Alternatively, in Properties, in the *Extents* area, select **Crop Region Visible**. **Annotation Crop** is also available in this area.

- It is best practice to hide a crop region before placing a view on a sheet. In the View Control Bar, click ⌕ (Hide Crop Region).

- Resize the crop region using the ○ control on each side of the region.

Breaking the crop region is typically used with sections or details.

- Click ∿ (Break Line) control to split the view into two regions, horizontally or vertically. Each part of the view can then be modified in size to display what is needed and be moved independently.

- The annotation crop region crops any annotation outside of the crop region and any annotations that it touches. If the model crop region crops an element that is tagged, the tag or annotation will automatically be cropped as well. You can turn on Annotation Crop and resize the crop region closer to the model crop region using the grip controls or by using the Crop Region Size dialog box, as shown in Figure 3–38. In the *Modify | Floor Plan* tab>Crop panel, click ⬐ (Size Crop) to open the dialog box.

Figure 3–38

Plan Regions

When you have a plan view with multiple levels of floors or ceilings, you can create plan regions that enable you to set a different view range for part of a view (as shown in Figure 3–39) for a set of clerestory windows.

Figure 3–39

How To: Create Plan Regions

1. In a plan view, in the *View* tab>Create panel, expand
    (Plan Views) and select (Plan Region).

2. In the *Modify | Create Plan Region Boundary* tab>Draw panel, select a draw tool and create the boundary for the plan region.

   - The boundary must be closed and cannot overlap other plan region boundaries, but the boundaries can be side by side.

3. Click (Finish Edit Mode).

4. In the *Modify | Plan Region* tab>Region panel, click (View Range).

5. In the View Range dialog box, specify the offsets for the plan region and click **OK**. The plan region is applied to the selected area.

- Plan regions can be copied to the clipboard and then pasted into other plan views.

- You can use shape handles to resize plan region boundaries without having to edit the boundary.

- If a plan region is above a door, the door swing displays, but the door opening does not display, as shown in Figure 3–40.

Figure 3–40

- Plan Regions can be toggled on and off in the Visibility/ Graphic Overrides dialog box on the *Annotation Categories* tab. If they are displayed, the plan regions are included when printing and exporting.

Hint: Depth Clipping and Far Clipping

Depth Clipping, shown in Figure 3–41, is a viewing option which sets how sloped walls are displayed if the *View Range* of a plan is set to a limited view.

Far Clipping (shown in Figure 3–42) is available for section and elevation views.

Figure 3–41   **Figure 3–42**

- An additional Graphic Display Option enables you to specify *Depth Cueing*, so that items that are in the distance will be made lighter.

Practice 3d

Add Callout Views in an Architectural Project

Practice Objectives

- Modify crop regions.
- Create callouts.
- Override visibility and graphic styles in views.

In this practice, you will create callout views of a guest room and make modifications to the visibility graphics so that one does not display the furniture and the other one does, as shown in Figure 3–43. You will also add callout views for other areas that need enlarged plans.

Figure 3–43

Task 1 - Modify the crop region of a view.

1. Open the project **Modern-Hotel-Callouts.rvt** from the practice files folder.

2. Open the **Floor Plans: Floor 1 - Overall** view.

3. In the View Control Bar, click ⊞ (Show Crop Region).

4. Select the crop region and drag the control on the top until the pool house displays, as shown in Figure 3–44.

5. Select one of the vertical grid lines and drag them so they are above the poolhouse, as shown in Figure 3–44.

Figure 3–44

6. In the View Control Bar, click ⬚ (Hide Crop Region).

7. Save the project.

Task 2 - Add callout views.

1. Open the **Floor Plans: Typical Guest Room Floor Plan** view.

2. Note that the *Scale* is set to **1/8" =1'-0"**.

3. In the *View* tab>Create panel, click ⬚ (Callout).

4. Place a callout around the guest room with furniture, as shown in Figure 3–45. Move the bubble as needed.

Guest room ———   **Callout** ———

Figure 3–45

5. Click in an empty space in the view to release the selection.

6. Double-click on the callout view bubble to display the view. Note that the *Scale* is automatically set to **1/4"= 1'-0"**, as it is a partial plan view.

7. Rename the view to **Typical Guest Room - Dimension Plan**.

8. Duplicate the callout view and rename it to **Typical Guest Room - Furniture Plan**.

9. Close all other views except the Dimension and Furniture Plans.

10. Type **WT** to tile the windows and **ZA** to zoom out in both of them, as shown in Figure 3–46.

Figure 3–46

11. Save the project.

Task 3 - Override graphics in views.

1. Click in the **Floor Plans: Typical Guest Room - Dimension Plan** view.

2. Open the Visibility/Graphic Overrides dialog box by typing **VV**.

3. In the dialog box, set the *Filter list* to **Architecture** (by clearing the checkmarks for the other options). In the *Visibility* column, clear **Casework**, **Furniture**, **Furniture Systems** (as shown in Figure 3–47) and **Plumbing Fixtures** (not shown).

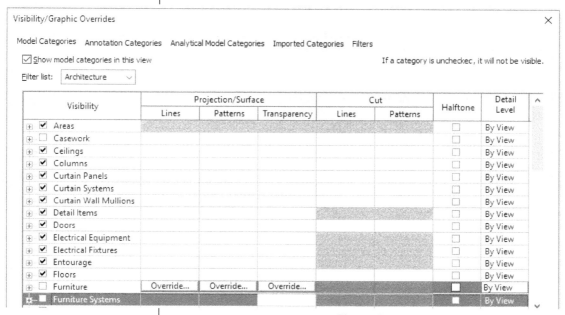

Figure 3–47

4. Click **OK**. The furniture is removed from the view.

5. Click in the **Floor Plans: Typical Guest Room - Furniture Plan** view.

6. Reopen the Visibility/Graphic Overrides dialog box. Below the table, click **All** and place a checkmark in one of the *Halftone* columns. All of the elements are set to halftone.

7. Click **None** to clear all categories.

8. In the *Halftone* column, clear the **Casework**, **Furniture**, **Furniture Systems**, and **Plumbing Fixtures** categories.

9. Click **Apply** to set the changes without exiting the dialog box.

10. In the *Annotation Categories* tab, clear **Show annotation categories in this view**. No annotations elements will display in this view even if they are added in other views of this part of the model.

11. Click **OK** to close the dialog box. The view should display with all existing elements in halftone, as shown in Figure 3–48.

Figure 3–48

12. Save the project.

Task 4 - Additional callouts.

1. Open the **Floor Plans: Floor 1 - Reference** view.

2. In the *View* tab>Create panel, click ⌀ (Callout) and add callouts to the stairs and restrooms. Name the views as shown in Figure 3–49.

Figure 3–49

- The view has been simplified for clarity.

3. Save and close the project.

Practice 3e

Add Callout Views in an MEP Project

Practice Objectives

- Create callouts.
- Adjust crop region display.

In this practice, you will create a callout view of one wing of the building. In the new callout view, you will then create an additional callout view, as shown in Figure 3–50.

Figure 3–50

1. In the practice files folder, open **Callout-School-MEP.rvt**.

2. Open the Mechanical>HVAC>Floor Plans>**01 Mechanical Plan** view.

3. In the *View* tab>Create panel, expand ⊙ (Callout) and select 🖉 (Sketch).

4. Sketch a boundary similar to that shown in Figure 3–51.

Figure 3–51

5. Click (Finish Edit Mode). Use the blue grip controls to move the bubble as shown in Figure 3–52.

Figure 3–52

6. In the Project Browser, double-click on the new callout view to open it. Rename the callout **01 Mechanical Plan-Area A**.

• In the View Control Bar, notice that the *Scale* is automatically increased to be two times the previous view.

7. In the View Control Bar, click ⬛ (Hide Crop Region).

8. In the *View* tab>Create panel, click ⌀ (Callout).

9. Draw a callout box around one set of two classrooms and move the bubble as shown in Figure 3–53.

Figure 3–53

10. In the Project Browser, rename the new callout **Typical Classroom Mechanical**. Open the view and you can see that the scale was doubled again from the previous callout view.

11. Reopen the **01 Mechanical Plan** view. Note that the larger callout displays, but the second callout created does not.

12. Save and close the project.

Practice 3f

Add Callout Views in a Structural Project

Practice Objective

- Create callouts.

In this practice, you will create a callout view of the elevator pit walls, as shown in Figure 3–54.

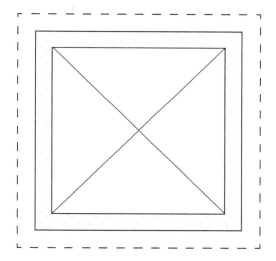

Figure 3–54

1. Open **Callouts Practice.rvt** from the practice files folder.

2. Ensure that you are in the **Structural Plans: Level 1** view.

3. In the View Control Bar, check the *Scale* and *Detail Level* of the view, as shown in Figure 3–55.

1/8" = 1'-0"

Figure 3–55

4. In the *View* tab>Create panel, click ⬚ (Callout).

5. Draw a callout around the elevator pit walls, as shown in Figure 3–56. Move the callout head as needed.

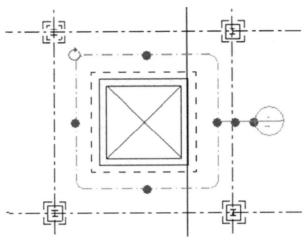

Figure 3–56

6. In the Project Browser, in the *Structural Plans* area, rename *Level 1- Callout* as **Elevator Pit Enlarged Plan**.

7. Open the view to display the callout.

8. In the View Control Bar, set the *Scale* to **1/4"=1'-0"** and the *Detail Level* to **Fine**.

9. In the View Control Bar, click 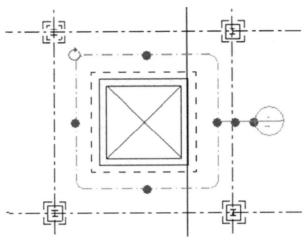 (Hide Crop Region).

10. Return to the **Level 1** view.

11. Save and close the project.

3.4 Creating Elevations and Sections

Elevations and sections are critical elements of construction documents and can assist you as you are working on a model. Any changes made in one of these views (such as the section in Figure 3–57), changes the entire model and any changes made to the project model are also displayed in the elevations and sections.

Figure 3–57

- In the Project Browser, elevations are separated by elevation type and sections are separated by section type, as shown in Figure 3–58.

Figure 3–58

- To open an elevation or section view, double-click on the marker arrow or on its name in the Project Browser.

- To give the elevation or section a new name, in the Project Browser, slowly double-click on the name or right-click on it and select **Rename...**.

Elevations

Elevations are *face-on* views of the interiors and exteriors of a building. Four Exterior Elevation views are defined in the default template: **North**, **South**, **East**, and **West**. You can create additional building elevation views at other angles or interior elevation views, as shown in Figure 3–59.

Figure 3–59

- Elevations markers must be placed in plan views.

- A framing elevation is set up to only capture framing elements that are behind other model elements in an elevation of a building.
    - By default, the framing elevation snaps and sets the extents along the grid lines by using **Attach to Grid** in the Options Bar.

- The most common use for a framing elevation is to generate braced frames and shear wall elevations.

- When you add an elevation or section to a sheet, the detail and sheet number are automatically added to the view title and elevation/section marker.

How To: Create an Elevation

1. In the *View* tab>Create panel, expand (Elevation) and click (Elevation).
2. In the Type Selector, select the elevation type. Two types come with the templates: **Building Elevation** and **Interior Elevation**.
3. Move the cursor near one of the walls that defines the elevation. The marker follows the angle of the wall.
4. Click to place the marker.

- The length, width, and height of an elevation are defined by the walls and ceiling/floor at which the elevation marker is pointing.

- When creating interior elevations, ensure that the floor or ceiling above is in place before creating the elevation or you will need to modify the elevation crop region so that the elevation markers do not show on all floors.

How To: Create Framing Elevations

1. Open a plan view.
2. In the *View* tab>Create panel, expand (Elevation) and click (Framing Elevation).
3. Hover the cursor over a grid line to display an elevation marker, as shown in Figure 3–60. Click to place the marker.

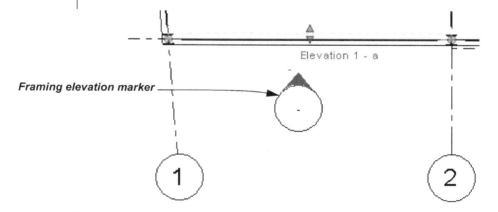

Framing elevation marker

Elevation 1 - a

Figure 3–60

Framing Elevations are listed in the Project Browser in the Elevations (Framing Elevation) area.

4. Click (Modify) and select the marker. The extents focus on the bracing bay only. You can use the round segment handles to expand the length of the elevation, as needed.

Sections

Sections are slices through a model. You can create a section through an entire building or through one wall for a detail. Sections can be created in plan, elevation, and other section views. You can flip, resize, or split a section. Figure 3–61 shows all the components of a section marker.

Cycle selection head

Section marker

Flip section

Shape controls

Gap in segment

Section line

Section crop region

Segment handle

Figure 3–61

How To: Create a Section

1. In the *View* tab>Create panel or in the Quick Access Toolbar, click (Section).

2. In the Type Selector, select **Section: Building Section** or **Section: Wall Section.** If you want a section in a Drafting view select **Detail View: Detail.**

3. In the view, select a point where you want to locate the crop region and section marker.

4. Select the second or end point that defines the section.
5. The shape controls display. You can flip the arrow and change the size of the cutting plane, as well as the location of the bubble and flag.

- When placing a section you can snap to other elements in the model as the start and end points of the section line. You can also use the Align command to reorient a section line to an element such as an angled wall.

- Section lines can also be used as an alignment object and can be snapped to when placing other geometry.

Modifying Elevations and Sections

There are two parts to modifying elevations and sections:

- To modify the markers (as shown in Figure 3–62), use the controls to change the length and depth of elevations and sections. There are other specific type options as well.

- To modify the view (as shown in Figure 3–63), use the controls to modify the size or create view breaks.

Figure 3–62

Figure 3–63

Modifying Elevation Markers

When you modify elevation markers, you can specify the length and depth of the clip plane, as shown in Figure 3–64.

- Select the arrowhead of the elevation marker (not the circle portion) to display the clip plane.

- Drag the round shape handles to lengthen or shorten the elevation.

- Adjust the ⏶⏷ (Drag) controls to modify the depth of the elevation.

To display additional interior elevations from one marker, select the circle portion (not the arrowhead) and place a checkmark in the Show Arrow box in the directions that you want to display, as shown in Figure 3–64.

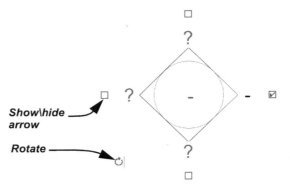

Figure 3–64

- Use the ↺ (Rotate) control to angle the marker (i.e., for a room with angled walls).

Modifying Section Markers

When you modify section markers, various shape handles and controls enable you to modify a section, as shown in Figure 3–65.

Figure 3–65

- Adjust the ▲▼ (Drag) controls to change the length and depth of the cut plane.

- Drag the segment handle controls at either end of the section line to change the location of the arrow or flag without changing the cut boundary.

- Click ‹› (Flip Section) to change the direction of the arrowhead, which also flips the entire section.

- Click ↻ (Cycle Section Head/Tail) to switch between an arrowhead, flag, or nothing on each end of the section.

- Click ↰ (Gaps in Segments) to create an opening in section lines, as shown in Figure 3–66. Select it again to restore the full section cut.

Figure 3–66

How To: Add a Jog to a Section Line

1. Select the section line you want to modify.

2. In the *Modify | Views* tab> Section panel, click ⬚ (Split Segment).

3. Select the point along the section line where you want to create the split, as shown in Figure 3–67.

4. Specify the location of the split line, as shown in Figure 3–68.

Figure 3–67   Figure 3–68

- If you need to adjust the location of any segment on the section line, modify it and drag the shape handles along each segment of the line, as shown in Figure 3–69.

Figure 3–69

To bring a split section line back into place, use the shape handle to drag the jogged line until it is at the same level with the rest of the line.

3D Section Views

There are two ways you can create section views of your 3D model: creating a selection box, as shown in Figure 3–70, and orienting to a view. Both of these are very helpful as you are working and also can be used in construction documents and presentations.

Figure 3–70

How To: Create a Selection Box

1. In a 3D view, select the elements you want to isolate. In the example shown in Figure 3–70, the front wall was selected.

2. In the *Modify* tab>View panel, click (Selection Box) or type **BX**.
3. The view is limited to a box around the selected item(s).
4. Use the controls of the Section Box to modify the size of the box to show exactly what you want.

- To toggle off a section box and restore the full model, in the view's Properties, in the *Extents* area, clear the check from **Section Box**.

How To: Orient a 3D View to a View

1. Open a 3D view.
2. Right-click on the ViewCube and select **Orient to View>Floor Plans, Elevations, Sections,** or **3D Views**, as shown in Figure 3–71, and select the view from the list.

Figure 3–71

3. The view displays as shown, in the partial floor plan view of a stair, in Figure 3–72. Use the 3D view rotation tools to navigate around the 3D model, as shown in Figure 3–73.

Figure 3–72

Figure 3–73

- **Orient to a Direction** allows you to rotate the view to a specific direction, as shown in Figure 3–74. This is similar to using the orientation planes of the ViewCube.

Figure 3–74

- **Orient to a Plane** opens the Select Orientation Plane dialog box and allows you to specify a Level, Grid, or named Reference Plane, or pick a plane or a line, as shown in Figure 3–75. The view is not cut at the plane but oriented in that direction.

Figure 3–75

Practice 3g

Create Elevations and Sections in an Architectural Project

Practice Objectives

- Create exterior and interior elevations.
- Add building sections and wall sections.

In this practice, you will create exterior elevations of the poolhouse and interior elevations of the restrooms. You will also add building sections, as shown in Figure 3–76, and several wall sections to the project.

Figure 3–76

Task 1 - Add exterior elevations.

1. Open the project **Modern-Hotel-Elevations.rvt** from the practice files folder.

2. Open the **Floor Plans: Floor 1 Overall** view.

3. In the View Control Bar, click ⬚ (Show Crop Region).

4. Ensure that there is enough space above the pool house to add an elevation mark at this scale, if not, move the crop region up.

5. In the *View* tab>Create panel, expand ⬆ (Elevation) and click ⬆ (Elevation). In the Type Selector, select **Elevation: Building Elevation**.

6. Place an elevation marker outside of the pool building, as shown in Figure 3–77.

Figure 3–77

7. Click ⬚ (Modify) and select the arrowhead on the new elevation marker.

8. Change the length and depth of the elevation crop region to just be around the poolhouse, as shown in Figure 3–78.

Grids are hidden to clarify the view.

Figure 3–78

9. Double-click on the arrowhead to open the elevation view.

10. In the elevation view, use the crop region segment handles to change the crop region so that the height is up to **Floor 3** and the bottom is just below the floor line. Bring the sides in close to the pool building.

11. Hide the grids and levels so that the elevation is similar to that shown in Figure 3–79.

Figure 3–79

12. Click ⊞ (Hide Crop Region).

In this project, North is considered the top of the project.

13. In the Project Browser, in the *Elevations (Building Elevation)* area), rename the elevation (Elevation 1 -a if you selected this direction first) as **Pool-North**.

14. Return to the **Floor Plans: Floor 1 Overall** view.

15. Add elevation markers to the other sides of the poolhouse.

16. Open the new elevations. Resize and rename them as needed.

17. Save the project.

Task 2 - Add interior elevations.

1. Open the **Floor Plans: Floor 1 - Restrooms** view.

2. Select the floor that shows the floor drain slopes and hide it.

3. In the *View* tab>Create panel, click ⬆ (Elevation).

4. In the Type Selector, select **Elevation: Interior Elevation**.

5. Place an elevation in both of the restrooms.

6. Click ⌖ (Modify and select the circle part of one of the elevation markers and check each of the boxes, as shown in Figure 3–80. This places an elevation in each direction.

Figure 3–80

7. Repeat for the other restroom.

8. In the Project Browser, under *Elevations (Interior Elevation)*, rename the top restroom elevations as **Men's Restroom-North**, **South**, **East**, **West** and the bottom restroom elevations as **Women's Restroom-North**, **South**, **East**, **West**.

9. Select all of the elevation marker arrows (not the circles) and, in Properties, set the *Hide at scales coarser than* to **1/4"=1'-0"**, as shown in Figure 3–81.

Doing this keeps these markers from showing up in other plans at larger scales.

Figure 3–81

10. Open the elevation **Men's Restroom-East**. The interior elevation should automatically stop at the boundaries of the walls and ceiling.

11. If the elevation is not bounded as expected, move the crop region so that it is tight against the walls, as shown in Figure 3–82.

Figure 3–82

12. Save the project.

Task 3 - Clean up a view and add building sections.

1. Open the **Floor Plans: Floor 1 - Reference** view.

2. Select the crop region and drag it below the poolhouse. Drag the annotation crop region down as needed.

3. Type **ZA** (Zoom All To Fit) to zoom out to the extents of the view.

4. In the *View* tab>Create panel, click ⌐ (Section).

5. In the Type Selector, select **Section: Building Section**.

6. Draw a horizontal section and a vertical section through the building, as shown in Figure 3–83.

North-South section   **East-West section**

Figure 3–83

7. In the Project Browser, under *Sections (Building Section)*, rename them to **East-West Section** and **North-South Section**.

8. View each of the building sections.

Task 4 - Add wall sections.

You are using the ***Floor 2*** *view to place the wall sections, as you want to ensure they go through certain features, such as doors and windows.*

1. Open the **Floor Plans: Floor 2** view.

2. Adjust the crop region so the poolhouse is not showing.

3. Type **ZA** (Zoom All To Fit) to zoom out to the extents of the view.

4. In the *View* tab>Create panel, click ⃔ (Section). In the Type Selector, select **Section: Wall Section**.

5. Draw four wall sections, as shown in Figure 3–84. Ensure that the front wall section passes through a window and the back wall section passes through a door.

Figure 3–84

6. Move any annotation elements so they do not interfere with the section cut.

7. View each of the wall sections.

8. Save and close the project.

Practice 3h

Create Elevations and Sections in an MEP Project

Practice Objectives

- Create exterior and interior elevations.
- Add building sections and wall sections.
- Apply a view template.

In this practice, you will create building and wall sections, as well as exterior and interior elevations, to show mechanical fixtures. Then, you will apply a view template to apply preset settings.

1. In the practice files folder, open **Elevations-School-MEP.rvt**.

2. Open the Mechanical>HVAC>Floor Plans>**01 Mechanical Plan** view.

3. In the *View* tab>Create panel, click ⟍ (Section).

4. In the Type Selector, select **Section: Building Section**.

5. Draw a section through the north wing, as shown in Figure 3–85.

Figure 3–85

6. Press <Esc> and then double-click on the section marker to open the section view.

7. Expand the crop region so that the first floor and the full height of the roof is displayed, as shown in Figure 3–86.

Figure 3–86

8. In the Project Browser, expand Mechanical>????>Sections (Building Section) and rename the new section **North Wing - HVAC**.

9. Right-click on the new section and select **Apply Template Properties**.

10. In the Apply View Template dialog box, select **Mechanical Section** and click **OK**.

11. In the 01 Mechanical Plan view, draw several other sections.

12. In the Project Browser, rename the sections and apply the **Mechanical Section** view template.

13. Save and close the project.

Practice 3i

Create Elevations and Sections in a Structural Project

Practice Objectives

- Add building sections and wall sections.
- Add a framing elevation.

In this practice, you will add a Building Section and a Wall Section to an existing project. You will also add a Framing Elevation as shown in Figure 3–87.

Figure 3–87

Task 1 - Create sections.

1. Open **Sections Practice.rvt** from the practice files folder.

2. In the Project Browser, open the **Structural Plans: Level 1** view.

3. In the *View* tab>Create panel or in the Quick Access Toolbar, click ⚲ (Section).

4. Place a vertical section offset slightly from the middle, between grids 2 and 3. Change the width of the section using the shape controls, as shown in Figure 3–88.

Shape control

Figure 3–88

5. In the Project Browser, expand *Sections (Building Section)*. Right-click on the new section and rename it **Building Section A**, as shown in Figure 3–89.

Figure 3–89

6. Open the new section by double-clicking on its name in the Project Browser. The entire Building displays as shown in Figure 3–90. Note that the view varies based on exactly where you placed the section.

Figure 3–90

7. Select the crop region and use the controls to shorten the section so that the curved walls to the left do not display, as shown in Figure 3–91.

Figure 3–91

8. Return to the Level 1 view. The boundary of the section has changed, as shown on the left in Figure 3–92. Use the segment control to move the section markers head down, as shown on the right in Figure 3–92.

Segment control

Before   After

Figure 3–92

9. Start the **Section** command again.

10. In the Type Selector, select **Section: Wall Section**.

11. Draw a short section through the wall as shown in Figure 3–93. Modify the section boundary so that it does not touch anything other than the wall.

Section boundary

Figure 3–93

12. In the Project Browser, expand *Sections (Wall Section)* and rename the section **Foundation Section**.

13. Open the new section view.

14. In the View Control Bar, change the *Scale* to **1/2"=1'-0"**.

15. By default, the section expands the entire height of the project. Use the controls to resize the section so that only the foundation displays as shown in Figure 3–94.

Figure 3–94

Task 2 - Add a framing elevation.

1. Open the **Structural Plans: Level 1** view.

2. Zoom in on the south wall of the building between grids D2 and D3.

3. In the *View* tab>Create panel, expand ⬆ (Elevation) and click ⚬ (Framing Elevation).

4. Hover the cursor over Grid D as shown in Figure 3–95. Pick a point when the framing elevation marker displays on the outside of the building.

Framing elevation marker

Grids : Grid : D

Figure 3–95

5. In the Project Browser, in the *Elevations (Framing Elevation)* area, rename the view as **Typical Bracing**.

6. Click on the arrowhead of the elevation marker to show the boundary. Using the controls, lengthen the elevation boundary so that it is just on each side of the columns, as shown in Figure 3–96.

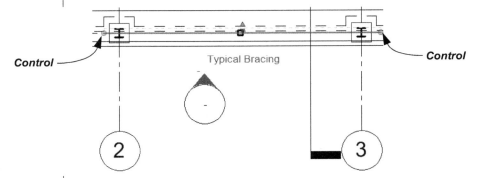

Control

Typical Bracing

Control

Figure 3–96

7. Open the framing elevation and in the View Control Bar, change the *Detail Level* to ▨ (Fine).

8. Modify the size of the elevation to only display the bracing as shown in Figure 3–97.

Figure 3–97

9. Return to the **Structural Plans: Level 1** view.

10. Zoom out to display the entire building.

11. In the Quick Access Toolbar, click ⬚ (Close Hidden Windows).

12. Save and close the project.

3.5 Working with Schedules

Schedules extract information from a project and display it in table form. Each schedule is stored as a separate view and can be placed on sheets, as shown in Figure 3–98. Any changes you make to the project elements that affect the schedules are automatically updated in both views and sheets.

Figure 3–98

- The Architectural Template (**Default.rte**) does not include any schedules. The **Construction-Default.rte**, **Residential-Default.rte**, and **Commercial-Default.rte** template files do include useful schedules.

How To: Work with Schedules

1. In the Project Browser, expand the *Schedules/Quantities* area, as shown in Figure 3–99, and double-click on the schedule you want to open.

Figure 3–99

2. Schedules are automatically filled out with the information stored in the instance and type parameters of related elements that are added to the model.
3. Fill out additional information in either the schedule or Properties.
4. From the *Modify Schedule | Quantities* tab>Appearance panel, you can select ▦ (Freeze Header) to keep the header row visible while you scroll through the schedule.
5. When selecting on a schedule's row, it will highlight in blue.
6. Drag and drop the schedule onto a sheet.

- You can zoom in to read small text in schedule views. Hold down the <Ctrl> key and scroll using the mouse wheel or press **<Ctrl>+<+>** to zoom in or **<Ctrl>+<->** to zoom out.

Modifying Schedules

Information in schedules is bi-directional:

- Make changes to elements and the schedule automatically updates.

- Make changes to information in the schedule cells and the elements automatically update.

How To: Modify Schedule Cells

1. Open the schedule view.
2. Select the cell you want to change. Some cells have drop-down lists, as shown in Figure 3–100. Others have edit fields.

If you change a Type Property in the schedule, it applies to all elements of that type. If you change an Instance Property, it only applies to that one element.

<Door Schedule>			
A	B	C	D
Mark	Type	Width	Height
101	36" x 84"	3' - 0"	7' - 0"
103	24" x 82"	3' - 0"	6' - 8"
104	30" x 80"	3' - 0"	6' - 8"
105	30" x 8...	3' - 0"	6' - 8"
106	32" x 84"	3' - 0"	6' - 8"
107	36" x 80"	3' - 0"	6' - 8"
108	36" x 84"	3' - 0"	7' - 0"

Figure 3–100

3. Add the new information. The change is reflected in the schedule, on the sheet, and in the elements of the project.

- If you change a Type Property, an alert box opens, as shown in Figure 3–101.

Figure 3–101

- When you select an element in a schedule, in the *Modify Schedule/Quantities* tab>Element panel, you can click

  (Highlight in Model). This opens a close-up view of the element with the Show Element(s) in View dialog box, as shown in Figure 3–102. Click **Show** to display more views of the element. Click **Close** to finish the command.

Figure 3–102

Hint: Customizing Schedules

Schedules are typically included in project templates, which are set up by the BIM Manager or other advanced users. They can be complex to create as there are many options.

- For more information about creating schedules, refer to the ASCENT guide *Autodesk Revit: BIM Management: Template and Family Creation*.

Modifying a Schedule on a Sheet

Once you have placed a schedule on a sheet, you can manipulate it to fit the information into the available space. Select the schedule to display the controls that enable you to modify it, as shown in Figure 3–103.

Figure 3–103

- The blue triangles modify the width of each column.

- The break mark splits the schedule into two parts.

- In a split schedule, you can use the arrows in the upper left corner to move that portion of the schedule table. The control at the bottom of the first table changes the length of the table and impacts any connected splits, as shown in Figure 3–104.

Figure 3–104

- To unsplit a schedule, drag the Move control from the side of the schedule that you want to unsplit back to the original column.

Practice 3j

Work with Schedules in an Architectural Project

Practice Objectives

- Update schedule information.
- Add a schedule to a sheet.

In this practice, you will add information to a door schedule and to elements that are connected to the schedule. You will then place the schedule on a sheet, as shown in Figure 3–105.

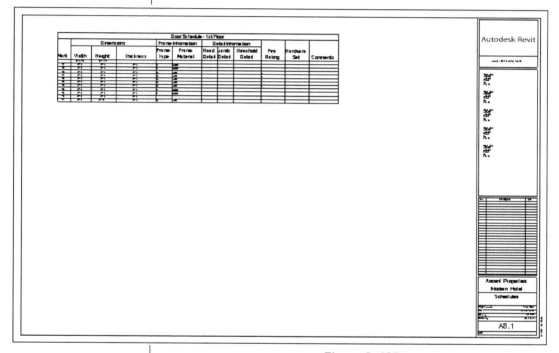

Figure 3–105

Task 1 - Fill in schedules.

1. Open the project **Modern-Hotel-Schedules.rvt** from the practice files folder.

2. Open the **Floor Plans: Floor 1** view.

3. In the Project Browser, expand *Schedules/Quantities*. Four schedules have been added to this project.

4. Double-click on **Door Schedule - 1st Floor** to open it. The existing doors in the project are already populated with some of the basic information included with the door, as shown in Figure 3–106.

<Door Schedule - 1st Floor>

A	B	C	D	E	F	G	H	I	J
		Dimensions		Frame Information			Detail Information		
Mark	Width	Height	Thickness	Frame Type	Frame Material	Head Detail	Jamb Detail	Threshold Detail	Fire Rating
101	3 - 0"	7 - 0"	0 - 2"						A
102	3 - 0"	7 - 0"	0 - 2"						A
103	3 - 0"	6 - 8"	0 - 2"						B
104	3 - 0"	6 - 8"	0 - 2"						B
105	3 - 0"	6 - 8"	0 - 2"						B
106	3 - 0"	6 - 8"	0 - 2"						B
107	3 - 0"	6 - 8"	0 - 2"						B
108	3 - 0"	7 - 0"	0 - 2"						A
109	3 - 0"	7 - 0"	0 - 2"						A
110	6 - 0"	7 - 0"	0 - 2"						D
111	6 - 0"	6 - 6"	0 - 2"						

Figure 3–106

5. Select Mark **101**.

6. In the *Modify Schedules/Quantities* tab>Element panel, click (Highlight in Model).

7. In the Show Element(s) In View dialog box click **Show** until you see a plan view of the door, as shown in Figure 3–107. Then, click **Close**.

Figure 3–107

8. The door is still selected and you are in a plan view. In Properties, set the following:
    - *Frame Type:* **A**
    - *Frame Material:* **Steel**
    - *Finish:* **Coated**

9. Click ⊞ (Edit Type).

10. In the Type Properties dialog box, in the *Identity Data* area, set the *Fire Rating* to **A**.

11. Click **OK** to finish.

12. Click on the *Door Schedule - 1st Floor* tab to open the view.

13. Note that the *Frame Type* and *Frame Material* display for one door and the matching exterior doors also have a fire rating. **Note:** The *Frame Type* and *Frame Material* did not populate on similar door types because the information you change was in the element property whereas the Fire Rating change was the elements type property so it changes for all similar door types.

14. Use the drop-down list and change the options for the matching doors, as shown in Figure 3–108.

A	B	C	D	E	F
	Dimensions			Frame Information	
Mark	Width	Height	Thickness	Frame Type	Frame Material
101	3 - 0"	7 - 0"	0 - 2"	A	Steel
102	3 - 0"	7 - 0"	0 - 2"	A	Steel
103	3 - 0"	6 - 8"	0 - 2"		Steel
104	3' - 0"	6' - 8"	0' - 2"		

Figure 3–108

15. In the Door Schedule view, specify the *Fire Rating* for some other doors in the schedule. When you change the fire rating, you are prompted to change all elements of that type. Click **OK**.

16. Open the **Floor Plans: Floor 1** view and zoom.

17. Select the door to the office, then right-click and click on **Select All Instances>In Entire Project**.

18. Look at the Status Bar beside ▽ (Filter) and note that more doors have been selected than are in the current view.

No visual changes to the door display because these are just text properties.

19. In Properties, set the *Construction and Materials* and the *Finishes* parameters as follows:
    - *Frame Type:* **B**
    - *Frame Material:* **Wood**
    - *Finish:* **Clear-coat**

20. Press <Esc> to clear the selection when you are finished.

21. Switch back to the schedule view to see the additions. Not all of the doors are showing because the schedule has been limited to the 1st floor doors.

22. Save the project.

Task 2 - Add schedules to a sheet.

1. In the Project Browser, open the sheet **A8.1 - Schedules**.

2. Drag and drop the **Door Schedule - 1st Floor** view onto the sheet, as shown in Figure 3–109.

	Dimensions			Frame Information		Detail Information			Fire Rating	Hardware Set	Comments
Mark	Width	Height	Thickness	Frame Type	Frame Material	Head Detail	Jamb Detail	Threshold Detail			
101	3'-0"	7'-0"	0'-2"	A	Steel				A		
102	3'-0"	7'-0"	0'-2"	A	Steel				A		
103	3'-0"	6'-8"	0'-2"	B	Wood				B		
104	3'-0"	6'-8"	0'-2"	B	Wood				B		
105	3'-0"	6'-8"	0'-2"	B	Wood				B		
106	3'-0"	6'-8"	0'-2"	B	Wood				B		
107	3'-0"	6'-8"	0'-2"	B	Wood				B		
108	3'-0"	7'-0"	0'-2"	A	Steel				A		
109	3'-0"	7'-0"	0'-2"	A	Steel				A		
110	6'-0"	7'-0"	0'-2"								
111	6'-0"	6'-10"	0'-2"	C	Clear-coat						

Table title: Door Schedule - 1st Floor

Figure 3–109

- Note that your schedule might look different than the one shown in Figure 3–109.

3. Zoom in and use the arrows at the top to modify the width of the columns so that the titles display correctly.

4. Click in an empty space on the sheet to finish placing the schedule.

5. Switch back to the **Floor Plans: Floor 1** view and select the double-swing door at the kitchen.

6. In the Type Selector, change the size to **72" x 82"**. In Properties, add a Frame Type, Frame Material, and Finish.

7. Return to the sheet **A8.1 - Schedules**. The information is automatically populated, as shown in Figure 3–110.

	Dimensions			Frame Information		
Mark	**Width**	**Height**	**Thickness**	**Frame Type**	**Frame Material**	
101	3' - 0"	7' - 0"	0' - 2"	A	Steel	
102	3' - 0"	7' - 0"	0' - 2"	A	Steel	
103	3' - 0"	6' - 8"	0' - 2"	B	Wood	
104	3' - 0"	6' - 8"	0' - 2"	B	Wood	
105	3' - 0"	6' - 8"	0' - 2"	B	Wood	
106	3' - 0"	6' - 8"	0' - 2"	B	Wood	
107	3' - 0"	6' - 8"	0' - 2"	B	Wood	
108	3' - 0"	7' - 0"	0' - 2"	A	Steel	
109	3' - 0"	7' - 0"	0' - 2"	A	Steel	
110	6' - 0"	7' - 0"	0' - 2"			
111	6' - 0"	6' - 10"	0' - 2"	C	Clear-coat	

The table header above also includes the partial title "Door Sched" at top right.

Figure 3–110

8. Save and close the project.

Practice 3k

Work with Schedules in an MEP Project

Practice Objectives

- Update schedule information.
- Add a schedule to a sheet.

In this practice, you will update a schedule and place it on a sheet, as shown in Figure 3–111.

MECHANICAL EQUIPMENT SCHEDULE					
Type Mark	Mark	Space: Name	Manufacturer	Model	Comments
AHU-1	1	CORRIDOR	ME Unlimited	AHU-24-M	
AHU-1	2	CORRIDOR	ME Unlimited	AHU-24-M	
AHU-1	3	CORRIDOR	ME Unlimited	AHU-24-M	
AHU-1	4	CORRIDOR	ME Unlimited	AHU-24-M	
AHU-1	5	CORRIDOR	ME Unlimited	AHU-24-M	
AHU-1	6	CORRIDOR	ME Unlimited	AHU-24-M	
AHU-1	7	CORRIDOR	ME Unlimited	AHU-24-M	
AHU-1	8	CORRIDOR	ME Unlimited	AHU-24-M	
AHU-3	9	CORRIDOR	ME Unlimited	AHU-36-L	
AHU-1	10	CORRIDOR	ME Unlimited	AHU-24-M	
AHU-1	11	CORRIDOR	ME Unlimited	AHU-24-M	
AHU-1	12	CORRIDOR	ME Unlimited	AHU-24-M	
AHU-2	13	CORRIDOR	ME Unlimited	AHU-12-S	
HW-1	14	STORAGE	ME Unlimited	HWH-10-M	
HW-1	15	STORAGE	ME Unlimited	HWH-10-M	
HW-1	16	JNTR.	ME Unlimited	HWH-10-M	
HW-1	17	JNTR.	ME Unlimited	HWH-10-M	

Figure 3–111

Task 1 - Fill in schedules.

1. In the practice files folder, open **Schedules-School-MEP.rvt**.

2. Open the Plumbing>Plumbing>3D Views>**3D Plumbing** view.

3. In the Project Browser, expand **Schedules/Quantities** and open **MECHANICAL EQUIPMENT SCHEDULE**. The schedule is already populated with some information, as shown in Figure 3–112.

<MECHANICAL EQUIPMENT SCHEDULE>					
A	B	C	D	E	F
Type Mark	Mark	Space: Name	Manufacturer	Model	Comments
AHU-1	1	CORRIDOR			
AHU-1	2	CORRIDOR			
AHU-1	3	CORRIDOR			
AHU-1	4	CORRIDOR			
AHU-1	5	CORRIDOR			
AHU-1	6	CORRIDOR			
AHU-1	7	CORRIDOR			

Figure 3–112

4. Several Type Marks are empty. Click in one of the empty *Type Mark* cells. In the *Modify Schedules/Quantities* tab> Element panel, click [icon] (Highlight in Model).

5. If a dialog box opens stating there is no open view that shows any of the highlighted elements, click **OK** to search through closed views.

6. In the view that comes up, if it is not showing the element you need to see, click **Show**. If you can see the element, click **Close** in the Show Element(s) in View dialog box.

7. Zoom out so that you can see the element (i.e., a hot water heater) in context.

8. In Properties, click [icon] (Edit Type).

9. In the Type Properties dialog box, in the *Identity Data* area, set the *Type Mark* to **HW-1**.

10. Click **OK** to finish.

11. Return to the Mechanical Equipment Schedule (select the tab or press <Ctrl>+<Tab> to switch between open windows).

12. All of the hot water heaters in the project now have a *Type Mark* set, as shown in Figure 3–113.

<MECHANICAL EQUIPMENT SCHEDULE>					
A	B	C	D	E	F
Type Mark	Mark	Space: Name	Manufacturer	Model	Comments
AHU-1	1	CORRIDOR			
AHU-1	2	CORRIDOR			
AHU-1	3	CORRIDOR			
AHU-1	4	CORRIDOR			
AHU-1	5	CORRIDOR			
AHU-1	6	CORRIDOR			
AHU-1	7	CORRIDOR			
AHU-1	8	CORRIDOR			
AHU-1	9	CORRIDOR			
AHU-1	10	CORRIDOR			
AHU-1	11	CORRIDOR			
AHU-1	12	CORRIDOR			
HW-1	49	STORAGE			
HW-1	50	STORAGE			
HW-1	51	JNTR.			
HW-1	52	JNTR.			
AHU-1	53	CORRIDOR			

Figure 3–113

13. In the *Mark* column you can see that the numbers are out of sequence. The numbering of hot water heaters and one air handling unit (AHU-1) is incorrect, starting at 49.

14. Change the *Mark* of the incorrectly numbered AHU-1 from **53** to **13**, then adjust each of the HW-1 to follow sequence.

15. In the schedule view, change the name of the Manufacturer of one of the AHUs to **ME Unlimited**. An alert displays warning that changing this changes all of the elements of this type, as shown in Figure 3–114. Click **OK**.

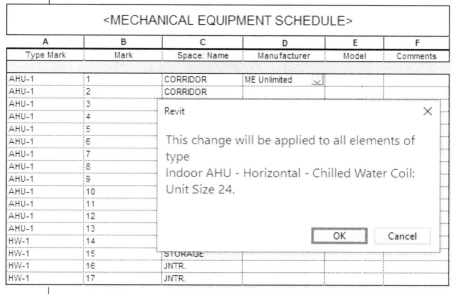

Figure 3–114

16. Open the Mechanical>HVAC>Floor Plans>**01 Mechanical Plan** view and zoom to the south wing and to the far right end of the hall in the office area.

17. Select the AHU that is connected to the Office duct system. In the Type Selector, change it to **Indoor AHU - Horizontal - Chilled Water Coil: Unit Size 12**.

18. While it is still selected, click **Edit Type** and set the *Type Mark* to **AHU-2**.

19. Switch back to the schedule view to see the change.

20. In the *Manufacturer* column, use the drop-down list to select the same *Manufacturer* for the modified AHU, as shown in Figure 3–115. Click **OK** in the dialog box notifying you of the change to any other elements of that type.

<MECHANICAL EQUIPMENT SCHEDULE>

A	B	C	D	E	F
Type Mark	Mark	Space: Name	Manufacturer	Model	Comments
AHU-1	1	CORRIDOR	ME Unlimited		
AHU-1	2	CORRIDOR	ME Unlimited		
AHU-1	3	CORRIDOR	ME Unlimited		
AHU-1	4	CORRIDOR	ME Unlimited		
AHU-1	5	CORRIDOR	ME Unlimited		
AHU-1	6	CORRIDOR	ME Unlimited		
AHU-1	7	CORRIDOR	ME Unlimited		
AHU-1	8	CORRIDOR	ME Unlimited		
AHU-1	9	CORRIDOR	ME Unlimited		
AHU-1	10	CORRIDOR	ME Unlimited		
AHU-1	11	CORRIDOR	ME Unlimited		
AHU-1	12	CORRIDOR	ME Unlimited		
AHU-2	13	CORRIDOR			
HW-1	14	STORAGE	ME Unlimited		
HW-1	15	STORAGE			
HW-1	16	JNTR.			
HW-1	17	JNTR.			

Figure 3–115

21. Fill in the other information.

22. Save the project.

Task 2 - Modify the plumbing fixture schedule.

1. In the Project Browser, expand **Schedules/Quantities** and open **PLUMBING FIXTURE SCHEDULE**. The schedule is already populated with some information.

2. From the *Modify Schedule | Quantities* tab>Appearance panel, select 	(Freeze Header). Scroll down the schedule and note that the schedule's headers stay at the top.

3. Note that the *Elevation from Level* column shows some of the sinks/lavatories at **0'-0"**. This means they have been orphaned.

4. Click on one of them. In the *Modify Schedules | Quantities* tab>Element panel, click 	(Highlight in Model).

5. Click **OK**, **Show**, or **Close** as needed.

6. Select the sink. From the *Modify | Plumbing Fixtures* tab> Work Plane panel, select (Pick Host). In the Placement panel, select 🖱 (Face). Hover over the linked architectural model's sink and use the midpoint to place the sink, as shown in Figure 3–116.

Figure 3–116

7. Switch back to the plumbing fixture schedule and notice that just the one sink updated. Each sink/lavatory and water closet would need to be rehosted to update.

8. Open the Plumbing>Plumbing>Floor Plans>**01 Plumbing Plan** view.

9. Select one sink in any classroom and right-click on it. Choose **Select All Instances>Visible in View**.

10. From Properties, change the *Schedule Level* to **Level 1**.

11. Switch back to the plumbing fixture schedule and notice that the *Elevation from Level* has changed without rehosting all of the sinks.

12. Continue to do this with the rest of the plumbing fixtures on Level 1.

Task 3 - Add schedules to a sheet.

1. In the Project Browser, right-click on Sheets (all) and select **New Sheet**. Select the E-sized title block and click **OK**.

2. In the Project Browser, right-click on the new sheet (which is bold) and select Rename. In the Sheet Title dialog box, set the *Number* to **M-801** and the *Name* to **Schedules** and click **OK**.

3. Drag and drop the **MECHANICALEQUIPMENT SCHEDULE** view onto the sheet, as shown in Figure 3–117.

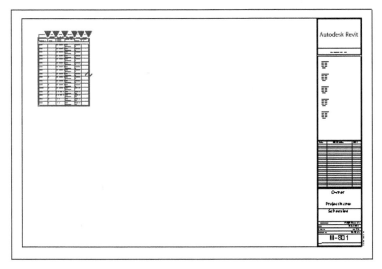

Figure 3–117

4. Zoom in and use the arrows at the top to modify the width of the columns so that the titles display correctly.

5. Click in an empty space on the sheet to finish placing the schedule.

6. Switch back to the **01 Mechanical Plan** view and select one of the Classroom AHUs.

7. In the Type Selector, change the size to **Unit Size 36**. In Type Properties add the *Model*, *Manufacturer*, and *Type Mark*.

8. Return to the Schedule sheet. The information is automatically populated.

9. Drag and drop the PLUMBING FIXTURE SCHEDULE view onto the sheet. Because it is itemized, it is toc long for the schedule. Place it anyway.

10. Using the split schedule table control, split the schedule as many times as you need to and use the length control to change the length so that they fit and look appropriate, as shown in Figure 3–118.

Figure 3–118

11. Save and close the project.

Practice 3I

Work with Schedules in a Structural Project

Practice Objectives

- Update schedule information.
- Add a schedule to a sheet.

In this practice, you will add Type Mark information to a structural elements schedule and the elements that are connected to that schedule. You will then place the schedule on a sheet and add elements in the project. The final information displays as shown in Figure 3–119.

Structural Elements Schedule		
Type Mark	Family and Type	Count

Structural Columns

P-1	Concrete-Rectangular-Column: 24 x 24	43
	W-Wide Flange-Column: W8X10	2
	W-Wide Flange-Column: W10X33	41

Structural Foundations

	Footing-Rectangular: 14'x14'x2'-0"	2
	Footing-Rectangular: 36" x 36" x 12"	43
	Foundation Slab: 6" Foundation Slab	1
W-1	Wall Foundation: Bearing Footing - 24" x 12"	17
W-2	Wall Foundation: Bearing Footing - 36" x 12"	4

Structural Framing

	HSS-Hollow Structural Section: HSS6X6X.500	28
	K-Series Bar Joist-Rod Web: 14K6	16
	K-Series Bar Joist-Rod Web: 16K7	100
	W-Wide Flange: W12X26	1558
	W-Wide Flange: W14X30	1023

Figure 3–119

Task 1 - Fill in schedules.

1. Open **Schedules-Syracuse-Suites.rvt** from the practice files folder.

2. Open the 3D Views: **3D Foundation** view. This view only displays the foundation elements, including concrete piers, footings, walls, and wall footings.

3. Rotate the view so you can see the stair and elevator shaft openings, as shown in Figure 3–120.

Figure 3–120

4. Close the {3D} view tab.

5. In the Project Browser, expand *Schedules/Quantities*. Note that four schedules have been added to this project.

6. Double-click on **Structural Elements Schedule** to open it. The existing structural elements in the project populate the schedule, as shown in Figure 3–121. Expand the width of the columns, as needed, to read the content.

<Structural Elements Schedule>		
A	B	C
Type Mark	Family and Type	Count
Structural Columns		
P-1	Concrete-Rectangular-Column: 24 x 24	42
	W-Wide Flange-Column: W8X10	2
	W-Wide Flange-Column: W10X33	41
Structural Foundations		
	Footing-Rectangular: 14'x14'x2'-0"	2
	Footing-Rectangular: 36" x 36" x 12"	42
	Foundation Slab: 6" Foundation Slab	1
	Wall Foundation: Bearing Footing - 24" x 12"	17
	Wall Foundation: Bearing Footing - 36" x 12"	4
Structural Framing		
	HSS-Hollow Structural Section: HSS6X6X.500	28
	K-Series Bar Joist-Rod Web: 14K6	16
	K-Series Bar Joist-Rod Web: 16K7	100
	W-Wide Flange: W12X26	1558
	W-Wide Flange: W14X30	1023

Figure 3–121

7. Note that only the *Concrete* columns have a **Type Mark**.

8. In the *Type Mark* column beside **Wall Foundation: Bearing Footing - 24" x 12"**, type **W-1.**

9. The warning dialog box shown in Figure 3–122 displays because the element is a type parameter; therefore, you are alerted before you make any changes. Click **OK**.

Figure 3–122

10. Select **Wall Foundation: Bearing Footing - 36" x 12"**.

11. In the *Modify | Schedule/Quantities* tab>Element panel, click (Highlight in Model).

12. In the Show Element(s) in View dialog box, click **Show** until you see a foundation element displayed in the **3D Foundations** view, as shown in Figure 3–123. Click **Close**.

Figure 3–123

13. With the elements highlighted, in Properties, click ⌗ (Edit Type).

14. In the Type Properties dialog box, in the *Identity Data* area, set the *Type Mark* to **W-2**.

15. Click **OK** to finish.

16. Return to the **Structural Elements Schedule** view, as shown in Figure 3–124. The **Type Mark** is now applied.

<Structural Elements Schedule>

A	B	C
Type Mark	Family and Type	Count
Structural Columns		
P-1	Concrete-Rectangular-Column: 24 x 24	42
	W-Wide Flange-Column: W8X10	2
	W-Wide Flange-Column: W10X33	41
Structural Foundations		
	Footing-Rectangular: 14'x14'x2'-0"	2
	Footing-Rectangular: 36" x 36" x 12"	42
	Foundation Slab: 6" Foundation Slab	1
W-1	Wall Foundation: Bearing Footing - 24" x 12"	17
W-2	Wall Foundation: Bearing Footing - 36" x 12"	4
Structural Framing		
	HSS-Hollow Structural Section: HSS6X6X.500	28
	K-Series Bar Joist-Rod Web: 14K6	16
	K-Series Bar Joist-Rod Web: 16K7	100
	W-Wide Flange: W12X26	1558
	W-Wide Flange: W14X30	1023

Figure 3–124

17. Open the other schedules and review the information.

18. Save the project.

Task 2 - Add schedules to a sheet.

1. In the Project Browser, open the sheet **S8.1 - Schedules**.

2. Drag and drop the **Structural Elements Schedule** view onto the sheet, as shown in Figure 3–125. Your schedule may look different then the one shown in Figure 3–125.

Structural Elements Schedule		
Type Mark	Family and Type	Count
Structural Columns		
P-1	Concrete-Rectangular-Column: 24 x 24	42
	W-Wide Flange-Column: W8X10	2
	W-Wide Flange-Column: W10X33	41
Structural Foundations		
	Footing-Rectangular: 14'x14'x2'-0"	2
	Footing-Rectangular: 36" x 36" x 12"	42
	Foundation Slab: 6" Foundation Slab	1
W-1	Wall Foundation: Bearing Footing - 24" x 12"	17
W-2	Wall Foundation: Bearing Footing - 36" x 12"	4
Structural Framing		
	HSS-Hollow Structural Section: HSS6X6X.500	28
	K-Series Bar Joist-Rod Web: 14K6	16
	K-Series Bar Joist-Rod Web: 16K7	100
	W-Wide Flange: W12X26	1558
	W-Wide Flange: W14X30	1024

Figure 3–125

3. Zoom in and use the arrows at the top of the schedule to modify the width of the columns to ensure that the titles display correctly.

4. In the schedule, note the number of Concrete Columns and their related footings.

5. Open the **Structural Plans: 00 T.O. Footing** view.

6. Zoom in and copy a concrete column and its footing to a nearby grid location that does not have an existing column, similar to that shown in Figure 3–126.

Figure 3–126

7. Switch back to the sheet view. Note that the numbers in the schedule have automatically updated to include the new column.

8. Switch to the **Structural Elements Schedule** view. Note that these column numbers have also been updated.

9. Save and close the project.

Chapter Review Questions

1. Which of the following commands creates a view that results in an independent view displaying the same model geometry and containing a copy of the annotation?

   a. Duplicate

   b. Duplicate with Detailing

   c. Duplicate as a Dependent

2. Which of the following is true about the Visibility/Graphic Overrides dialog box?

   a. Changes made in the dialog box only affect the current view.

   b. It can only be used to toggle categories on and off.

   c. It can be used to toggle individual elements on and off.

   d. It can be used to change the color of individual elements.

3. If you want to hide just one of the elevation markers in a view, what do you have to do?

   a. Select the elevation marker, then right-click and select **Hide in View>By Filter**.

   b. Select the elevation marker, then right-click and select **Hide in View>Category**.

   c. Select the elevation marker, then right-click and select **Hide in View>Elements**.

   d. In the Visibility/Graphics Overrides dialog box, uncheck **Elevations**.

4. What is the purpose of creating a callout?

   a. To create a boundary around part of the model that needs revising, similar to a revision cloud.

   b. To create a view of part of the model to export to the AutoCAD® software for further detailing.

   c. To create a view of part of the model that is linked to the main view from which it is taken.

   d. To create a 2D view of part of the model.

5. You placed dimensions in a view but only some of them display, as shown on the left in Figure 3–127. You were expecting the view to display as shown on the right in Figure 3–127. What do you need to modify to see the missing dimensions?

Figure 3–127

a. Dimension Settings

b. Dimension Type

c. Visibility Graphic Overrides

d. Annotation Crop Region

6. How do you create multiple interior elevations in one room?

a. Using the **Interior Elevation** command, place the elevation marker.

b. Using the **Elevation** command from the Properties Type Selector, change to **Interior Elevation** and place the first marker, select it and select the appropriate Show Arrow boxes.

c. Using the **Interior Elevation** command, place an elevation marker for each wall of the room you want to display.

d. Using the **Elevation** command, select a Multiple Elevation marker type, and place the elevation marker.

7. How do you create a jog in a building section, such as that shown in Figure 3–128?

Figure 3–128

a. Use the **Split Element** tool in the *Modify* tab>Modify panel.

b. Select the building section and then click **Split Segment** in the contextual tab.

c. Select the building section and click the blue control in the middle of the section line.

d. Draw two separate sections, and use the **Section Jog** tool to combine them into a jogged section.

8. What happens when you delete a door in an Autodesk Revit model?

a. You must delete the door on the sheet.

b. You must delete the door from the schedule.

c. The door is removed from the model, but not from the schedule.

d. The door is removed from the model and the schedule.

9. In a schedule, if you change type information (such as a Type Mark) all instances of that type update with the new information.

a. True

b. False

Command Summary

Button	Command	Location
Views		
	Elevation	• **Ribbon:** *View* tab>Create panel> expand Elevation
	Callout: Rectangle	• **Ribbon:** *View* tab>Create panel> expand Callout
	Callout: Sketch	• **Ribbon:** *View* tab>Create panel> expand Callout
	Duplicate	• **Ribbon:** *View* tab>Create panel> expand Duplicate View
		• **Right-click:** *(on a view in the Project Browser)* expand Duplicate View
	Duplicate as Dependent	• **Ribbon:** *View* tab>Create panel> expand Duplicate View
		• **Right-click:** *(on a view in the Project Browser)* expand Duplicate View
	Duplicate with Detailing	• **Ribbon:** *View* tab>Create panel> expand Duplicate View
		• **Right-click:** *(on a view in the Project Browser)* Duplicate View
	Plan Region	• **Ribbon:** *View* tab>Create panel> expand Plan Views
	Section	• **Ribbon:** *View* tab>Create panel
		• **Quick Access Toolbar**
	Split Segment	• **Ribbon:** *(when the elevation or section marker is selected) Modify	Views* tab> Section panel
Crop Views		
	Crop View	• **View Control Bar**
		• **View Properties:** Crop View *(check)*
	Do Not Crop View	• **View Control Bar**
		• **View Properties:** Crop View *(clear)*
	Edit Crop	• **Ribbon:** *(when the crop region of a callout, elevation, or section view is selected) Modify	Views* tab>Mode panel
	Hide Crop Region	• **View Control Bar**
		• **View Properties:** Crop Region Visible *(clear)*
	Reset Crop	• **Ribbon:** *(when the crop region of a callout, elevation or section view is selected) Modify	Views* tab>Mode panel

	Show Crop Region	• **View Control Bar** • **View Properties:** Crop Region Visible (*check*)
	Size Crop	• **Ribbon:** (*when the crop region of a callout, elevation or section view is selected*) Modify | Views tab>Mode panel

View Display

	Hide in View	• **Ribbon:** *Modify* tab>View Graphics panel>Hide>Elements *or* By Category • **Right-click:** (*when an element is selected*) Hide in View>Elements *or* Category
	Override Graphics in View	• **Ribbon:** *Modify* tab>View Graphics panel>Hide>Elements *or* By Category • **Right-click:** (*when an element is selected*) Override Graphics in View>By Element *or* By Category • **Shortcut:** (*category only*) VV or VG
	Plan Region	• **Ribbon:** *View* tab>Create panel expand Plan Views.
	Selection Box	• **Ribbon:** *Modify* tab>View panel • **Shortcut: BX.**
	Reveal Hidden Elements	• **View Control Bar**
	Temporary Hide/Isolate	• **View Control Bar**
	Temporary View Properties	• **View Control Bar**

Printing and Sharing

The accurate creation of construction documents in the Autodesk® Revit® software ensures that the design is correctly communicated to downstream users. Construction documents are created primarily in special views called sheets. Selecting title blocks, assigning title block information, placing views, and printing the sheets are essential steps in the construction documentation process. You can also export Autodesk Revit projects so they can be used in vector-based programs for collaboration with clients or team members using other CAD programs.

Learning Objectives in This Chapter

- Add sheets with title blocks and views of a project.
- Enter the title block information for individual sheets and for an entire project.
- Place and organize views on sheets.
- Print sheets using the default Print dialog box.
- Export Autodesk Revit projects to other file formats, including CAD formats and DWF files.

4.1 Setting Up Sheets

While you are modeling a project, the foundations of the working drawings are already in progress. Any view (such as a floor plan, section, callout, or schedule) can be placed on a sheet, as shown in Figure 4–1.

Figure 4–1

- Company templates can be created with standard sheets using the company (or project) title block and related views already placed on the sheet.

- The sheet size is based on the selected title block family.

- Sheets are listed in the *Sheets* area in the Project Browser.

- Most information on sheets is included in the views. You can add general notes and other non-model elements directly to the sheet, though it is better to add them using drafting views or legends, as these can be placed on multiple sheets.

How To: Set Up Sheets

1. In the Project Browser, right-click on the *Sheets* area header and select **New Sheet...** or in the *View* tab>Sheet Composition panel, click (Sheet).

2. In the New Sheet dialog box, select a title block from the list as shown in Figure 4–2. Alternatively, if there is a list of placeholder sheets, select one or more from the list.

*Click **Load...** to load a sheet from the Library.*

Hold <Ctrl> to select multiple placeholder sheets.

Figure 4–2

3. Click **OK**. A new sheet is created using the preferred title block.
4. Fill out the information in the title block as needed.
5. Add views to the sheet.

*   When you create sheets, the next sheet is incremented numerically.

*   Double-click on the sheet name to change the name and number in the Sheet Title dialog box.

*   When you change the *Sheet Name* and/or *Number* in the title block, it automatically changes the name and number of the sheet in the Project Browser.

*   The plot stamp on the side of the sheet automatically updates according to the current date and time. The format of the display uses the regional settings of your computer.

- The Scale is automatically entered when a view is inserted onto a sheet. If a sheet has multiple views with different scales, the scale displays **As Indicated.**

Sheet (Title Block) Properties

Each new sheet includes a title block. You can change the title block information in Properties, as shown in Figure 4–3, or by selecting any blue label you want to edit (Sheet Name, Sheet Number, Drawn by, etc.), as shown in Figure 4–4.

Figure 4–3

Figure 4–4

Properties that apply to all sheets can be entered in the Project Information dialog box (as shown in Figure 4–5). In the *Manage* tab>Settings panel, click (Project Information).

Figure 4–5

4.2 Placing and Modifying Views on Sheets

The process of adding views to a sheet is simple. Drag and drop a view from the Project Browser onto the sheet. The new view on the sheet is displayed at the scale specified in the original view. The view title displays the name, number, and scale of the view, as shown in Figure 4–6.

Figure 4–6

How To: Place Views on Sheets

Alignment lines from existing views display to help you place additional views.

1. Set up the view as you want it to display on the sheet, including the scale and visibility of elements.
2. Create or open the sheet where you want to place the view.
3. Select the view in the Project Browser, and drag and drop it onto the sheet.
4. The center of the view is attached to the cursor. Click to place it on the sheet.

Placing Views on Sheets

- Views can only be placed on a sheet once. However, you can duplicate the view and place that copy on a sheet.

- Views on a sheet are associative. They automatically update to reflect changes to the project.

- Each view on a sheet is listed under the sheet name in the Project Browser, as shown in Figure 4–7.

Figure 4–7

- You can also use two other methods to place views on sheets:

  - In the Project Browser, right-click on the sheet name and select **Add View...**

  - In the *View* tab>Sheet Composition panel, click (Place View).

  Then, in the Views dialog box (shown in Figure 4–8), select the view you want to use and click **Add View to Sheet.**

This method lists only those views which have not yet been placed on a sheet.

Figure 4–8

- To remove a view from a sheet, select it and press <Delete>. Alternatively, in the Project Browser, expand the individual sheet information to show the views, right-click on the view name and select **Remove From Sheet**.

Hint: Setting Up the Project Browser

To view and change the Project Browser's types, select the top level node of the Project Browser (which is set to *Views (all)* by default) and select the type you want to use from the Type Selector. For example, you can set the Browser to only display views that are not on sheets, as shown in Figure 4–9.

Figure 4–9

Moving Views and View Titles

*You can also use the **Move** command or the arrow keys to move a view.*

- To move a view on a sheet, select the edge of the view and drag it to a new location. The view title moves with the view.

- To move only the view title, select the title and drag it to the new location.

- To modify the length of the line under the title name, select the edge of the view and drag the controls, as shown in Figure 4–10.

North-South Entry
1   1/8" = 1'-0"

Figure 4–10

- To change the title of a view on a sheet without changing its name in the Project Browser, in Properties, in the *Identity Data* area, type a new title for the *Title on Sheet* parameter, as shown in Figure 4–11.

Figure 4–11

Rotating Views

- When creating a vertical sheet, you can rotate the view on the sheet by 90 degrees. Select the view and set the direction of rotation in the Rotation on Sheet drop-down list in the Options Bar, as shown in Figure 4–12.

Figure 4–12

- To rotate a view to an angle other than 90 degrees, open the view, toggle on and select the crop region and use the **Rotate** command to change the angle.

Working Inside Views

To make small changes to a view while working on a sheet:

- Double-click *inside* the view to activate it.
- Double-click *outside* the view to deactivate it.

Only use this method for small changes. Significant changes should be made directly in the view.

Only elements in the viewport are available for modification. The rest of the sheet is grayed out, as shown in Figure 4–13.

Figure 4–13

- You can activate and deactivate views by right-clicking on the edge of the view or by using the tools found on the *Modify | Viewports* and *Views* tab>Sheet Composition panel.

- Changes you make to elements when a view is activated also display in the original view.

- If you are unsure which sheet a view is on, right-click on the view in the Project Browser and select **Open Sheet**. This item is grayed out if the view has not been placed on a sheet and is not available for schedules and legends which can be placed on more than one sheet.

Resizing Views on Sheets

Each view displays the extents of the model or the elements contained in the crop region. If the view does not fit on a sheet (as shown in Figure 4–14), you might need to crop the view or move the elevation markers closer to the building.

If the extents of the view change dramatically based on a scale change or a crop region, it is easier to delete the view on the sheet and drag it over again.

Figure 4–14

Hint: Add an Image to a Sheet

Company logos and renderings saved to image files (such as .JPG and .PNG) can be added directly on a sheet or in a view.

1. In the *Insert* tab>Import panel, click (Image).
2. In the Import Image dialog box, select and open the image file. The extents of the image display, as shown in Figure 4–15.

Figure 4–15

3. Place the image where you want it.
4. The image is displayed. Pick one of the grips and extend it to modify the size of the image.

- In Properties, you can adjust the height and width and also set the *Draw Layer* to either **Background** or **Foreground**, as shown in Figure 4–16.

Dimensions		☆
Width	1' 5 185/256"	
Height	1' 1 41/64"	
Horizontal Scale	1.000000	
Vertical Scale	1.000000	
Lock Proportions	☑	
Other		☆
Draw Layer	Background	

Figure 4–16

- You can select more than one image at a time and move them as a group to the background or foreground.

- In the *Modify | Raster Images* tab (as shown in Figure 4–17), you can access the Arrange options and Manage Images.

Figure 4–17

Practice 4a

Work with Sheets in an Architectural Project

Practice Objectives

- Set up project properties.
- Create sheets individually.
- Modify views to prepare them to be placed on sheets.
- Place views on sheets.

In this practice, you will complete the project information, add new sheets and use existing sheets. You will fill in title block information and then add views to sheets, such as the Wall Sections sheet shown in Figure 4–18. Complete as many sheets as you have time for.

- This practice follows the steps for working with a full set of construction documents. The process is the same for half- or full-size documentation sheets.

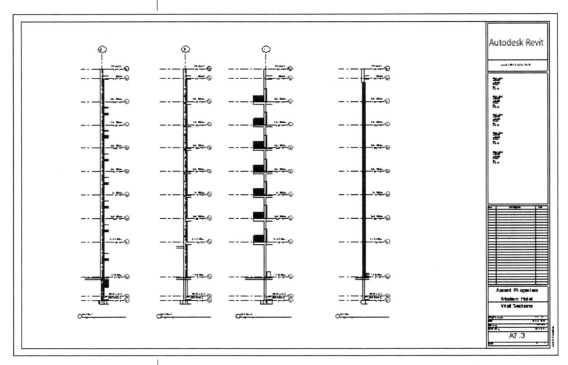

Figure 4–18

Task 1 - Complete the project information.

1. Open the project **Modern-Hotel-Sheets.rvt** from the practice files folder.

2. In the *Manage* tab>Settings panel, click ⬛ (Project Information).

3. In the Project Information dialog box, in the *Other* area, set the following parameters:
   - *Project Issue Date:* **Issue Date**
   - *Project Status:* **Design Development**
   - *Client Name:* **Ascent Properties**
   - *Project Address:* Click **Edit...** and enter your address
   - *Project Name:* **Modern Hotel**
   - *Project Number:* **1234-567**

4. Click **OK**.

5. Save the project.

Task 2 - Create a cover sheet and floor plan sheets.

1. In the *View* tab>Sheet Composition panel, click ⬛ (Sheet).

2. In the New Sheet dialog box, select the **D 22 x 34 Horizontal** title block.

3. Click **OK**.

4. Zoom in on the lower right corner of the title block. The Project Properties filled out earlier are automatically added to the sheet.

These properties are used across the entire sheet set and do not need to be entered on each sheet.

5. Continue filling out the title block, as shown in Figure 4–19.

Figure 4–19

6. Zoom back out to display the whole sheet.

7. In the Project Browser, expand the **3D Views** node. Drag and drop the **Exterior Front Perspective** view on to the sheet, as shown in Figure 4–20. There are two items that are not required on the cover sheet, the viewport title and crop region.

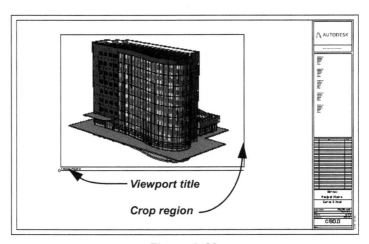

Viewport title

Crop region

Figure 4–20

8. Select the edge of the viewport. In the Type Selector, select **Viewport: No Title**.

9. Double-click inside the viewport, the title block grays out and you can modify the actual view.

10. In Properties, in the *Extents* area, clear the check from **Crop Region Visible**. (This could also be done in the View Control Bar.)

11. Double-click outside the viewport to return to the sheet.

12. In the Project Browser, right-click on the **Sheets (all)** node and select **New Sheet**.

13. Using the D-sized title block, create the following new sheets:

Sheet Number and Name	View Name
A2.1: Ground Floor Plan	Floor 1
A2.2: Upper Floor Plan (Typical)	Typical Guest Room Floor Plan
A2.3: Roof Plan	Roof

14. Save the project.

Task 3 - Set up and add views to sheets.

1. Duplicate (no detailing) the **Floor Plans: Floor 1** and **Floor 2** views and name them **Floor 1 - Life Safety Plan** and **Floor 2-8 - Life Safety Plan**.

2. Open the new views and do the following:
   - Hide all elements except the actual building elements.
   - Toggle on the crop region and ensure it is tight up against the building.
   - Toggle the crop region off.
   - In the Floor 2-8 plan, turn off the roof on the front of the building.

3. Open the sheet **A1.1 - Floor 1 - Life Safety Plan**.

4. In the Project Browser, right-click on that sheet and select **Add View...**.

The crop region defines the extent of the view on the sheet.

5. In the Views dialog box scroll down and select **Floor Plan: Floor 1 - Life Safety Plan**, as shown in Figure 4–21. Click **Add View to Sheet** and place the view on the sheet.

Figure 4–21

6. Repeat the process for the other floor and rename sheet **Floor 2 - Life Safety Plan** as **Floor 2-8 - Life Safety Plan**.

   • The **Floor 1 - Life Safety Plan** is no longer available because it has already been added to a sheet.

7. Repeat the process of adding views to sheets using the views you have available. For example, modify and add elevations Pool-East and Pool-North and place them on one of the sheets (rename the sheet to identify what is placed on it).

   • Modify crop regions and hide unnecessary elements in the views, as shown in Figure 4–22. Toggle off crop regions after you have modified them.

Figure 4–22

- Verify the scale of a view in Properties before placing it on a sheet.
- Use alignment lines to help place multiple views on one sheet, as shown in Figure 4–23.

Figure 4–23

- Change the view title, if needed, to more accurately describe what is on the sheet.
- To make minor changes to a view once it is on a sheet, double-click inside the viewport to activate the view. To return to the sheet, double-click outside the viewport to deactivate the view.

8. Once you have added callout, section, or elevation views to sheets, switch back to the **Floor Plans: Floor** 1 view. Zoom in on one of the markers. Note that it has now been automatically assigned a detail and sheet number, as shown in Figure 4–24.

Your numbers might not exactly match the numbers in the example.

Figure 4–24

9. Save and close the project.

Practice 4b

Work with Sheets in an MEP Project

Practice Objectives

- Set up project properties.
- Create sheets individually.
- Modify views to prepare them to be placed on sheets.
- Place views on sheets.

In this practice, you will complete the project information, add new sheets and use existing sheets. You will fill in title block information and then add views to sheets, such as the Lighting Plan sheet shown in Figure 4–25. Complete as many sheets as you have time for.

- This practice follows the steps for working with a full set of construction documents. The process is the same for half- or full-size documentation sheets.

Viewport

View title

Figure 4–25

Task 1 - Complete the project information.

1. In the practice files *Documents* folder, open
   Documents-School-MEP.rvt.

2. In the *Manage* tab>Settings panel, click (Project
   Information).

3. In the Project Properties dialog box, add the following values,
   as shown in Figure 4–26.
   * *Client Name:* **School District ABC**
   * *Project Name:* **Elementary School**
   * *Project Number:* **1234.56**

These values are added automatically to any sheet you create.

Project Information			✕
Family:	System Family: Project Information	⌄	Load...
Type:		⌄	Edit Type...

Instance Parameters - Control selected or to-be-created instance

Parameter	Value	^
Identity Data		⌄
Organization Name		
Organization Description		
Building Name		
Author		
Energy Analysis		⌄
Energy Settings	Edit...	
Route Analysis		⌄
Route Analysis Settings	Edit...	
Other		⌄
Project Issue Date	Issue Date	
Project Status	Project Status	
Client Name	School District ABC	
Project Address	Enter address here	
Project Name	Elementary School	
Project Number	1234.56	

Figure 4–26

4. Click **OK**.

5. In the Project Browser, expand the *Sheets (all)* area and
   open **M-101 - 01 Mechanical Schematic**. There is already a
   view placed on the sheet.

6. Zoom in on the title block and review the contents. The Project Parameters that you added are automatically applied to the sheet, as shown in Figure 4–27.

*The Scale is automatically entered when a view is inserted onto a sheet. If a sheet has multiple scales, the scale reads **As Indicated**.*

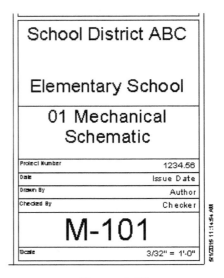

Figure 4–27

7. Set *Drawn by* to your initials. Leave the *Checked by* and *Issue Date* parameters as is.

8. Open another sheet. The project parameter values are repeated but note that the *Drawn By* value is not added because it is a parameter that is set per sheet.

9. Review the other existing Mechanical sheets and save the project.

Task 2 - Add sheets.

1. In the *View* tab>Sheet Composition panel, click (Sheet).

2. In the New Sheet dialog box, select the title block **E1 30 x42 Horizontal** and click **OK**.

3. In the Project Browser, select the new sheet, right-click, and select **Rename**.

4. In the Sheet Title dialog box, set *Number* as **C-101**, *Name* as **Cover Sheet**, and click **OK**. The title block updates as shown in Figure 4–28.

Figure 4–28

5. In the Project Browser, right-click on *Sheets (all)* and select **New Sheet...**.

6. Using the same title block, create the following sheets:
   - E-301 - 1st Floor Lighting Plan
   - E-302 - 2nd Floor Lighting Plan
   - E-303 - Power Panel Plan Detail
   - P-509 - Plumbing 3D

7. In the Project Browser, in the *Sheets (all)* area, note that these new sheets, the other sheets that you created, and the M-# sheets that were already created for you are displayed.

8. Save the project.

Task 3 - Set up and add views to sheets.

1. In the Project Browser, in the **Electrical>Lighting>Floor Plans**, right-click on the **01 Lighting Plan** view and using **Duplicate as Dependent**, create two copies of dependent views. Name them **01 Lighting Plan - North** and **01 Lighting Plan - South**.

You can change the sheet number and name in the title block or by renaming it in the Project Browser.

2. Open the **01 Lighting Plan - North** view, zoom out to see the crop region (toggle it on, if needed), and resize it to fit the north classroom wing, as shown in Figure 4–29.

Figure 4–29

3. Toggle the crop region off.

4. Repeat the steps with the **01 Lighting Plan - South** view.

5. Open the sheet **E-301 - 1st Floor Lighting Plan** and drag and drop the **1st Floor Lighting Plan North** and **South** views you just created onto it.

6. Open the **E-303 - Power Panel Plan Detail** sheet and drag and drop the **Power Panel Callout** view onto it.

7. On the sheet, double-click on the **Power Panel Callout** to activate the view.

8. Open Visibility Graphics and expand **Site**. Uncheck **Internal Origins**.

9. Double-click anywhere outside the active view to deactivate it.

You must first select the viewport on the sheet, then click on the view title to adjust it.

10. Select the **Power Panel Callout** view on the sheet and use the controls to adjust the view title so it fits under the callout, as shown in Figure 4–30. Hint: Use <Tab> to select the grip and not the view title bubble or name.

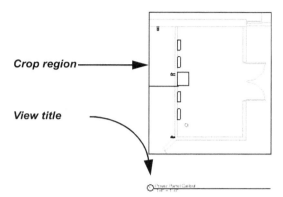

Crop region

View title

Figure 4–30

11. Switch to the **01 Power Plan** view. Zoom in on the callout marker by the power panels. Notice that it has now been automatically assigned a detail and sheet number, as shown in Figure 4–31.

Figure 4–31

12. Repeat the process of adding views and schedules to sheets using the views and schedules you have available.

- Modify crop regions and hide unnecessary elements in the views. Toggle off crop regions after you have modified them.

- Verify the scale of a view in Properties before placing it on a sheet.

- Use alignment lines to help place multiple views on one sheet.

- Change the view title if needed, to more accurately describe what is on the sheet.

- To make minor changes to a view once it is on a sheet, right-click on the view and select **Activate View.** To return to the sheet, right-click on the view and select **Deactivate View**.

- To make larger changes to a view on a sheet, return to the original view.

- If you modify the size of a view that is already placed on a sheet, delete the view from the sheet and replace it with the updated view.

13. Save the project.

Practice 4c

Work with Sheets in a Structural Project

Practice Objectives

- Set up project properties.
- Create sheets individually.
- Place views on sheets.

In this practice, you will complete project information, create a cover sheet, and add views to the sheet. You will then create a foundation plan sheet, as shown in Figure 4–32, and as many other sheets as time permits, modifying the scales as required.

- This practice follows the steps for working with a full set of construction documents. The process is the same for half- or full-size documentation sheets.

Figure 4–32

Task 1 - Complete the project information.

1. Open **Sheets-Syracuse-Suites.rvt** from the practice files folder.

2. In the *Manage* tab>Setting panel, click (Project Information).

These properties are used across the entire sheet set and do not need to be entered on each sheet.

3. In the Project Properties dialog box, in the *Other* section, set the following parameters (or use your own information based on your company standards):
   - *Project Issue Date:* current date
   - *Project Status:* **Design Development**
   - *Client Name:* **CITY OF SYRACUSE**
   - *Project Address:* (click **...**)**1234 Clinton St. Syracuse, NY 13066**
   - *Project Name:* **SYRACUSE SUITES**
   - *Project Number:* **1234-567**

4. Click **OK**.

5. Save the project.

Task 2 - Create a cover sheet.

1. In the Project Browser, right-click on *Sheets (all)* and select **New Sheet**, as shown in Figure 4–33, or in the *View* tab> Sheet Composition panel, click ⬜ (New Sheet).

Some sheets already exist in the project.

Schedules/Quantities
Pier Schedule
Sheet List
Steel Column Takeoff
Structural Foundation Schedule

New Sheet...

Browser Organization...

Search...

Figure 4–33

2. In the New Sheet dialog box, *Select Titleblocks* area, select **Syracuse Suites Cover Sheet: E1 30x42 Horizontal** and click **OK**.

3. In the Project Browser, *Sheets* category, right-click on new sheet and select **Rename**.

4. In the Sheet Title dialog box, set *Number* to **S-000** and *Name* to **COVER SHEET**, as shown in Figure 4–34.

Figure 4–34

5. In the Project Browser, expand **3D Views**.

6. Select the **Isometric** view and drag it to the coversheet.

7. Delete the view because it is too large.

8. Open the **Isometric** view and set the *Scale* to **1/16"=1'-0"**.

9. Switch to the cover sheet and place the view on the sheet.

10. In the *Legends* category, add the Symbol Legend to the sheet as shown in Figure 4–35.

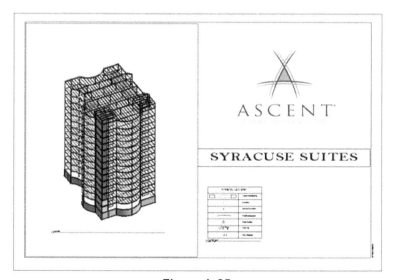

Figure 4–35

Task 3 - Create additional sheets.

1. In the *View* tab>Sheet Composition panel, click (Sheet).

2. In the New Sheet dialog box, select the title block **Syracuse Suites E1: 30x42 Horizontal** and click **OK**.

3. In the Project Browser, right-click on **S-001 – Unnamed** and rename it as **S-201: FOUNDATION PLAN**, as shown in Figure 4–36.

Figure 4–36

4. Click **OK**.

5. In the Project Browser, find the **T.O. FOOTING** structural plan view and drag it onto the sheet, centering it in the view as shown in Figure 4–37.

Figure 4–37

6. Several sheets already exist in the project. Place the Structural Plans: **00 GROUND FLOOR PLAN** view on the sheet **S-202-Ground Floor Plan.**

7. Zoom in to see the title of the view. It displays as **00 GROUND FLOOR PLAN**, as shown in Figure 4–38.

Figure 4–38

8. In the Project Browser, select the view and then, in Properties, scroll down to the *Identity Data* section. Change the *Title on Sheet* to **GROUND FLOOR - STRUCTURAL PLAN**, as shown in Figure 4–39.

Identity Data		⌃
View Template	<None>	
View Name	00 GROUND FLOOR PLAN	
Dependency	Independent	
Title on Sheet	GROUND FLOOR - STRUCTURAL PLAN	
Sheet Number	S-202	
Sheet Name	Ground Floor Plan	

Figure 4–39

9. Click **Apply**. The title changes on the sheet, as shown in Figure 4–40.

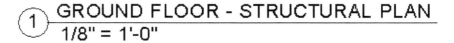

Figure 4–40

10. (Optional) Add views to the other sheets.

    • If any views do not fit on the sheet, change the scale.

11. When the sheets have been created, browse through them separately and note that all of the tags are filled out, as shown in Figure 4–41. This enables you to verify whether the tags point to the sheets correctly. If a tag does not display detail and sheet numbers, the view has not been dragged onto a sheet.

Figure 4–41

12. Save the project.

4.3 Printing Sheets

With the **Print** command, you can print individual sheets or a list of selected sheets. You can also print an individual view or a portion of a view for check prints or presentations. To open the Print dialog box (shown in Figure 4–42), in the *File* tab, click

🖶 (Print) or press **<Ctrl>+<P>**.

Figure 4–42

Printing Options

The Print dialog box is divided into the following areas: *Printer*, *File*, *Print Range*, *Options*, and *Settings*. Modify them as needed to produce the plot you want.

- **Printing Tips**: Opens Autodesk WikiHelp online, in which you can find help with troubleshooting printing issues.

- **Preview**: Opens a preview of the print output so that you can see what is going to be printed.

Printer

Select from the list of available printers, as shown in Figure 4–43. Click **Properties...** to adjust the properties of the selected printer. The options vary according to the printer. Select the **Print to file** option to print to a file rather than directly to a printer. You can create .PLT or .PRN files.

Figure 4–43

- You must have a .PDF print driver installed on your system to print to PDF.

File

The *File* area is only available if the **Print to file** option has been selected in the *Printer* area or if you are printing to an electronic-only type of printer. You can create one file or multiple files depending on the type of printer you are using, as shown in Figure 4–44. Click **Browse...** to select the file location and name.

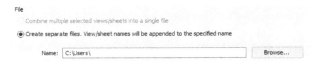

Figure 4–44

Print Range

The *Print Range* area enables you to print individual views/sheets or sets of views/sheets, as shown in Figure 4–45.

Figure 4–45

- **Current window**: Prints the entire current sheet or view you have open.

- **Visible portion of current window**: Prints only what is displayed in the current sheet or view.

- **Selected views/sheets**: Prints multiple views or sheets. Click **Select...** to open the View/Sheet Set dialog box to choose what to include in the print set. You can save these sets by name so that you can more easily print the same group again.

Options

If your printer supports multiple copies, you can specify the number in the *Options* area, as shown in Figure 4–46. You can also reverse the print order or collate your prints. These options are also available in the printer properties.

Figure 4–46

Settings

Click **Setup**... to open the Print Setup dialog box, as shown in Figure 4–47. Here, you can specify the *Orientation* and *Zoom* settings, among others. You can also save these settings by name.

Figure 4–47

- In the *Options* area, specify the types of elements you want to print or not print. Unless specified, all of the elements in a view or sheet print.

- Sheets should always be printed at **Zoom** set to **100%** size unless you are creating a quick markup set that does not need to be exact.

4.4 Exporting Files

If your company uses multiple CAD programs or works with consultants who use other CAD programs, prepare your Autodesk Revit files so that the other programs can use them as well. The Autodesk Revit software provides ways to export Autodesk Revit vector data to CAD formats, DWF/DWFx, Images and Animations, Reports, FBX, gbXML, IFC (Industry Foundation Classes), and ODBC databases, as shown in Figure 4–48.

Scroll down the Export list to see additional options.

Figure 4–48

- Find out if the users for which you are exporting need a 2D or 3D view. You can export any view, but only 3D views export the entire building model; other views create 2D files.

- Text character size, location, and other text related properties is rendered faithfully when exported to other CAD file formats.

Export Types

- **CAD Formats:** Exports projects to AutoCAD DWG or DXF, MicroStation DGN, or ASIC SAT files for 3D modeling.

- **DWF/DWFx:** Exports views and sheets to DWF or DWFx files to be used in Autodesk® Design Review for review and redlining.

- **FBX:** Exports 3D files for Autodesk® MotionBuilder®, as well as Autodesk® Maya®, Autodesk® 3ds Max®, and Viz plug-ins. You must be in a 3D view for this to display.

- **Family Types:** Exports family type information to a text (.txt) file that can be imported into a spreadsheet program to verify that all of the parameters for each type are correct. You must be in a family file for this to display.

- **gbXML:** Exports model information that can be used in other programs for energy or load analysis.

- **IFC:** Exports the Autodesk Revit model to Industry Foundation Class objects. These can be used by CAD programs that do not use RVT file formats. It uses established standards for typical objects in the building industry. For example, an Autodesk Revit wall element translates to an IfcWall object. Additional mapping for specialty items can be set up.

- **ODBC Database:** Exports Autodesk Revit information to an Open Database Connectivity database file. It creates tables of the model element types and instances, levels, rooms, key schedules, and assembly codes.

- **Images and Animations:** Exports walkthroughs, solar studies, and images.

- **Reports:** Exports information from Schedules and Room/Area. Schedules are exported as delimited text files that can be imported into a spreadsheet. You must be in a schedule view to export. Room/Area reports are saved as HTML files.

- **Options:** Sets up the options for Export Setups for DWG/DXF, DGN, and IFC options.

- **NWC:** (Autodesk Navisworks or Navisworks NWC Export Utility installs only) If you have Autodesk Navisworks 2021 or the Navisworks NWC Export Utility 2021 installed, you will see the option to export to an NWC file type.

Exporting CAD Format Files

Exporting Autodesk Revit Projects to various CAD file formats is a common need in collaboration with consultants and engineers. Using this process, you can export individual views or sheets, or sets of views or sheets to DWG, DXF, DGN, and SAT files. You can also create and save sets of views/sheets.

- To improve performance and file size of the exported file, you will want to use Visibility/Graphic Overrides to turn off objects that are not being seen in the view you are exporting.

- Use a section box or crop region to minimize elements outside the region.

- Reduce the amount of detail by setting the view's detail level to Coarse or Medium.

How To: Export a CAD Format File

1. If you are exporting only one view, open the view you want to export. If you are exporting the model, open a 3D view.

2. In the *File* tab, expand ⬛ (Export), click

   ⬛ (CAD Formats), and select the type of format you want to export as shown in Figure 4–49.

Figure 4–49

- The examples in this section show the process for DWG files. It is the same for other types of files.

3. The Export CAD Formats dialog box displays, as shown in Figure 4–50.

Figure 4–50

4. If you have an existing export setup, you can select it from the drop-down list as shown in Figure 4–51, or click ⎯ (Modify Export Setup) to create a new one.

Figure 4–51

5. Select the view(s) you want to export from the Export drop-down list as shown in Figure 4–52.

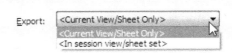

Figure 4–52

- To export only the active view, select **<Current View/ Sheet Only>**.
- To export any views or sheets that are open in the session of the Autodesk Revit software, select **<In session view/sheet set>**.
- To export a predefined set of views or sheets, select the name from the list if it is available. You can create new sets of views and sheets to export.

6. When everything is set up correctly, click **Next....**.
7. In the Export CAD Formats - Save to Target Folder dialog box, select the folder location and name. If you are exporting to DWG or DXF, select the version in the Files of type drop-down list.
8. Click **OK.**

- The Project Base Point of the Autodesk Revit project becomes the 0,0 coordinate point in other CAD formats.

How To: Create an Export Setup

1. In the DWG, DXF, or DGN Export dialog box, next to the Select Export Setup list, click [...] (Modify Export Setup) or in the *File* tab, expand (Export), scroll down to (Options), expand it, and select (Export Setups DWG/DXF) or (Export Setups DGN).
2. The Modify DWG/DXF or Modify DGN Export Setup dialog box contains all of the elements and types you can export. You can select an existing Layer standard provided with the program (as shown in Figure 4–53), or create a new one.

Figure 4–53

3. Select each of the tabs and apply the appropriate information.

- In the *Layers* tab, map the Categories in the Autodesk Revit software to the Layers (or Levels).
- In the *Lines*, *Patterns*, and *Text & Fonts* tabs map the styles required.
- In the *Colors* tab, select to export either Index colors (255 colors) or True color (RGB values).
- In the *Solids* tab (3D views only), select to export to either Polymesh or ACIS solids.
- In the *Units & Coordinates* tab, specify what unit type one DWG unit is and the basis for the coordinate system.
- In the *General* tab, you can set up how the rooms and room boundaries are exported, what to do with any non-plottable layers, how scope boxes, reference planes, coincident lines, and unreferenced view tags are handled, how views on sheets and links are treated, and which version of the DWG file format to use.

- Export setups can be created in a template file or shared between open projects using Transfer Project Standards.

How To: Create a New Set of Views/Sheets to Export

1. Start the appropriate Export CAD Formats command.

2. In the Export CAD Formats dialog box, click ⬚ (New Set).
3. In the New Set dialog box, type a name and click **OK**.

4. The tab displays with the new set active and additional information, as shown in Figure 4–54.

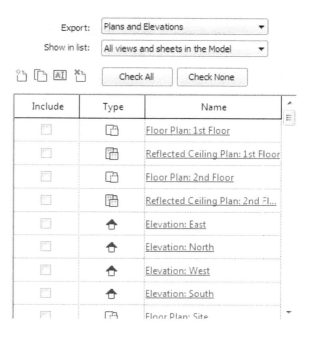

Figure 4–54

5. Use *Show in List* to limit the number of items that display in the table.
6. Select the views and/or sheets that you want to export from the project.
   - Use **Check all** or **Check none** to aid in selection.
7. When you finish with the set, continue the export process.

Exporting to DWF

Exporting DWF/DWFx (Design Web Format) files gives you a safe and easy way to share Autodesk Revit project information without sending the actual file. For example, a client does not have to have the Autodesk Revit software on their machine to view the file and they cannot make any changes directly to it. DWF/DWFx files are also much smaller than project files and are therefore easier to email or post on a website. DWF/DWFx files can include element data that can be viewed in Autodesk Design Review.

The process of exporting a DWF file is similar to CAD Format exports. You can export individual views or sheets, as shown in Figure 4–55, or you can create sets of multiple views/sheets by clicking on (New Set) and selecting from all the views/sheets in the project.

Figure 4–55

- In the *DWF Properties* tab, set up the export object data, the graphics settings, and print setup.

- The *Project Information* tab, shown in Figure 4–56, can be updated and included in a DWF export.

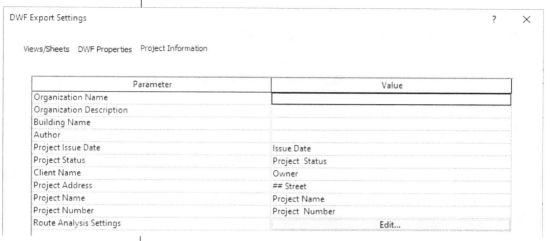

DWF Export Settings   ?   ✕

Views/Sheets   DWF Properties   Project Information

Parameter	Value
Organization Name	
Organization Description	
Building Name	
Author	
Project Issue Date	Issue Date
Project Status	Project Status
Client Name	Owner
Project Address	## Street
Project Name	Project Name
Project Number	Project Number
Route Analysis Settings	Edit...

Figure 4–56

- Files can be exported to the DWF or DWFx format.

- You can mark up (redline) DWF/DWFx files using other programs. The markups can then be linked back into the Autodesk Revit project, using the (DWG Markup) command so the original user can make the changes noted.

- Textures, line patterns, line weights, and text are included in 3D DWF exports.

Practice 4d | Export Files

Practice Objective

- Export views to AutoCAD drawing files and DWF viewing files.

In this practice, you will export several views to AutoCAD drawing files and to DWF files, as shown in Autodesk Design Review in Figure 4–57.

Figure 4–57

Task 1 - Set up and export a set of 2D views to a DWG file.

1. In the practice files folder, open the **Office Phases** project that matches your discipline.

   - The views shown in this practice use the original version of **Office-Export.rvt**. Your practice file will vary according to the project you select and the work that has been done in the file.

2. In the *File* tab, expand 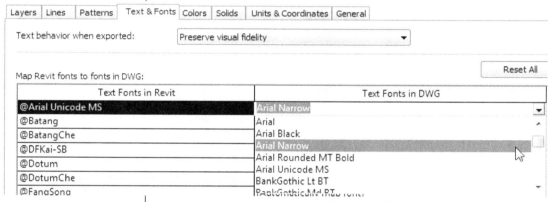 (Export), expand
    (CAD Formats), and click (DWG).

3. In the DWG Export dialog box, in the *Select Export Setup*
    area, click [...] (Modify Export Setup).

4. In the Modify DWG/DXF Export Setup dialog box, *Layers* tab,
    Load layers from standards list, select the standard you are
    most likely to use.

5. In the *Text & Fonts* tab for *Text behavior when exported*,
    select **Preserve visual fidelity**.

6. Scroll down in the list of fonts and map *Arial* to **Arial Narrow**,
    as shown in Figure 4–58.

Figure 4–58

7. In the *General* tab, select **Export rooms, spaces and areas
    as polylines**. Click **OK**.

8. In the DWG Export dialog box, click (New Set).

9. In the New Set dialog box, type the name **Plans** and click
    OK.

10. Select at least two floor/structural plan views, as shown in Figure 4–59.

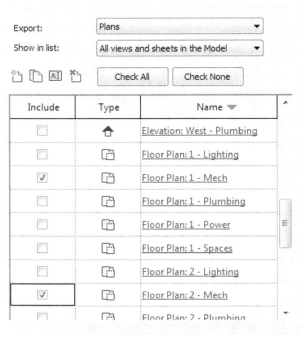

Figure 4–59

11. Click **Next...**.

12. In the Export CAD Formats - Save to Target Folder dialog box, set the *Save In:* to the practice files folder. Set the *Files of Type:* to **AutoCAD 2018 DWG Files (*.dwg)**.

13. Set the *Naming* to **Automatic-Long (Specify prefix)** and type **Plans** in the *File name/Prefix* field.

14. Click **OK**. The software generates DWG files for the each selected view using the setup you defined.

Task 2 - Export a 3D view to AutoCAD.

---

1. Switch to a 3D view from the 3D Views section in the Project Browser.

2. In the *File* tab, expand (Export), expand (CAD Formats), and click (DWG Files).

3. In the DWG Export dialog box, set *Export:* to **<Current View/Sheet only>**, as shown in Figure 4–60.

Figure 4–60

4. Click **Next...**. In the Export CAD Formats - Save to Target Folder dialog box, type a file name, and click **OK**.

5. If you have access to AutoCAD, you can open the files to see the exported geometry or view them in Windows Explorer, as shown in Figure 4–61 in the Extra Large Icons view.

Office-Phases-MEP - Floor Plan - 1 - Mech.dwg   Office-Phases-MEP - Floor Plan - 1 -   Office-Phases-MEP - 3D View - 3D HVAC.dwg
Mech-Office-Link-MEP-M-rvt-1-1 - Mech.dwg

Figure 4–61

Task 3 - Export to DWF.

1. In the *File* tab, expand (Export) and click

   (DWF/DWFx).

2. In the DWF Export Settings dialog box, click (New Set).

3. In the New Set dialog box, type the name **Sheets** and click **OK**.

4. Change the *Show in list:* to **Sheets in the Model** and select the sheets, as shown in Figure 4–62.

Figure 4–62

5. Switch to the *DWF Properties* tab and verify that **Element properties** is selected.

6. Click **Next...**.

7. In the Export DWF - Save to Target Folder dialog box, type in the *File name/prefix*: **Sheets**. Note that **Combine selected views and sheets into a single dwf file** is selected by default and grayed out because the *Naming*: is set to **Manual (Specify file name)**.

8. Click **OK**.

9. If you have Autodesk Design Review, you can open and view the file.

10. If you have time, create a 3D DWF of the model and view the file.

11. Save and close all open files.

Chapter Review Questions

1. How do you specify the size of a sheet?

   a. In the Sheet Properties, specify the **Sheet Size**.

   b. In the Options Bar, specify the **Sheet Size**.

   c. In the New Sheet dialog box, select a title block to control the Sheet Size.

   d. In the Sheet view, right-click and select **Sheet Size**.

2. How is the title block information filled in as shown in Figure 4–63? (Select all that apply.)

Figure 4–63

   a. Select the title block and select the label that you want to change.

   b. Select the title block and modify it in Properties.

   c. Right-click on the Sheet in the Project Browser and select **Information**.

   d. Some of the information is filled in automatically.

3. On how many sheets can a floor plan view be placed?

   a. 1

   b. 2-5

   c. 6+

   d. As many as you want.

4. Which of the following is the best method to use if the size of a view is too large for a sheet, as shown in Figure 4–64?

Figure 4–64

a. Delete the view, change the scale and place the view back on the sheet.

b. Change the scale of the sheet.

5. How do you set up a view on a sheet that only displays part of a floor plan, as shown in Figure 4–65?

Figure 4–65

a. Drag and drop the view to the sheet and use the crop region to modify it.

b. Activate the view and rescale it.

c. Create a callout view displaying the part that you want to use and place the callout view on the sheet.

d. Open the view in the Project Browser and change the View Scale.

6. Which of the following settings can be specified when you export a project to DWG/DXF? (Select all that apply.)

   a. Line Weight to Color

   b. Text

   c. Units

   d. Patterns

Command Summary

Button	Command	Location
Sheets and Printing		
	Activate View	• **Ribbon:** *(select the view) Modify | Viewports* tab>Viewport panel • **Double-click:** *(in viewport)* • **Right-click:** *(on view)* Activate View
	Deactivate View	• **Ribbon:** *View* tab>Sheet Composition panel>expand Viewports • **Double-click:** *(on sheet)* • **Right-click:** *(on view)* Deactivate View
	Place View	• **Ribbon:** *View* tab>Sheet Composition panel
	Print	• **File tab**
	Sheet	• **Ribbon:** *View* tab>Sheet Composition panel
Exporting		
	ACIS (SAT)	• *File* tab: Expand Export>CAD Formats
	Building Site	• *File* tab: Expand Export
	CAD Formats	• *File* tab: Expand Export
	DGN	• *File* tab: Expand Export>CAD Formats
	DWF/DWFx	• *File* tab: Expand Export
	DWG	• *File* tab: Expand Export>CAD Formats
	DXF	• *File* tab: Expand Export>CAD Formats
	Export	• *File* tab
	Export Setups DGN	• *File* tab: Expand Export>Options
	Export Setups DWG/DWF	• *File* tab: Expand Export>Options

	Family Types	• *File* tab: Expand Export
	FBX	• *File* tab: Expand Export
	gbXML	• *File* tab: Expand Export
	IFC	• *File* tab: Expand Export
	IFC Options	• *File* tab: Expand Export>Options
	Images and Animations	• *File* tab: Expand Export
	Mass Model gbXML	• *File* tab: Expand Export
	ODBC Database	• *File* tab: Expand Export
	Options	• *File* tab: Expand Export
	Reports	• *File* tab: Expand Export

Starting Multidiscipline Projects

Files from other CAD programs can be imported (and in some cases linked) into an Autodesk® Revit® project. These elements can be traced over or used as is to create a hybrid project. Imported CAD files can be manipulated and even exploded into individual elements, which can then take on Revit properties. Autodesk Revit models can be linked into other projects. Linking models can be used to create multiple copies of one building that are placed in a site plan, or to link an architectural model into a structural or MEP project.

Learning Objectives in This Chapter

- Import or link files that were created in other CAD programs into an Autodesk Revit project.
- Link Autodesk Revit models into a host project.
- Modify link display settings in views.

5.1 Importing and Linking Vector Files

You can print a hybrid drawing - part Autodesk Revit project and part imported/linked drawing.

Many firms have legacy drawings from vector-based CAD programs and could be working with consultants that use them. For example, you may want to link a DWG plan into your project, as shown in the Link CAD Formats dialog box in Figure 5–1, that you would then trace over using Autodesk Revit tools. Other non-CAD specific file formats, including coordination models from Navisworks, IFC files and point clouds, can also be opened or linked into Autodesk Revit projects.

Figure 5–1

CAD file formats that can be imported or linked include AutoCAD® (DWG and DXF), MicroStation® (DGN), 3D ACIS modeling kernel (SAT), and Trimble® SketchUp® (SKP). Note that files from Rhinoceros® (3DM) can only be imported.

Linking vs. Importing

- **Link:** A connection is maintained with the original file and the link updates if the original file is updated.
- **Import:** No connection is maintained with the original file. It becomes a separate element in the Autodesk Revit model.

How To: Import or Link a CAD File

1. The dialog boxes for Link CAD and Import CAD formats are the same except for the Positioning method. Proceed as follows:

To...	Then...
Import a CAD file	In the *Insert* tab>Import panel, click 🔲 (Import CAD).
Link a CAD file	In the *Insert* tab>Link panel, click 🔲 (Link CAD).

2. Fill out the Import CAD (or Link CAD) dialog box. The top part of the dialog box holds the standard select file options. The bottom outlines the various options for importing or linking, as shown in Figure 5–2.

Figure 5–2

3. Click **Open**.

Depending on the selected Positioning method, the file is automatically placed or you can place it with the cursor.

Link and Import Options

Current view only	If selected, the file is imported/linked into the current view and not into other views. You might want to enable this option if you are just working on a floor plan and do not want the objects to display in 3D and other views.
Colors	The Autodesk Revit software works mainly with black lines of different weights on a white background to describe elements, but both AutoCAD and MicroStation use a variety of colors. To make the move into the Autodesk Revit software easier, you can select to turn all colors to Black and White, Preserve colors, or Invert colors
Layers	You can select which layers from the original drawing are imported/linked. The options are All, Visible (those that are not off or frozen), and Select. Select opens a list of layers or levels from which you can select when you import the drawing file.
Import units	Autodesk Revit software can auto-detect the units in the imported/linked file. You can also specify the units that you want to use from a list of typical Imperial and Metric units or set a Custom scale factor.
Correct lines that are slightly off axis	Corrects lines that are less than 0.1 degree of axis so that any elements based on those line are created correctly. It is on by default. Toggle it off if you are working with site plans.
Positioning	Select from the methods to place the imported/linked file in the Autodesk Revit host project. If linking the file, Auto - By Shared Coordinates is available.
Place at:	Select a level in the drop-down list to specify the vertical positioning for the file. This is grayed out if you have selected Current view only.
Orient to View	Select this to place the file at the same orientation as the current view.

- The default positioning is **Auto - Origin to Internal Origin**. The software remembers the most recently used positioning type as long as you are in the same session of Autodesk Revit. (The CAD Links dialog box remembers the last positioning used separately from the RVT Links dialog box.)

- If you are linking a file, an additional Positioning option, **Auto-By Shared Coordinates**, is available. It is typically used with linked Autodesk Revit files. If you use it with a CAD file, an alert box opens, as shown in Figure 5–3, containing information about the coordinate systems and what the Autodesk Revit software does.

Figure 5–3

- When you link a DWG file that includes reference files (XREFs), as shown in AutoCAD's External References palette in Figure 5–4, only files whose *Type* is set to **Attach** will display. Files whose *Type* is set to **Overlay** do not display.

Figure 5–4

- When you import a DWG file, all XREFs display no matter how they are set up in the DWG file.

Importing Line Weights

One significant setting for imported drawings is the line weight. Both AutoCAD and MicroStation can use line weights as well as colors. Typically, AutoCAD line weights are associated with a color. Therefore, the Autodesk Revit software imports them by color.

How To: Import Line Weights

Clicking ⌖ in the title bar of a panel typically opens a settings dialog box related to the commands in the panel.

1. Before you import a CAD file, in the *Insert* tab>Import panel, click ⌖ (Import Line Weights), as shown in Figure 5–5.

Import Line Weights

Maps pen numbers from layers of a DWG or DXF file to Revit line weights.

Press F1 for more help

Figure 5–5

2. In the Import Line Weights dialog box, shown in Figure 5–6, load a text file that holds the relationships or type them in the dialog box. You can then save them for later use.

Figure 5–6

3. Click **OK** and then import the CAD file.

- To load information from an existing text file, click **Load...** and select the file that you want to use. Several files are included in the *Data* folder, as shown in Figure 5–7.

Figure 5–7

- To create a custom text file for specific projects, set up a sequence and click **Save As...**.

- Save your custom import line weight text files to a folder that is accessible to everyone that might need to use it. Do not save any custom files to the Autodesk Revit folders because they might be deleted if the program is upgraded or reinstalled.

Hint: Linking Autodesk Civil 3D DWG Files

Autodesk Civil 3D creates DWG files but the process of using them accurately in Autodesk Revit requires some extra steps. The Project Base Point in Revit is basically the same as the 0,0,0 origin point in an AutoCAD DWG. However, Civil 3D files typically use real world site locations established by surveyors. You can request a reference point (Northing, Easting, Elevation) from the civil engineer and add that information to the Survey Point in the Revit project before linking the site into the model.

Working with Other File Formats

There are additional file formats that can be opened or linked into Autodesk Revit projects, including IFC (Industry Foundation Class) elements, point clouds and coordination models. ADSK (Autodesk Exchange) files can be loaded and used as a family.

IFC (Industry Foundation Classes)

The IFC specification is an international data neutral format. Models created in any building design program can be saved or exported to this file format. You can open IFC files directly (*File* tab>Open> (IFC)) or link them into the current project (in the *Insert* tab>Link panel, click (Link IFC)).

- If you are opening an IFC file, first set up the default template and manage the mapping of IFC classes to Revit Categories (*File* tab>Open> (IFC Options)).

- Autodesk Revit models can be exported to IFC.

Autodesk Exchange Files

Building Component files, such as the blower created in Inventor shown in Figure 5–8, can be loaded and used as a family into an Autodesk Revit project. They display the real size of the equipment and can also include connectors to related MEP elements. They must first be saved in the original program as an Autodesk® Exchange (ADSK) file.

Supply air connector

Figure 5–8

- To use an ADSK file, first load it into the project (*Insert* tab> Load from Library panel, click 🔽 (Load Family)) and then use the **Component** command to place it.

- ADSK files can be saved as an RFA family file. In the *File* tab, expand 🗁 (Open), expand 🗀 (Building Component) and select the ADSK file to open. Then, in the *File* tab, expand 💾 (Save As) and click 🗗 (Family).

Point Clouds

Point clouds are created using 3D laser scanners and are frequently used to establish accurate existing information. Once you link a point cloud (in the *Insert* tab>Link panel click

🔵 (Point Cloud)) into a project, as shown in Figure 5–9, you can snap to alignment planes and individual points.

Figure 5–9

There are three file formats that you can link:

- **RCS** - Individual indexed scanned models.
- **RCP** - Groups of indexed scanned models.
- Raw format point clouds must first be converted to RCS or RCP files using Autodesk® Recap® before being imported into Autodesk Revit.

How To: Link a Point Cloud

1. In the *Insert* tab>Link panel, click 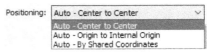 (Point Cloud).
2. In the Link Point Cloud dialog box, specify the Positioning (Auto - Center to Center, Auto - Origin to Internal Origin, or Auto - By Shared Coordinates), as shown in Figure 5–10, and click **Add...**.

Positioning: Auto - Center to Center

- Auto - Center to Center
- Auto - Origin to Internal Origin
- Auto - By Shared Coordinates

Figure 5–10

- In the Visibility/Graphic Overrides dialog box, in the P*oint Clouds* tab, you can change the visibility and set a color mode. Each individual scan can be controlled individually.

Coordination Models

Many construction projects include designs from a variety of software programs. Autodesk® Navisworks® enables you to link together files from these different programs to create a coordination model. You can then link the models saved in Navisworks as a NWD or NWC file into your Autodesk Revit model, to help you coordinate the larger project, as shown in Figure 5–11.

Figure 5–11

How To: Link a Coordination Model

1. In the *Insert* tab>Link panel, click (Coordination Model).
2. In the Coordination Model dialog box, specify the *Positioning* (**Origin to Internal Origin** or **By Shared Coordinates**), as shown in Figure 5–12, and click **Add...**.

Positioning:	Origin to Internal Origin	⌄
Add...		Place Instance

Figure 5–12

3. Navigate to the correct file folder, select the Navisworks document (NWD or NWC), and click **Open**.
4. In the Coordination Model dialog box (shown in Figure 5–13), modify the *Path Type* if required and click **Apply** if you want to remain in the dialog box. Otherwise, click **OK**.

Figure 5–13

- You can add copies of the coordination model if needed. Select the *Model Name*, specify the *Positioning* and click **Place Instance**.

- You can also use the buttons to **Reload From...**, **Reload**, **Unload**, and **Remove** coordination models.

Practice 5a

Work with Vector Files - Architectural

Practice Objective

- Link an AutoCAD file into an Autodesk Revit project and use it as a basis to add elements for a hybrid drawing.

In this practice, you will create a hybrid CAD/Autodesk Revit project for an addition to an existing building. You will link an AutoCAD file into a project and add some Autodesk Revit elements, as shown in Figure 5–14.

New Autodesk Revit elements

Figure 5–14

1. Start a new project based on the default Architectural template.

2. Save the project as **Bank Addition Architectural.rvt** in your practice files folder.

3. Verify that you are in the **Floor Plans: Level 1** view.

4. In the *Insert* tab>Link panel, click (Link CAD).

5. In the Link CAD dialog box, in the practice files folder, select the AutoCAD drawing file **Bank-Existing.dwg** and set the following options:

- Select **Current View Only**
- *Colors*: **Black and White**
- *Layers:* **All**
- *Import Units:* **Auto-Detect**
- Select **Correct lines that are slightly off axis**
- *Positioning*: **Auto - Center to Center**

6. Click **Open**.

7. Switch to an elevation view. No elements are in that view—the imported information is 2D only. Switch to **Floor Plans: Level 2**. You will not see the linked file because it was linked in **Floor Plans: Level 1** with **Current View Only** selected.

8. Switch back to the **Floor Plans: Level 1** view.

9. Use the outline in front of the lobby and vestibule to draw exterior walls (with a Height to Level 2). Add doors (you will need to load a double door) and windows in front of the existing entrance of the building as a new entrance, similar to that shown in Figure 5–15.

Figure 5–15

10. Switch to the **Elevations (Building Elevations): South** view. You should see the Autodesk Revit objects in the view.

11. Save the project.

Practice 5b

Work with Vector Files - MEP

Practice Objectives

- Import an AutoCAD file into an Autodesk Revit project and use it as a basis to add elements for a hybrid drawing.

In this practice, you will create a hybrid CAD/Autodesk Revit project for an addition to an existing building. You will link an AutoCAD file and an Autodesk Revit model into a project and add some Autodesk Revit elements, as shown in Figure 5–16.

New Autodesk Revit elements

Figure 5–16

1. Start a new project based on the Electrical or Systems template. (To access these templates, in the New Project dialog box, click **Browse...** and select the required template from the Autodesk Revit templates library.)

2. Save the project as **Bank Addition-MEP.rvt** in your practice files folder.

3. Open the Electrical>Lighting> **Floor Plans: 1- Lighting** view.

4. In the *Insert* tab>Link panel, click 🔲 (Link CAD).

5. In the Link CAD dialog box, in the practice files folder, select the AutoCAD drawing file **Bank-MEP.dwg** and set the following options:

    - Select **Current View Only**
    - *Colors*: **Black and White**
    - *Layers:* **All**
    - *Import Units:* **Auto-Detect**
    - Select **Correct lines that are slightly off axis**
    - *Positioning*: **Auto - Origin to Internal Origin**

6. Click **Open**.

7. Switch to an elevation view. No elements are in that view—the imported information is 2D only. Switch to **Floor Plans: Lighting 2**. You will not see the linked file because it was linked in **Floor Plans: Lighting 1** with **Current View Only** selected.

8. Switch back to the **Floor Plans: 1 - Lighting** view.

9. Link in the Autodesk Revit model **Bank-Addition-A.rvt** from your practice files folder using **Auto - Internal Origin to Internal Origin** positioning.

10. Open the Electrical>Lighting>Ceiling Plans>**1 - Ceiling Elec** view. The linked Autodesk Revit elements display in this view but the imported CAD elements do not.

11. Add several new lights in the new entry area similar to that shown in Figure 5–17. (This example uses pendant lights placed on the ceiling face.)

Figure 5–17

12. Verify that in the *Modify | Place Fixture* tab>Placement panel,
    (Place on Face) is selected.Switch to the **Elevations (Building Elevations): North- Elec** view. You should see the Autodesk Revit objects in the view.

13. Save the project.

Practice 5c

Work with Vector Files - Structural

Practice Objectives

- Link an AutoCAD file into an Autodesk Revit project and use it as a basis to add elements for a hybrid drawing.

In this practice, you will create a hybrid CAD/Autodesk Revit project for an addition to an existing building. You will link an AutoCAD file into a project and add some Autodesk Revit elements, as shown in Figure 5–18.

New Autodesk Revit elements

Figure 5–18

1. Start a new project based on the default Structural template.

2. Save the project as **Bank Addition Structural.rvt** in your practice files folder.

3. Verify that you are in the **Structural Plans: Level 2** view.

4. In the *Insert* tab>Link panel, click (Link CAD).

5. In the Import CAD dialog box, in the practice files folder, select the AutoCAD drawing file **Bank-Existing.dwg** and set the following options:

   - Select **Current View Only**
   - *Colors*: **Black and White**
   - *Layers:* **All**
   - *Import Units:* **Auto-Detect**
   - Select **Correct lines that are slightly off axis**
   - *Positioning*: **Auto - Center to Center**

6. Click **Open**.

7. Switch to an elevation view. No elements are in that view—the imported information is 2D only. Switch to **Structural Plans: Level 1**. You will not see the linked file because it was linked in **Structural Plans: Level 2** with **Current View Only** selected.

8. Switch back to the **Structural Plans: Level 2** view.

9. Change the imported CAD file to halftone in the Visibility/Graphic Overrides dialog box.

10. Add structural columns (with a *Depth* set to **Level 1**) and beams to the top of them using the outline in front of the vestibule and lobbies for a new entrance, similar to that shown in Figure 5–19.

Figure 5–19

11. Switch to the **Elevations (Building Elevations): South** view. You should see the Autodesk Revit objects in the view.

12. Save the project.

5.2 Linking Models

You can link an Autodesk® Revit® project into any other project. A linked model automatically updates if the original file is changed. This method can be used in many ways. For example, use this method when you have a number of identical buildings on one site plan, as shown in Figure 5–20. When you link one Revit model into another, the model that you are working in is called the *host* or *hosting* model, and the model that has been linked into the host model is called the *linked* model.

Figure 5–20

It is important to understand that when models are linked into a Revit project, that project remembers the paths so that the user does not have to relink the models every time they reopen their own model. This saves the user a great deal of time over the course of a project; however, it can also increase the amount of time it takes to open a model. The more linked models in a project, the longer it will take to open.

It is best practice, when linking models into one another, to use the same Revit version across all of the models.

Structural and MEP projects typically use the architectural model as the base for their projects. But there are times when an architect will link consultants' files into the architectural file as well.

- Architectural, structural, and MEP models created in the Autodesk® Revit® software can be linked to each other as long as they are from the same release cycle.

- When you use linked models, clashes between disciplines can be detected, and information can be passed between disciplines.

- Elements can be copied and monitored for even better coordination.

Linked models can be constrained to elements in the host project and to each other. You can select references in linked models as a work plane and can schedule elements from the linked model in the host project.

Hint: Project Base Point

The origin of a project coordinate system is specified by the project base point, as shown in Figure 5–21. This should be set early in the project and before you start linking files together. It can be (but is not always) connected with the Survey Point, a secondary coordinate system used with shared coordinates. The internal origin, or startup location, never moves and is the internal coordinate system used for the base position for all of the model's elements.

Figure 5–21

- Project base points and survey points are visible in the Site view of the default architectural template. You can toggle them on in any view. In the Visibility/Graphic Overrides dialog box, in the *Model Category* tab, expand the **Site** category.

- The Internal Origin is typically off in all views, but it can be toggled on through the Visibility/Graphic Overrides dialog box, in the *Model Category* tab under the **Site** category.

- A linked model's project base, survey, and internal origin points will be grayed out in the view, indicating they belong to the linked model. The host model's points display in color, as shown in Figure 5–22.

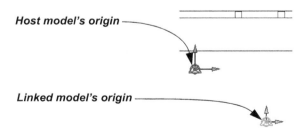

Figure 5–22

- Spot Coordinates and Spot Elevations are relative to the project base point.

How To: Add a Linked Model to a Host Project

1. In the *Insert* tab>Link panel, click 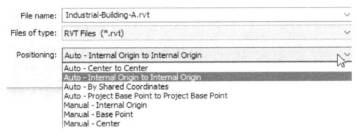 (Link Revit).
2. In the Import/Link RVT dialog box, select the file that you want to link. Before opening the file, set the *Positioning*, as shown in Figure 5–23, and click **Open**.

File name: Industrial-Building-A.rvt

Files of type: RVT Files (*.rvt)

Positioning: Auto - Internal Origin to Internal Origin
- Auto - Center to Center
- Auto - Internal Origin to Internal Origin
- Auto - By Shared Coordinates
- Auto - Project Base Point to Project Base Point
- Manual - Internal Origin
- Manual - Base Point
- Manual - Center

Figure 5–23

- Depending on how you decide to position the file, it is automatically placed in the file or you can manually place it with the cursor.

- The default positioning is **Auto - Internal Origin to Internal Origin**. The center of a linked model is the center of the geometry. Therefore, if you modify the extents of the original model, its exact location changes in the host project if you link **Center to Center**.

- **Auto - Project Base Point to Project Base Point** aligns the base points of the projects rather than the default origins.

- The software remembers the most recently used positioning type as long as you are in the same session of Autodesk Revit. (The CAD Links dialog box remembers the last positioning used as well, but separately from RVT Links)

- As the links are loading, do not click on the screen or click any buttons. The more links that are present in a project, the longer it takes to load.

- Linked models can be moved once you have placed them in the project. If you want to return them to the original location, right-click on the link and select either **Reposition to Project Base Point** or **Reposition to Internal Origin**, as shown in Figure 5–24

Figure 5–24

Hint: Preventing Linked Model from Being Moved

Once a linked model is in the correct location, you can lock it in place to ensure that it does not get moved by mistake, or prevent the linked model from being selected.

- To toggle off the ability to select links, in the Status Bar, click (Select Links).

- To pin the linked model in place, select it and in the *Modify* tab>Modify panel, click (Pin).

- To prevent pinned elements from being selected, in the Status Bar, click (Select Pinned Elements).

Multiple Copies of Links

Copied instances of a linked model are typically used when creating a master project with the same building placed in multiple locations, such as a university campus with several identical student residences, or with identical units, such as hospital rooms used multiple times within one building.

- Linked models can be copied, rotated, arrayed, and mirrored.

- You only link a model once, but you can place as many copies as are required into the host project. The copies are numbered automatically, and the name can be changed in Properties when the instance is selected. There is only one linked model, and the copies are additional instances of that link.

- When you have placed a link in a project, you can use the Project Browser, as shown in Figure 5–25, to drag and drop additional copies of the link into the project.

Revit Links
Warehouse Layout.rvt

Figure 5–25

Annotation and Linked Models

Many annotations can be added to the host model that reference elements in the linked model. For example, in Figure 5–26, the walls columns and grids are part of the linked model but the dimensions and tags are placed in the host project.

Figure 5–26

- Elements in the linked model can also be scheduled in the host project.

- The information annotated or scheduled for elements in a linked model cannot be controlled through the host model. Therefore, it is best to coordinate what information needs to be used in the hosting model annotation at the beginning of the project rather than waiting until it is necessary.

Managing Links

A linked model reloads each time the host project is opened. You can also reload the model by right-clicking on the Revit Link in the Project Browser, and then selecting **Reload** or **Reload From**, as shown in Figure 5–27.

Figure 5–27

The Manage Links dialog box (shown in Figure 5–28) enables you to reload, unload, add, and remove links. Additionally, it provides access to other options. To open the Manage Links dialog box, in the *Insert* tab>Link, panel click ▣ (Manage Links). The Manage Links dialog box also displays when you select a link in the *Modify | RVT Links* tab.

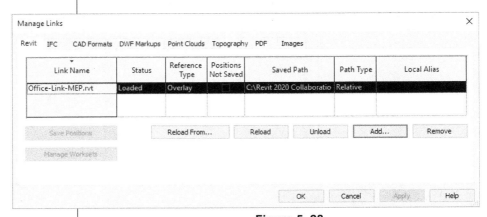

Figure 5–28

The options available in the Manage Links dialog box include the following:

- **Reload From:** Opens the Add Link dialog box, which enables you to select the file you want to reload. Use this if the linked file location or name has changed.

- **Reload:** Reloads the file without additional prompts.

- **Unload:** Unloads the file so that it the link is kept, but the file is not displayed or calculated in the project. Use **Reload** to restore it.

- **Add:** Opens the Import/Link RVT dialog box, which enables you to link additional models into the host project.

- **Remove:** Deletes the link from the file.

Links can be nested into one another. How a link responds when the host project is linked into another project depends on the option in the *Reference Type* column:

- **Overlay:** The nested linked model is not referenced in the new host project.

- **Attach:** The nested linked model displays in the new host project.

The option in the *Path Type* column controls how the location of the link is remembered:

- **Relative**

  - Searches the root folder of the current project.
  - If the file is moved, the software still searches for it.

- **Absolute**

  - Searches the entire file path where the file was originally saved.
  - If the original file is moved, the software is not able to find it.

- Other options control how the linked file interfaces with Worksets and Saved Positioning.

- In the Manage Links dialog box, when you have multiple links, you can sort rows by clicking the column header.

Linked Model Properties

Linked models have both instance properties and type properties. Instance Properties, as shown in Figure 5–29, include the *Name* for the individual copy of the link. This is automatically updated as you insert more than one. You can also change the name to help you identify it later. It also shows if it is part of a *Design Option* and if it is set to a *Shared Site*.

Figure 5–29

Type Properties, as shown in Figure 5–30, include *Room Bounding* which is required if you want to be able to place rooms or spaces from the information in the linked model. It also includes *Reference Type* (Overlay or Attachment) and *Phase Mapping* as well as workset information if the project is workshared.

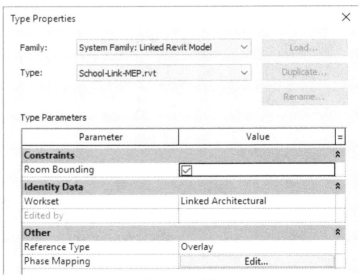

Figure 5–30

The phases in linked models can be mapped to the host project phasing so that the phasing schemes from different projects can be displayed consistently. Edit the Type Properties of the linked model and next to *Phase Mapping*, click **Edit...**. In the Phases dialog box, as shown in Figure 5–31, select the Phase from the linked model to match the corresponding phase in the host project.

Figure 5–31

Practice 5d | Link Models

Practice Objectives

- Link several models into a host project.
- Make copies of linked models in a project.

In this practice, you will link architectural, structural, and MEP models into a host building site project. You will make copies of the linked models and place them on the site, as shown in Figure 5–32.

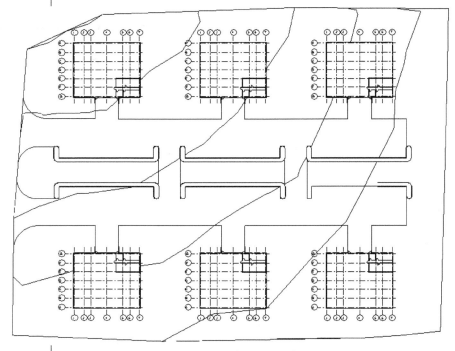

Figure 5–32

1. In the practice files folder, open **Industrial-Park.rvt**. The site has six rectangular pads for warehouse buildings.

2. In the *Insert* tab>Link panel, click (Link Revit).

3. In the Import/Link RVT dialog box, select the file **Industrial-Building-A.rvt**. Verify that the Positioning is set to **Auto - Internal Origin to Internal Origin.**

4. Click **Open**.

5. Select the new link. In Properties, verify that the *Name* of this instance is **1**. This makes tracking the rest of the instances easier.

6. Click (Link Revit) again and link in **Industrial-Building-MEP.rvt** at the same position.

7. An alert box opens, warning you that the model has another model linked to it and that it is not visible in this project. This is because it was linked in that file as an overlay rather than an attachment. Close the dialog box.

8. Repeat the process one more time and link in **Industrial-Building-S.rvt** at the same position.

9. The links do not come in directly on a pad. They need to be moved to the correct location. Select all of the linked models that are on top of each other and move them to one of the pads at the top of the site. You might need to zoom in to place it precisely.

10. Copy the linked models to the other pads on the same side of the parking lot.

11. Mirror the links from the north side of the parking to the south side and move them into place, as shown above in Figure 5–32.

12. Save the project.

Chapter Review Questions

1. Which of the following types of vector files can you import into the Autodesk Revit software? (Select all that apply.)

   a. DGN

   b. DWG

   c. DOC

   d. DXF

2. Which of the following settings can be specified before you import AutoCAD files or Microstation files into a project?

   a. Color to Line Weight

   b. Text and Dimension Styles

   c. Units

   d. Patterns

3. When linking an Autodesk Revit model into another project, which of the positioning methods keeps the model in the same place if the extents of the linked model changes in size?

   a. Auto - Center to Center

   b. Auto - Internal Origin to Internal Origin

   c. Manual - Base Point

   d. Manual - Center

Command Summary

Button	Command	Location
	Import CAD	• **Ribbon**: *Insert* tab>Import panel
	Link CAD	• **Ribbon**: *Insert* tab>Link panel
	Link Revit	• **Ribbon**: *Insert* tab>Link Panel>Link Revit
	Manage Links	• **Ribbon**: *Insert* tab>Link panel> Manage Links or *Modify RVT Links* tab> Link panel>Manage Links (if selected)

Project Team Collaboration

Project team collaboration happens on many levels in a firm and between disciplines. When you have a very large project with more than one person working on that project at one time, you need to enable worksharing, then create and use worksets. Worksets enable you to work in one part of a project while someone else is working in another part of the same project. Not everyone needs to know how to create a central model or set up worksets, but everyone needs to learn how to work with them.

Learning Objectives in This Chapter

- Understand worksharing workflow and definitions.
- Set up worksets in a project.
- Place elements in worksets.
- Create a central model.
- Create and open a local file based on the central model.
- Control workset visibility by view.
- Synchronize a local file with the central model.
- Set the active workset and work in the local file.
- Request and approve permission to edit elements.
- Temporarily enable the display of worksets.
- Close the workshared project correctly.
- Investigate tips for using worksets.

- The methodologies covered in this chapter focus on using server-based tools within Autodesk Revit. If you are using BIM 360 to access files, you can still use most of the processes covered in this chapter, such as setting up worksets. To learn more about BIM 360, refer to the ASCENT guide *Autodesk®️ BIM 360™️: Fundamentals*.

6.1 Introduction to Worksharing

NOTE: *All images in the upcoming sections refer to users as "User1" or "User2". In your working environment, you will see your unique Revit username in these dialog boxes.*

Autodesk® Revit® projects include the entire building model in one file. A process called *worksharing* is used when the file needs to be separated into logical components (as shown in Figure 6–1) without losing the connection to the whole. The main component of worksharing is worksets.

Worksharing gives multiple team members who are connected on the same network the ability to co-author a single project model (one RVT file).The appropriate team member creates a central model and worksets. Team members open and work in a local copy of the central model that is linked back to the central model through saving and synchronizing.

Figure 6–1

A workshared project consists of one central model (also known as a central file) and individual models for each user known as local files, as shown in Figure 6–2. Each team member will work in their local file and use a function called *synchronizing with central* to send and receive updates with the central model.

Figure 6–2

- The central model is created by the BIM manager, project manager, or project lead, and is stored on a server or in the cloud, enabling multiple user access.

Collaborate Tab

The tools found in the *Collaborate* tab, shown in Figure 6–3, are designed to help you and your team work more effectively in a workshared environment. Many of these tools are also available in the Quick Access Toolbar and Status Bar.

Figure 6–3

Worksharing Definitions

Worksharing: This is a functionality that, when enabled, allows multiple members of the team to access a project stored in one centralized location, which gives multiple users the ability to work on the same project simultaneously.

Workshared file: This is a project that has worksets enabled. If the project has no worksets enabled, it is called a *non-workshared file*.

Workset: This is a collection of elements that are related geometrically, parametrically, or by location within an overall project that are subdivided so they can be worked on while isolated from the rest of the model. When worksharing is enabled, worksets are automatically activated and the *Workset1* and *Shared Grids and Levels* worksets are added to the project by default.

Central model: Also called the central file, this is the main project file that is stored on a local network that all users can access. Using a central model is called *file-based worksharing*. The central model stores workset and element information in the project and is the file to which everyone saves and synchronizes their changes. The central model updates all the local files with the latest model information. This file should not be edited directly.

Local file: This is a copy of the central model that is saved to your local computer. This is the file that you modify and work in. As you work, you save the file locally and synchronize it with the central model.

Element borrowing: This refers to the process of modifying items in the project that are not part of the workset you have checked out. This either happens automatically (if no one else has checked out a workset) or specifically, when you request to have control of the elements (if someone else has a workset checked out).

Active workset: The workset that displays in the Status Bar is the active workset. Any new elements that are added will be placed on this workset. As you work, you will change the active workset accordingly.

Relinquish: This releases or returns a checked-out workset so that others can work on the elements within that workset. If you do not release or relinquish your checked-out worksets, other users will get a warning that they cannot edit the workset until you relinquish it, and they are given the option to request to borrow the workset. **Relinquish All Mine** allows you to relinquish worksets without synchronizing to the central model.

Reload Latest: This updates your local file without you needing to synchronize with the central model.

General Process of Worksharing and Worksets

1. Wait for the appropriate team member to enable worksharing, set up worksets, and create the central model.
2. Create a local file from the central model.
3. Work in your local file and select the worksets that you need to work on by verifying the active workset.
   - Work in your local model by adding, deleting, and modifying elements.
   - You may need to request to borrow elements in worksets that are currently checked out by other team members.
4. Save the local file as frequently as you would save any other project.
5. Synchronize the local file with the central model several times a day or as required by company policy or project status.
   - This reloads any changes from the central model to your local file and vice versa.
   - If the option to **Save Local File before and after synchronizing with central** is checked, your local file will be saved, but it is always recommended to save the local file yourself every time you synchronize to the central model.

6.2 Enabling Worksharing

Once it has been established that a project will need to be workshared, a designated person will enable worksharing, create worksets, and create the central model. The central model will be placed in a shared centralized network location and each user will create their own local file to work from. The central model will host all updated information for the project so that it can be distributed to each user as it is updated.

How To: Enable Worksharing

1. Open an existing project that will become your workshared file or start a new project.
2. In the *Collaborate* tab>Manage Collaboration panel, click ⬚ (Collaborate).

   - If this file has never been saved or if changes have been made and not yet saved, the Collaborate - Revit Model Not Saved dialog box will display, as shown in Figure 6–4. Select **Save the model and continue**.

Figure 6–4

   - The model needs to be saved to a shared network location for everyone to access it.

3. In the Collaborate dialog box, select **Within your network**, as shown in Figure 6–5. Then, click **OK**.

Figure 6–5

4. Once worksharing is enabled, default worksets will be created in the model.

• Worksharing in the cloud can be done through BIM 360 Document Management, but this guide focuses on collaborating within your local area network. For BIM 360, refer to the ASCENT guide *Autodesk® BIM 360™: Fundamentals*.

6.3 Setting Up Worksets

After a project has worksharing enabled, worksets need to be created. Individual worksets are subsets of a project with only specific elements available to view or edit per team member. Worksets are created in the Worksets dialog box, as shown in Figure 6–6. There are four categories of worksets: User-Created, Families, Project Standards, and Views.

Figure 6–6

- It is important to have one user start a project and develop most of the views, families, and other settings before sharing.

- If you have multiple buildings in a project, use linking to show the relationships between the buildings. Each Revit model can have its own worksets.

- Determining how to divide a project into worksets depends on the complexity of the project, the need to be able to load only parts of the model, and the need to control visibility by workset.

- If your company's BIM standards are to primarily check out worksets rather than borrowing on the fly, dividing the project depends on the different tasks to be done and the number of people working on the project. See "Best Practices for Worksharing" on page 91.

- User-Created worksets should be based on areas of the building that can be worked on when isolated from the rest of the model, such as the exterior shell, building core, or certain sections of the building that can be worked on by a single user at a time.

- You can also have worksets for electrical, site, and structural work that are not visible to other users, and separate worksets for linked Autodesk Revit files.

How To: Create Worksets

1. In the *Collaborate* tab>Manage Collaboration panel, click

   (Worksets). Alternatively, in the Status Bar, click

   (Worksets).

   - Two default User-Created worksets are created: *Shared Levels and Grids* and *Workset1*.
   - Four categories of worksets are created by default, as described below:

Workset Category	Definition
User-Created	User-Created worksets are used to divide the overall model into collections of elements that are related, usually geometrically, so that the elements can be edited by a user as if they were isolated from the rest of the model.
Families	Each family type loaded into a project will have its own workset. This prevents type changes from being made to a family that is also being used by another user, even if you are using separate worksets. Family worksets cannot be renamed or deleted.
Project Standards	Project Standards are overall project settings, such as system family types (walls, ceilings, roofs, etc.), filters, fill patterns, line styles, materials, or text types. Project Standards worksets help keep these things consistent while multiple people are working on a collaborated model and allow more than one user to work with them at the same time.
Views	Every view that exists in a project will also have its own workset, which allows for any annotation or drafting elements to be placed in the View workset rather than in a workset with model elements. This happens automatically, so there is no need to specify the correct workset when you are placing annotation elements.

2. In the Worksets dialog box, click **New** and type a name for the workset in the New Workset dialog box, as shown in Figure 6–7.

Figure 6–7

- As they are created, the worksets are open and editable by the person who set them up.

- Select or clear the **Visible in all views** option, as needed. For example, a workset showing the exterior of the building is required in all views, while a furniture layout is only required in specific views.

3. Click **OK**.
4. Continue to create new worksets, as needed.
5. Set the *Active workset*. This designates which workset will be active, meaning any new elements added to the project will be part of this workset.

- Selecting the **Gray Inactive Workset Graphics** check box allows users to have a visual understanding of which elements in a project are active and inactive by graying out inactive worksets.

- The new worksets are automatically made **Editable**.

- You can change existing workset names in the Worksets dialog box. Select the workset and click **Rename**.

  - You can rename the default Workset1 workset.
  - You cannot rename the default Project Standards, Families, or Views worksets.

- If you delete a workset and there are elements in the workset, the dialog box shown in Figure 6–8 displays, prompting you to choose what to do with any elements in the workset. They can either be deleted or moved to another workset.

Figure 6–8

- To rename or delete a workset, it must first be made editable.

  - The Workset1, Project Standards, Families, and Views worksets cannot be deleted.

6. Click **OK** to close the dialog box.

Placing Elements in Worksets

When you are working with an existing model that has worksharing enabled and worksets created, you will want to place existing building elements into the appropriate worksets. For example, move any furniture already in a project to a furniture workset, as shown in Figure 6–9.

Figure 6–9

- Worksets can span levels; therefore, you can select elements on each level and move them into the appropriate workset.

- Whatever elements are not moved will remain in the default workset, which is Workset1.

How To: Move Elements to the Appropriate Worksets

1. Open a view that displays the elements you need to move to a different workset.
2. Select the element(s).
3. In Properties, change the *Workset* parameter to the workset in which you want the elements to be, as shown above in Figure 6–9.

- You can select multiple types of building elements and move them to a workset. However, you will need to filter out any annotation elements, such as views and tags, that are automatically assigned to the related View workset.

- Curtain wall subcomponents (grids, mullions, and panels) must be filtered out of a selection set. Select just the base curtain wall element when you want to move it to a workset.

- If you have added elements to a workset that is not visible in the current workset, the elements do not display in the view. If you need elements to be visible, open the Visibility/Graphic Overrides dialog box. Select the *Worksets* tab and modify the *Visibility Setting* for the worksets you want to be visible in the current view, as shown in Figure 6–10.

Worksets	Visibility Setting
Exterior Shell	Use Global Setting (Visible)
Furniture	Use Global Setting (Visible)
Plumbing	Use Global Setting (Not Visible)
Shared Levels and Grids	Use Global Setting (Visible)

Figure 6–10

Hint: Setting a Starting View

To save time when opening a complex model with worksharing activated, you can specify a *starting view*. This could be a cover sheet or a drafting view with information about the project. The idea is that the contents of the starting view are simple elements rather than model elements.

- To set the starting view, in the *Manage* tab>Manage Project panel, click 🔲 (Starting View). In the Starting View dialog box, select the view name, as shown in Figure 6–11.

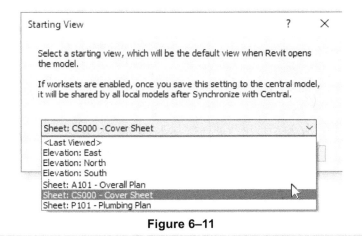

Figure 6–11

6.4 Create a Central Model

The central model keeps track of available worksets and coordinates the changes made in each one with the rest of the worksets. It needs to be accessible to all team members, but should not be worked in directly. The central model maintains a connection to all local files and distributes updated information when a user syncs or reloads latest.

How To: Create a Central Model

1. In the workshared project's *File* tab, click 🖼 (Save As)> 🖼 (Project).
2. In the Save As dialog box, navigate to the network location and click the **Options...** button.
3. In the File Save Options dialog box, **Make this a Central Model after save** is selected and grayed out (as shown Figure 6–12) because worksets have been enabled and the next step is to create the central model. Click **OK**.

Figure 6–12

4. In the Quick Access Toolbar or the *Collaborate* tab>Synchronize panel, click ⚙ (Synchronize and Modify Settings).

5. In the Synchronize with Central dialog box, select **User-created Worksets** so that worksets you checked out are relinquished and available to everyone, as shown in Figure 6–13. You can also add a comment. Click **OK**.

Figure 6–13

6. Close the central model.

Practice 6a

Set Up a Workshared File - Architectural

Practice Objectives

- Enable worksharing on an existing project.
- Set up worksets and move existing elements to the worksets.
- Create a central model.

In this practice, you will set up a workshared file from an existing project, create worksets, move building elements to different worksets, and create a central model.

Task 1 - Set up a workshared file.

1. In the practice files folder, open **Midrise-A.rvt**.

2. In the *Collaborate* tab>Manage Collaboration panel, click (Collaborate).

3. In the Collaborate dialog box, select **Within your network** and click **OK**.

4. In the *Collaborate* tab>Manage Collaboration panel or in the Status Bar, click (Worksets).

Owner "User1" will differ for each user and will be your Revit username, found in Options in the General pane.

5. In the Worksets dialog box, rename Workset1 to **Exterior**, then create the new worksets shown in Figure 6–14. The **Visible in all views** option should be off for all new worksets, except for **Vertical Circulation** and **Plumbing Fixtures**.

- When you have an existing project and you are creating worksets, you want to rename Workset1 to something that the project has a majority of. For example, an architectural project will have a lot of walls, doors, and windows; therefore, you would want all the elements to start out in this workset instead of trying to pick all the elements individually to put in the appropriate workset.

Worksets

Active workset:

Vertical Circulation ☑ Gray Inactive Workset Graphics

Name	Editable	Owner	Borrowers	Opened	Visible in all views
Exterior	Yes	User1		Yes	☑
Furniture Level 1	Yes	User1		Yes	☐
Interior Level 1	Yes	User1		Yes	☐
Interior Level 2	Yes	User1		Yes	☐
Plumbing Fixtures	Yes	User1		Yes	☑
Shared Levels and Grids	Yes	User1		Yes	☑
Vertical Circulation	Yes	User1		Yes	☑

Figure 6–14

6. Verify that the *Active workset* is **Exterior**. Select **Gray Inactive Workset Graphics** and click **OK** to close the Worksets dialog box.

7. If prompted to change the active workset, click **No**. Elements on the Shared Levels and Grids workset and the view-specific room tags are grayed out. Everything in the Exterior workset displays in black.

- Note which workset shows as active either in the *Collaborate* tab>Manage Collaboration panel>Active Workset or in the Status Bar.

Task 2 - Move building elements to worksets.

1. In the **Floor Plans: Level 1** view, select all of the interior walls, columns, and doors. Use 🔽 (Filter) to remove other items from the selection set. Ensure that you do not select any exterior doors, rooms, room tags, and especially the curtain wall door.

2. In Properties, change the *Workset* for the selected elements to **Interior Level 1**. The items should be removed from the view if you toggled off the **Visible by default** option when you created the workset.

3. Repeat the same procedure to move the furniture and furniture systems to the **Furniture Level 1** workset.

4. Repeat the same procedure and move the elevators (Specialty Equipment), stairs, and railing to the **Vertical Circulation** workset, and the bathroom items to the **Plumbing Fixtures** workset. These elements are still visible but grayed out, as shown in Figure 6–15.

Figure 6–15

Task 3 - Create a central model.

1. In the *File* tab, expand (Save As) and click (Project).

2. Click **Options...** and verify that **Central file** is checked.

   • The **Make this a Central Model after save** option is selected but grayed out. This project must become the central model because you have initiated worksets. Click **OK** to close the dialog box.

For this practice, you will be saving to your local drive, but central models must always be saved to a network location.

3. Name the file **Midrise-A.rvt** and be sure that you are saving it within your practice files folder. Click **Save**.

4. In the Status Bar, click 🔲 (Worksets). All of the files are now *Editable* with your username listed as the *Owner*, as shown in Figure 6–16.

Name	Editable	Owner	Borrowers	Opened	Visible in all views
Exterior	Yes	User1		Yes	☑
Furniture Level 1	Yes	User1		Yes	☐
Interior Level 1	Yes	User1		Yes	☐
Interior Level 2	Yes	User1		Yes	☐
Plumbing Fixtures	Yes	User1		Yes	☑
Shared Levels and Grids	Yes	User1		Yes	☑
Vertical Circulation	Yes	User1		Yes	☑

Figure 6–16

5. Click **OK** to close the dialog box.

6. In the *Collaborate* tab>Synchronize panel, click

   🔲 (Synchronize and Modify Settings). In the Synchronize with Central dialog box, select the option to relinquish **User-created Worksets** so that they are available to everyone, as shown in Figure 6–17.

Since no local file has been created from this model, the "Save Local File before and after synchronizing with central" option is grayed out.

Figure 6–17

7. Click **OK** to synchronize with central and close the file.

Practice 6b

Set Up a Workshared File - MEP

Practice Objectives

- Enable worksharing on an existing project.
- Set up worksets and move existing elements to the worksets.
- Create a central model.

In this practice, you will set up a workshared file from an existing project, set up worksets, move building elements to different worksets, and create a central model.

Task 1 - Set up a workshared file.

1. In the practice files folder, open **Olethe-Building-MEP.rvt**.

2. In the *Collaborate* tab>Manage Collaboration panel, click 🖳 (Collaborate).

3. In the Collaborate dialog box, select **Within your network** and click **OK**.

4. In the *Collaborate* tab>Manage Collaboration panel or in the Status Bar, click 🗑 (Worksets).

5. In the Worksets dialog box, rename Workset1 to **HVAC** (the majority of the existing elements, which are ducts and duct fittings, need to be in this workset).

   - When you have an existing project and you are creating worksets, you want to rename Workset1 to something that the project has a majority of. For example, a mechanical project will have a lot of ducts and duct fittings; therefore, you would want all the elements to start out in this workset instead of trying to pick all elements individually to put in the appropriate workset.

Owner "User1" will differ for each user and will be your Revit username, found in Options in the General pane.

6. In the Worksets dialog box, create the new worksets shown in Figure 6–18. The **Visible in all views** option should be off for all new worksets, except for **Architectural Link**.

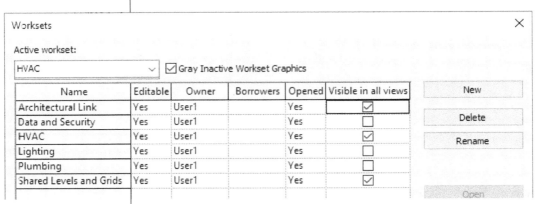

Figure 6–18

7. Verify that the active workset is **HVAC**. Select the **Gray Inactive Workset Graphics** option and click **OK** to close the Worksets dialog box.

8. If prompted to change the active workset, click **No** to keep the HVAC workset active.

   • Note which workset shows as active either in the *Collaborate* tab>Manage Collaboration panel>Active Workset or in the Status Bar.

Task 2 - Move building elements to worksets.

1. In the 3D view, select some of the ducts and equipment. In Properties, you can see that the *Workset* is **HVAC**.

2. Select the linked architectural model. It is also set to HVAC. Change the *Workset* to **Architectural Link**.

   • If the link is not selected, in the Status Bar, click

   (Select Links) to toggle it on.

3. Open the Electrical>Lighting>Floor Plans>**1-Lighting** view.

4. Select all of the lighting fixtures and move them to the **Lighting** workset. The elements are removed from the view because the Lighting workset is set to not visible.

5. Open the Mechanical>Plumbing>Floor Plans>**1-Plumbing** view and move the plumbing fixtures to the **Plumbing** workset. These elements are also removed from the view because the Plumbing workset is set to not visible.

6. Open the Coordination>MEP>Floor Plans>**1 - MEP** view.

7. Open the Worksets dialog box and make the Lighting and Plumbing worksets visible. Click **OK**. The view displays with the HVAC workset in color but the other worksets grayed out, as shown in Figure 6–19.

Figure 6–19

Task 3 - Create a central model.

1. In the *File* tab, expand (Save As), and click (Project).

2. In the Save As dialog box, click **Options...**. The **Make this a Central Model after save** option is selected but grayed out. This project must become the central model because you have initiated worksets. Click **OK** to close the dialog box.

3. Make sure the name is **Olethe-Building-MEP.rvt** and that you are saving it within your practice files folder. Click **Save**.

For this practice, you will be saving to your local drive, but central models must always be saved to a network location.

4. Click (Worksets). All of the files are now *Editable* with your username listed as the *Owner*. Clear **Visible in all views** for Lighting and Plumbing, as shown in Figure 6–20.

Name	Editable	Owner	Borrowers	Opened	Visible in all views
Architectural Link	Yes	User1		Yes	✓
Data and Security	Yes	User1		Yes	☐
Electrical	Yes	User1		Yes	☐
HVAC	Yes	User1		Yes	✓
Lighting	Yes	User1		Yes	☐
Plumbing	Yes	User1		Yes	☐
Shared Levels and Grids	Yes	User1		Yes	✓

Figure 6–20

5. Click **OK** to close the dialog box.

6. Click (Synchronize and Modify Settings). In the Synchronize with Central dialog box, select the option to relinquish **User-created Worksets** so that they are available to everyone, as shown in Figure 6–21.

Synchronize with Central ✕

Central Model Location:

Revit 2020 Collaboration Tools Practice Files\Olethe-Building-MEP.rvt   Browse...

☐ Compact Central Model (slow)

After synchronizing, relinquish the following worksets and elements:

☐ Project Standard Worksets   ☐ View Worksets
☐ Family Worksets   ☑ User-created Worksets
☐ Borrowed Elements

Comment:

Start of Central Model

☐ Save Local File before and after synchronizing with central

[OK]   [Cancel]   [Help]

Figure 6–21

7. Click **OK** to synchronize with central and close the file.

Practice 6c

Set Up a Workshared File - Structural

Practice Objectives

- Enable worksharing on an existing project.
- Set up worksets and move existing elements to the worksets.
- Create a central model.

In this practice, you will set up a workshared file from an existing project, set up worksets, move elements to different worksets, and create a central model.

Task 1 - Set up a workshared file.

1. In the practice files folder, open **Bon-Air-Office-S.rvt**.

2. In the *Collaborate* tab>Manage Collaboration panel, click ⬚⬚ (Collaborate).

3. In the Collaborate dialog box, select **Within your network** and click **OK**.

4. In the *Collaborate* tab>Manage Collaboration panel or in the Status Bar, click 🐾 (Worksets).

5. In the Worksharing dialog box, rename Workset1 as **Columns, Beams & Bracing** and click **OK**.

   - When you have an existing project and you are creating worksets, you want to rename Workset1 to something that the project has a majority of. For example, a structural project will have a lot of columns, beams, and bracing; therefore, you would want all the elements to start out in this workset instead of trying to pick all columns, beams, and bracing to put in the appropriate workset.

Owner "User1" will differ for each user and will be your Revit username, found in Options in the General pane.

6. In the Worksets dialog box, create the new worksets shown in Figure 6–22. The **Visible in all views** option should be off for all new worksets. (The Shared Levels and Grids workset has already been created.)

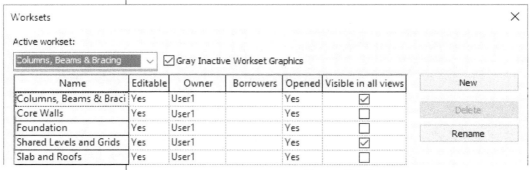

Figure 6–22

7. Verify that the *Active workset* is **Columns, Beams & Bracing**. Select **Gray Inactive Workset Graphics** and click **OK** to close the Worksets dialog box.

8. If prompted to change the active workset, click **No** because you want to keep the active workset as Columns, Beams & Bracing and not the last workset you created.

   • Note which workset shows as active either in the *Collaborate* tab>Manage Collaboration panel>Active Workset or in the Status Bar.

9. Open the **Structural Plans: Level 1** view. Elements in the Shared Levels and Grids workset and the view-specific view and section markers are grayed out. Everything else is black because they are in the Columns, Beams & Bracing workset that was formerly named Workset1.

Task 2 - Move building elements to worksets.

---

1. Open the **Elevations (Building Elevation): East** view.

2. Select all of the elements from Level 1 down to the lowest footing, as shown in Figure 6–23.

Figure 6–23

3. In Properties, change the workset for the selected elements

    to **Foundation**. Use ▽ (Filter) to remove slab edges. (The elements should be removed from the view if you toggled off the **Visible in all views** option when you created the workset.)

    •   Although you are changing the workset for the wall foundations, analytical wall foundations do not automatically follow and it is not possible to manually change their workset. When starting a project from scratch, as would typically be the case, it is important to set the right workset before creating the wall foundations.

4. In the East Elevation, select everything in the view. Use

    ▽ (Filter) to only select the slabs (floors) and roofs. Move them to the **Slabs & Roofs** workset. Ensure that you include the slab edge.

5. Repeat the procedure by opening the appropriate views and moving the elevator walls to the **Core Walls** workset.

Task 3 - Create a central model.

1. In the *File* tab, expand (Save As) and click (Project).

For this practice, you will be saving to your local drive, but central models must always be saved to a network location.

2. In the Save As dialog box, click **Options...**. The **Make this a Central Model after save** option is selected but grayed out. This project must become the central model because you have initiated worksets. Click **OK** to close the dialog box.

3. Name the file **Bon-Air-Office-S.rvt** and be sure that you are saving it within your practice files folder. Click **Save**.

4. Click (Worksets). All of the files are listed as *Editable* with your username listed as the *Owner*, as shown in Figure 6–24.

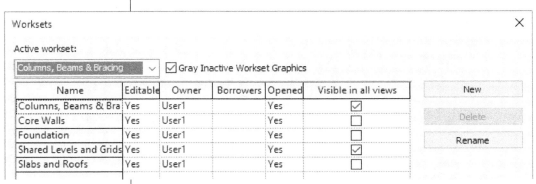

Figure 6–24

5. Click **OK** to close the dialog box.

6. Click (Synchronize and Modify Settings). In the Synchronize with Central dialog box, select the option to relinquish **User-created Worksets** so that they are available to everyone, as shown in Figure 6–25.

Figure 6–25

7. Click **OK** to synchronize with central and close the file.

6.5 Create a Local File from a Central Model

After a central model has been saved to a shared local network location, you will use the Open dialog box to create a local copy, as shown in Figure 6–26. Doing this creates a link between your local file and the central model.

Figure 6–26

• You always work directly in your local file and synchronize your changes to the central model.

• Synchronizing to central will also update your local file with any changes from other users working on the project.

Hint: Notifications and Default File Location

In the *File* tab, click **Options**. In the Options dialog box, in the *General* tab, you can set reminders to save and synchronize the local file with the central model, as shown in Figure 6–27.

Figure 6–27

- This pane is also where your local file pulls your username from.

In the *File Locations* tab, set the *Default path for user files*, as shown in Figure 6–28.

Figure 6–28

- This pane is also where you set the location for project template files, family template files, and point cloud files.

How To: Create a Local File

1. From the Quick Access Toolbar, click 📂 (Open).
2. In the Open dialog box, navigate to the central model and verify that **Create New Local** (shown previously in Figure 6–26) is checked.

    There are two other options available in the Open dialog box:

    - **Detach from Central:** Opens the file and detaches it from the central model. This should only be done by the administrator of the central model.
    - **Audit:** Scans and fixes corrupt elements in a model when working with workshared files.

3. Click **Open**. You can also expand the **Open** button for other options, as shown in Figure 6–29 and explained in the following table.

Figure 6–29

All	Opens all worksets.
Editable	Opens all worksets that are editable (not checked out by someone else).
Last Viewed	Opens the worksets that were viewed the last time you saved the local file. This is the default setting after the local file has been saved once.
Specify	Opens the Opening Worksets dialog box (once you click **Open**), where you select the worksets you want opened or closed.

If you select **Specify...** and click **Open**, the Opening Worksets dialog box displays, as shown in Figure 6–30, where you can do the following:

- Select the name of the workset(s) and click **Close** if a workset is opened and you want it closed.
- Select the name of the workset(s) and click **Open** if a workset is closed and you want it opened.
- Select more than one workset by holding <Ctrl> or <Shift>.
- Select all of the worksets by pressing <Ctrl>+<A>.

Figure 6–30

4. Click **OK** in the Opening Worksets dialog box after making your selections.
5. A copy of the project is created. It will have the same name as the central model with your Autodesk Revit username added to the end.
6. From the *Collaborate* tab>Synchronize panel, expand the Synchronize with Central drop-down list and select (Synchronize and Modify Settings).

7. In the Synchronize with Central dialog box, verify that the *Central Model Location* path is correct and that **Save Local File before and after synchronizing with central** is checked, as shown in Figure 6–31. You can add a comment if needed.

Figure 6–31

8. Click **OK** to close the dialog box.

- After your local file is created, you will not open the central model again unless a new local file is needed. You will always work from your local file.

- Save the local file as frequently as you would save any other project.

- Synchronize the local file with the central model several times a day or as required by company policy or project status.

  - If your company policy is to create a new local file daily or weekly, when you open the central model with **Create New Local** checked, you will get the Duplicate name dialog box. Click **Overwrite existing copy**, as shown in Figure 6–32, to continue.

Figure 6–32

- **Append timestamp to existing copy** creates a new local file but adds the date and time to the end of the file name in your local file location, as shown in Figure 6–33.

Figure 6–33

- When you open a local file, select only the worksets you need to open. Limiting the number of worksets speeds up the opening and saving process and frees up elements for other project team members to edit.

Saving and Synchronizing Your Local File

To save your local file, you can click (Save) in the Quick Access Toolbar. You can also make sure that within the Synchronize with Central dialog box, you have the check box selected for **Save Local File before and after synchronizing with central**, as shown in Figure 6–34.

Figure 6–34

- Save the local file frequently (every 15 to 30 minutes).

- Synchronize to the central model periodically (every hour or two) or after you have made major changes to the project. At the end of the day, make sure you synchronize with central and relinquish worksets.

Synchronizing to the Central Model

There are two methods for synchronizing to the central model. In the Quick Access Toolbar or *Collaborate* tab>Synchronize panel, expand (Synchronize with Central) and click (Synchronize Now) or (Synchronize and Modify Settings). The last-used command is active if you click the top-level icon.

- **Synchronize Now:** Updates the central model and then the local file with any changes to the central model since the last synchronization without prompting you for any settings. It automatically relinquishes elements borrowed from any workset but retains worksets used by the current user.
- **Synchronize and Modify Settings:** Opens the Synchronize with Central dialog box so you can set the options for relinquishing worksets and elements, add comments, and specify to save the file locally before and after synchronization.

- Always keep **Save Local File before and after synchronizing with central** checked to ensure your local copy is up to date with the latest changes from the central model.

- When you close a local file without saving to the central model, you are prompted to do so, as shown in Figure 6–35.

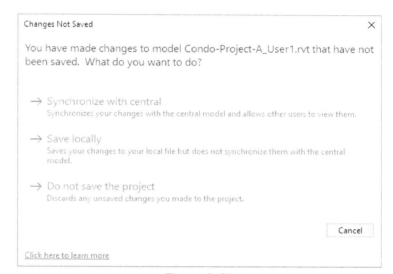

Figure 6–35

6.6 Working in a Workshared File

The key to successfully working in a workshared project is coordinating and communicating with the other members of your team. However, the majority of the work you will do in a workshared project will be no different than any other project. Only check out worksets that you need to work in (as shown in Figure 6–36) and borrow elements as you work.

Figure 6–36

When new elements are added to the project, they are placed in the active workset, as shown in Figure 6–37. It is therefore important to set the active workset correctly before adding new elements. Not doing so can result in visibility and permissions-related issues.

(Workset: Element name) ⟶
Status Bar showing active workset ⟶

Figure 6–37

How To: Set the Active Workset

1. Open your local file.
2. In the Status Bar (or *Collaborate* tab>Manage Collaboration panel), expand the *Active Workset* list and select a workset, as shown in Figure 6–38.

Figure 6–38

- It does not matter if the workset says **(Not Editable)**; you can still add elements to it. **Not Editable** means that you have not checked out the workset but are working on the basis of borrowing elements.

- You can gray out inactive worksets in a view to easily distinguish between active and inactive worksets, as shown in Figure 6–39. In the *Collaborate* tab>Manage Collaboration panel, toggle (Gray Inactive Workset Graphics) on. You can also select **Gray Inactive Workset Graphics** in the Worksets dialog box.

Figure 6–39

Hint: Worksharing Monitoring

Worksharing monitoring displays information about the workshared model you are working in or have opened, as shown in Figure 6–40. It shows you who is working in the project, if there are any issues, if your local file is up to date, and information about requests for borrowing elements. You can also set up options on what information you would like displayed in desktop notifications that appear above your computer's system tray (Date and Time). You can click on the History icon to display the action from all team members working in the project.

Click to open the Central File History dialog box

Figure 6–40

- From the *Collaborate* tab>Synchronize panel, click (Worksharing Monitor).

  - You can open System Performance to monitor your computer's resources, like hard drive space, memory, and CPU load.
  - The Worksharing Monitor for Autodesk Revit 2021 dialog box needs to remain open while you work in order to receive desktop notifications.

- To specify notification options, click (Options).

  - Worksharing Monitor options include General, Central File Access, Editing Request, and Notifications.

Editing Elements in Worksets

There are two different ways to edit elements in worksets.

- **Borrow elements:** If you *borrow* the elements as you make changes, no one has to wait for permission to make modifications. After the interior wall is moved (as shown in Figure 6–41), it will show that you have borrowed the workset that the element is on (as shown in Figure 6–42). This method allows others to modify elements on the same workset without requesting permission.This can speed up the work if you have a fairly small group of people working on the project, especially when there is some overlap between the purposes of the users or when the project has only been divided into a few worksets.

Figure 6–41

Worksets

Active workset:

Interior Level 1 (Not Editable) ∨ ☐ Gray Inactive Workset Graphic

Name	Editable	Owner	Borrowe	Opened
Exterior	No			Yes
Furniture	No			Yes
Interior Level 1	No		User2	Yes
Plumbing	No			Yes
Shared Levels and Grids	No			Yes
Vertical circulation	No			Yes

Figure 6–42

Check with your project coordinator to see which method your office uses.

- **Check out a workset:** When you *check out* a specific workset and make it editable, no one else can modify elements in that workset without placing a request to borrow an element.

Borrowing Elements

When you select an element and see the **Make element editable** icon, as shown in Figure 6–43, it means that you have not checked out that particular workset or that you are not currently borrowing the element.

Figure 6–43

- It is not necessary to click the icon; simply proceed to edit the element.

  - If you modify the element and it enables you to do so, then no one else has that workset checked out and you were given automatic permission to modify this element.
  - If someone else has borrowed the element or checked out the workset to which it belongs, you are prompted to request permission to edit the element.

How To: Check Out Worksets

You can also open the Worksets dialog box from the Status Bar.

1. In the *Collaborate* tab>Manage Collaboration panel, click
   (Worksets).
2. In the Worksets dialog box, select **Yes** in the *Editable* column next to the workset name that you want to check out and edit, as shown in Figure 6–44. More than one workset can be checked out and made editable at a time, but ensure that you only check out the ones that you really need.

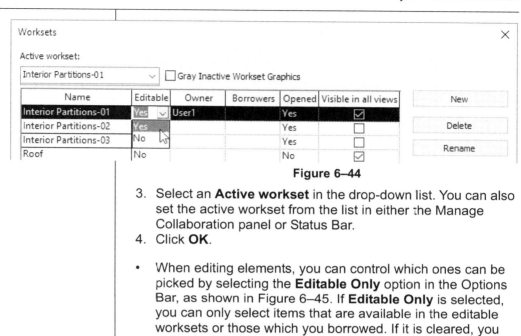

Figure 6–44

3. Select an **Active workset** in the drop-down list. You can also set the active workset from the list in either the Manage Collaboration panel or Status Bar.
4. Click **OK**.

- When editing elements, you can control which ones can be picked by selecting the **Editable Only** option in the Options Bar, as shown in Figure 6–45. If **Editable Only** is selected, you can only select items that are available in the editable worksets or those which you borrowed. If it is cleared, you can select anything.

Figure 6–45

Permissions to Edit

If you try to edit an element that is owned by someone else, an alert box opens stating that you cannot edit the element without their permission, as shown in Figure 6–46. First, you must request an edit. Second, the owner of the workset either grants or denies the request. If the request is granted, update your local file and you will have control of the element until you relinquish it.

Figure 6–46

How To: Request an Edit

1. When the alert box opens stating that you need to have permission to modify an element (as shown previously in Figure 6–46), click **Place Request** to ask to borrow the element.
2. An alert box opens stating the request has been made, as shown in Figure 6–47. If you expect a quick reply, leave the message in place. If you want to continue working, click **Close** and cancel out of the alert box. The request is still active.

Figure 6–47

How To: Grant or Deny an Editing Request

1. When a user sends an editing request for an element you are currently borrowing or which belongs to a workset that you have checked out (editable), an alert displays, as shown in Figure 6–48.

Figure 6–48

2. In the Editing Request Received dialog box, click **Show** to zoom into the element requested, **Grant** to allow the other user to modify the element, or **Deny** to stop the other user from modifying the element.

3. If you do not respond right away to the editing request, you can always access it again. In the *Collaborate* tab> Synchronize panel, click 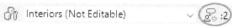 (Editing Requests) or in the Status Bar, click (Editing Requests). The information in the Status Bar includes the number of requests outstanding, as shown in Figure 6–49.

Interiors (Not Editable)

Figure 6–49

4. In the Editing Requests dialog box, as shown in Figure 6–50, select the pending request. Click on the date.

Figure 6–50

*   When you select the editing request date, the elements included in the request are highlighted in the project. Click **Show** to zoom in on the elements, if needed.

5. Click **Grant** to enable the other user to make the changes or **Deny/Retract** to deny the request. (The original user can also retract the request with this button.) You can also grant the request by saving the entire workset back to the central model and relinquishing the items.

Applying an Editing Request

When an editing request is granted, a confirmation alert box opens in the program of the user who requested it, as shown in Figure 6–51. Close the alert box.

Figure 6–51

- If the requesting user canceled out of the Edit Request dialog box, when they are notified that they have permission, they can click (Reload Latest) or type **RL** to make the ownership modification.

- If the Error dialog box is still open, the Editing Request Placed dialog box displays that the request has been granted, as shown in Figure 6–52. Click **Close** and the element is modified.

Figure 6–52

Editing Request Frequency

To control the frequency of updates to editing requests (and worksharing display modes), in the Options dialog box, in the *General* tab, move the slider bar between *Less Frequent* and *More Frequent*, as shown in Figure 6–53.

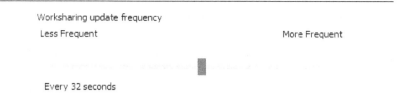

Figure 6–53

- If the bar is moved to the far side of *Less Frequent*, it changes to manual and updates only when you borrow elements or synchronize with the central model. This can improve the performance of the program but also causes the other user to wait until you receive the request.

Relinquishing Worksets

After you have been working with borrowed elements or have checked out worksets, you should return them to the central model when you are finished. In the Quick Access Toolbar or *Collaborate* tab>Synchronize panel, click (Synchronize and Modify Settings). The Synchronize with Central dialog box displays, as shown in Figure 6–54. In this dialog box, select the worksets and/or borrowed elements you want to relinquish. Only those which you have ownership of are available.

Figure 6–54

Synchronize with Central Options

- The **Borrowed Elements** option will be selected by default. This relinquishes any elements you borrowed from another workset.

- Select the **Save Local File before and after synchronizing with central** option to save extra steps.

- Periodically, use the **Compact Central Model (slow)** option when you save to the central model. This reduces the file size, but also increases the time required to save.

Adding comments at key points and for significant changes in the project is useful in case the project backup needs to be restored in the future.

- You can add comments to the central model for others to see. To view the comments, in the *Collaborate* tab>Synchronize panel, click (Show History) and select the central model whose history you want to view. The History dialog box displays with the *Date/Time Stamp*, *Modified by*, and *Comments* columns populated with information, as shown in Figure 6–55.

Date/Time Stamp	Modified by	Comments
10/17/2020 3:07:34 PM	User1	Moved air terminals and light fixtures
10/17/2020 3:07:27 PM	User2	
10/17/2020 3:05:00 PM	User2	
10/17/2020 3:04:51 PM	User1	

Figure 6–55

6.7 Visibility and Display Options with Worksharing

While using worksets, there are certain display tools to help you as you work. Worksets can be toggled off and on in the Visibility/Graphic Overrides dialog box. You can use the Worksharing Display settings to graphically differentiate by color, such as indicating the Owners of different elements or the elements that need to be updated.

Controlling Workset Visibility

Not all worksets need to be visible in every view. For example, the exterior shell of a building should display in most views, but interior walls or the site features only need to be displayed in related views. The default workset visibility is controlled when the workset is first created, but can be managed in the Visibility/Graphic Overrides dialog box, as shown in Figure 6–56.

Figure 6–56

How To: Change the Visibility of Worksets

1. Type **VV** or **VG** to open the Visibility/Graphic Overrides dialog box.

2. Select the *Worksets* tab. Modify the *Visibility Setting* for each workset, as required. Changing the setting to **Show** or **Hide** only impacts the current view.

3. Click **OK** to close the dialog box.

• Worksets marked with an asterisk (*) have not been opened in this session of the Autodesk Revit software and are therefore not visible in any view.

Limiting the number of worksets speeds up the process of opening and saving the file. It is recommended that you close a workset that is not required rather than change its visibility.

- Closing worksets toggles off element visibility in all views. It also saves more computer memory than just toggling off the display of worksets.

- The *Worksets* tab in the Visibility/Graphic Overrides dialog box is only available when worksets have been enabled.

- These overrides can also be set up in a view template.

Worksharing Display Options

A handy way to view the status of elements in worksharing is to set the Worksharing Display. For example, when you set the Worksharing Display to Worksets, as shown in Figure 6–57, the elements in each workset are highlighted in a different color.

Figure 6–57

There are several types of worksharing displays: Checkout Status, Owners, Model Updates, and Worksets. You can access them in the Status Bar, as shown in Figure 6–58.

Figure 6–58

- As you hover the cursor over elements in a view with Worksharing Display selected, information about the element displays, depending on the type you selected (as shown in Figure 6–59).

Toggling on Gray Inactive Worksets while using Worksharing Display might change the display status of elements in two tones of the same color.

Figure 6–59

- You can modify the colors in the Worksharing Display Settings dialog box, as well as select which items you want to display, as shown in Figure 6–60.

Figure 6–60

6.8 Worksharing and Linked Models

NOTE: All images in the upcoming sections refer to users as "User1" or "User2". in your working environment, you will see your unique Revit username in these dialog boxes.

When you are working in a workshared project, each linked model should be in a separate workset. For example, before linking in a structural model, specify and set the appropriate workset, as shown in Figure 6–61. When you open a local file, you can specify which worksets you want to display, as shown in Figure 6–62.

Figure 6–61	Figure 6–62

The same is true if you are linking in a model that has been workshared. You can control which worksets are open and which worksets display. In this case, the worksets from the linked model are not available for modification or use in the host project (which might have its own worksets).

- Remember that limiting the number of worksets you open and display speeds up the process of opening and saving the file. It is recommended that you close a workset that is not required rather than change its visibility. When working with linked files, you can also close them, as shown in Figure 6–63.

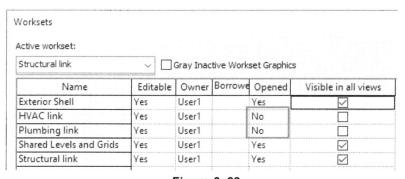

Worksets

Active workset:

Structural link ☐ Gray Inactive Workset Graphics

Name	Editable	Owner	Borrowe	Opened	Visible in all views
Exterior Shell	Yes	User1		Yes	☑
HVAC link	Yes	User1		No	☐
Plumbing link	Yes	User1		No	☐
Shared Levels and Grids	Yes	User1		Yes	☑
Structural link	Yes	User1		Yes	☑

Figure 6–63

Managing Links in Local Files

When you open a local file that includes linked models set up in separate worksets, you can choose to unload each link for just yourself or for all users. In the Manage Links dialog box, as shown in Figure 6–64, select the link and in the *Unload* area, select either **For all users** or **For me**.

Figure 6–64

- If you unload for all users, the link will still be available but will be unloaded by default anytime someone else opens a local file. You will need to place a request to reload it if the original person that unloaded the link has not relinquished it.

- If you unload a link just for yourself, this action is remembered when you synchronize with the central model. If you want to reload the link, select it and click **Clear my override**.

Managing Worksets in Linked Models

Linked models that include worksets can be managed at two levels. You can load and unload the entire link or you can open and close the individual worksets in the linked model. For example, you might want the Site workset turned on in some views but not in others, as shown in Figure 6–65.

- Worksets can also be set as visible in some views and not visible in other views.

Figure 6–65

How To: Open and Close Worksets in a Linked Model

1. Open the Manage Links dialog box.
2. In the Manage Links dialog box, select the link that includes worksets, as shown in Figure 6–66, and click **Manage Worksets**.

Figure 6–66

- The **Manage Worksets** button will be grayed out if there are no worksets associated with a link.

3. In the Manage Worksets for Link dialog box, select the workset(s) you want to close and click **Close** or the workset(s) you want to open and click **Open**. For example, in Figure 6–67, the linked Roof and Site worksets have been closed.

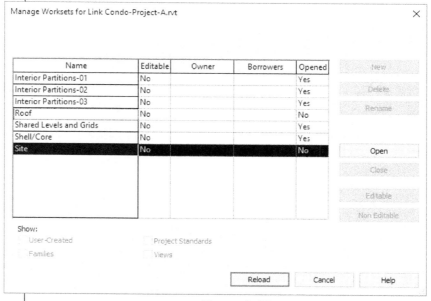

Figure 6–67

4. Click **Reload** and the link displays only the worksets that are opened.

How To: Change the Visibility of Worksets in a Linked Model

1. Type **VV** to open the Visibility/Graphic Overrides dialog box.
2. Click on the *Revit Links* tab. This tab only displays if there are links in the project.
3. In the *Display Settings* column, beside the link, click **<By Host View>**.
4. In the RVT Link Display Settings dialog box, in the *Basics* tab, select **Custom**, as shown in Figure 6–68.

RVT Link Display Settings

Basics   Model Categories   Annotation Categories   Analytical Model Categories   Import Categories   Worksets

○ By host view   ○ By linked view   ◉ Custom

Figure 6–68

5. Select the *Worksets* tab and set the *Worksets* to **<Custom>**. This enables you to modify the visibility of individual worksets as needed. For example, in Figure 6–69, the **Interior Partitions** worksets are cleared, indicating that they are not visible in the current view.

   • Worksets that display with **(Closed)*** do not display in any view.

Figure 6–69

6. Click **OK** to close the dialog boxes.

Practice 6d

Working in a Workshared Project - Architectural

Practice Objectives

- Work in pairs to simulate a worksharing environment.
- Update an existing central model for use in the practice.
- Create a local file of the central model from each copy of the software.

In this practice, you will need to work in pairs to simulate a worksharing environment. On your individual machines, User1 and User2 will each create a local file and select specific worksets to open in each project, as shown in Figure 6–70. One user within the pair will create the central model.

*A video called **Intro to Worksharing.mp4** is located in the practice files Videos folder.*

- Instructors: You will need to create a shared network folder for students to work in pairs to simulate the work environment.
- Students: If this is self-paced training and you are not able to work in pairs or save a central model to a shared network location, videos are available in the practice files *Videos* folder for each of the tasks in Practice 6d.

"User1" and "User2" are referenced throughout the practice but you will see your unique Revit username instead.

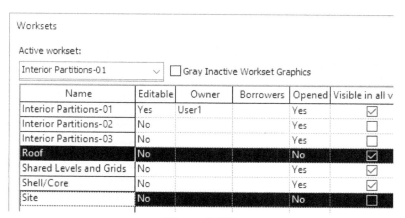

Name	Editable	Owner	Borrowers	Opened	Visible in all v
Interior Partitions-01	Yes	User1		Yes	☑
Interior Partitions-02	No			Yes	☐
Interior Partitions-03	No			Yes	☐
Roof	No			No	☑
Shared Levels and Grids	No			Yes	☑
Shell/Core	No			Yes	☑
Site	No			No	☐

Figure 6–70

This practice uses a project that has been subdivided into worksets. To simulate a worksharing environment, work in groups of two. To keep the practices simple, the terms "User1" and "User2" will be used to indicate which user is to do certain tasks.

- **User1** updates the central model and focuses on the interiors of the condo units.

- **User2** focuses on the exterior and core.

Task 1 - Update the central model.

*A video called **Task1.mp4** is located in the practice files Videos folder.*

1. **User1**, in the Quick Access Toolbar, click (Open). In the practice files folder, open **Condo-Project-A.rvt**.

2. Alert boxes about a Copied Central Model and Cannot find Central Model display. Read and then close the alert boxes.

3. In the *File* tab, expand (Save As) and click (Project).

A central model needs to be repathed if it has been relocated. You will typically not have to do this in a work environment, but will need to do it for this practice to work.

4. In the Save As dialog box, click **Options...**.

5. In the File Save Options dialog box, select **Make this a Central Model after save** and then click **OK**.

6. Verify that the name is still set to **Condo-Project-A.rvt**, navigate to the shared network folder location and click **Save**.

   - If the Workset File Already Exists dialog box displays, click **Yes** to replace the existing file.

7. Close the project.

Task 2 - Create the local file for User1.

*A video called **Task2.mp4** is located in the practice files Videos folder.*

1. **User1** continues working within Revit.

2. In the Quick Access Toolbar, click (Open). In the practice files folder, open **Condo-Project-A.rvt**.

   - Do not select central models from the startup screen, as that opens the central model itself. Instead, use the Open command to create a new local file.

3. Verify that **Create New Local** is selected and click **Open**, as shown in Figure 6–71.

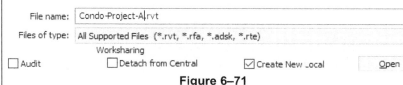

Figure 6–71

4. The file opens and displays the name
    Condo-Project-A_User1.rvt at the top of the interface.

    *   Note what the file name is at the top of your Revit user
        interface. It should have the file name with your unique
        username at the end.

5. In the *Collaborate* tab>Manage Collaboration panel or in the
    Status Bar, click (Worksets).

6. In the Worksets dialog box, do the following, as shown in
    Figure 6–72:

    *   Set the *Active workset* to **Interior Partitions-01**.
    *   For **Interior Partitions-01**, set *Editable* to **Yes** and select
        Visible in all views.
    *   Select the worksets **Roof** and **Site**. Click **Close** so that
        the worksets are not open in this session.

Figure 6–72

7. Click **OK** to finish.

8. In the Quick Access Toolbar, click (Save) to save the local file.

Task 3 - Create the local file for User2.

A video called
Task3.mp4 *is located in the practice files Videos folder.*

1. **User2**, in the Quick Access Toolbar, click (Open), navigate to the shared network folder location and select the file **Condo-Project-A.rvt**. Verify that **Create New Local** is selected.

2. Click the arrow next to **Open** and select **Specify...** in the drop-down list, as shown in Figure 6–73.

Figure 6–73

3. Click **Open** to open the project.

4. In the Opening Worksets dialog box, select the three **Interior Partitions** worksets and click **Close** so that these worksets are not opened in this session, as shown in Figure 6–74.

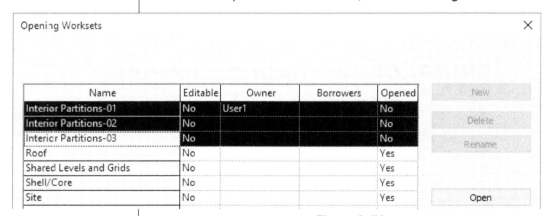

Name	Editable	Owner	Borrowers	Opened	
Interior Partitions-01	No	User1		No	New
Interior Partitions-02	No			No	Delete
Interior Partitions-03	No			No	Rename
Roof	No			Yes	
Shared Levels and Grids	No			Yes	
Shell/Core	No			Yes	
Site	No			Yes	Open

Figure 6–74

5. Click **OK** to finish.

- Note what the file name is at the top of your Revit user interface. It should have the file name with your unique username at the end.

6. Save the local file. Keep the file open.

The local file name should be Condo-Project-A_your unique username.rvt.

Task 4 - Add and modify elements in worksets.

A video called **Task4.mp4** *is located in the practice files Videos folder.*

1. **User1,** in your local file for Condo-Project-A, verify that you are in the **Floor Plans: First Floor** view.

2. Zoom in on Unit 1C and add several walls using an interior wall type with the *Height* set to **Second Floor**. Include one that butts up against an existing window, as shown in Figure 6–75. A warning displays, noting that the insert conflicts with the joined wall.

Figure 6–75

3. Close the warning.

4. Click ⌖ (Modify) and select the window. It has an icon connected to it, as shown in Figure 6–76, indicating that it belongs to another workset. Click the **Make element editable** icon.

Figure 6–76

5. Move the window so it does not conflict with the wall.

6. Open the Worksets dialog box. **User1** will be noted as the *Owner* of the **Interior Partitions-01** workset and a *Borrower* of the **Shell/Core** workset, as shown in Figure 6–77.

Figure 6–77

7. Click **OK** to close the dialog box.

8. In the *Collaborate* tab>Synchronize panel or in the Quick Access Toolbar, click (Synchronize and Modify Settings) to open the Synchronize with Central dialog box. The **Borrowed Elements** option should be selected. Add a comment about moving the window and select the **Save Local File before and after synchronizing with central** option, as shown in Figure 6–78.

Figure 6–78

9. Click **OK**.

Task 5 - Check out a workset.

A video called ***Task5.mp4*** *is located in the practice files Videos folder.*

1. **User2**, open the **Floor Plans: First Floor** view if it is not already open. None of the changes show in the local file.

2. In the *Collaborate* tab>Synchronize panel, click (Reload Latest or type **RL**. The window location changes but you might not see the new walls if that workset is not open and visible.

3. Click (Worksets) to open the dialog box.

4. In the *Visible in all views* column, select the check box for **Interior Partitions-01**, if it is not already showing. Make sure the *Opened* column for **Interior Partitions-01** is set to **Yes**.

5. Select **Shell/Core** in the *Active workset* drop-down list and make it editable (select **Yes** in the *Editable* column). The *Owner* should display as **User 2**, as shown in Figure 6–79.

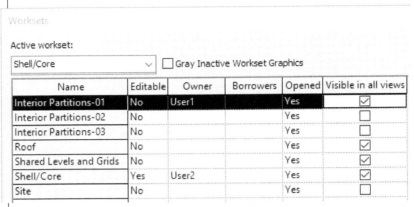

Worksets

Active workset:

Shell/Core ⌄   ☐ Gray Inactive Workset Graphics

Name	Editable	Owner	Borrowers	Opened	Visible in all views
Interior Partitions-01	No	User1		Yes	☑
Interior Partitions-02	No			Yes	☐
Interior Partitions-03	No			Yes	☐
Roof	No			Yes	☑
Shared Levels and Grids	No			Yes	☑
Shell/Core	Yes	User2		Yes	☑
Site	No			Yes	☐

Figure 6–79

6. Click **OK** to close the dialog box.

7. Move door number 5 in Unit 1A down in the wall so that it is no longer opposite to door number 6.

8. In the Quick Access Toolbar, click 🖫 (Save) to save the local file.

9. **User1**, type **RL** (Reload Latest). There are no new changes to load, as shown in Figure 6–80, because User2 has not saved back to the central model. Close the dialog box.

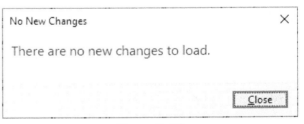

No New Changes   ✕

There are no new changes to load.

Close

Figure 6–80

10. **User2** will click 🗗 (Synchronize Now). This saves the changes to the central model without relinquishing the Shell/Core workset.

Task 6 - Request permission to edit.

A video called
Task6.mp4 *is located in the practice files Videos folder.*

1. **User1**, type **RL** (Reload Latest) again. This time, the door moves in response to the change made in the central model.

2. Try to move the door back where it was. This time, an error message displays that cannot be ignored, as shown in Figure 6–81. **User2** has made the Shell/Core workset editable. Therefore, other users cannot edit elements in it without permission.

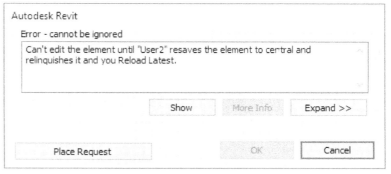

Figure 6–81

3. Click **Place Request**. The Editing Request Placed dialog box opens. Leave it open.

4. **User2** now has an alert box displayed, as shown in Figure 6–82.

Figure 6–82

5. Hover the cursor over the **Show** button to highlight the door. Move the dialog box out of the way if needed to see the door.

6. Click on **Grant** to give the other user permission to modify the placement of this door. By doing this, you enable the other user full control over this one element in the workset.

7. **User1** will get an Editing Request Granted dialog box, as shown in Figure 6–83.

Figure 6–83

8. Close the Editing Request Granted dialog box. Because your request was granted, the door moves.

9. Move the door again to exactly where you want it. This time, you are not prompted to ask to move the door because you are still borrowing it.

10. Try to move another door. You do not have permission to move this door. Click **Cancel** rather than place the request. The door returns to its original location.

Task 7 - View information about the worksets.

*A video called **Task7.mp4** is located in the practice files Videos folder.*

1. **User1,** in the View Control Bar, expand the Worksharing Display and click ⚌ (Owners). Different colors highlight the elements and their respective owners. Hover the cursor over one of the walls to display information about the owner, as shown in Figure 6–84.

Figure 6–84

- The color on your display might be different.

2. Zoom out so you can see the full floor plan.

3. Click (Synchronize and Modify Settings) and relinquish **User-created Worksets** and **Borrowed Elements.**

4. The new interior walls once displayed as owned by **User1** are now not in color and the door that was borrowed returns to the original owner **User2**.

5. Toggle the Worksharing Display off.

6. Save the local file.

7. **User2**, click (Synchronize Now). The door moves to the location where **User1** moved it. When you save to the central model, it also reloads the latest changes.

8. Close the project. When the Editable Elements dialog box opens, as shown in Figure 6–85, click **Relinquish elements and worksets**.

Editable Elements   ✕

You still have elements editable within your model
Condo-Project-A_User2.rvt. What do you want to do?

→ Relinquish elements and worksets
Resaves the local file and allows others to gain access to these elements and worksets.

→ Keep ownership of elements and worksets
Prevents others from gaining access to these elements and worksets.

Cancel

Figure 6–85

9. **User1**, close the project and synchronize with central.

Practice 6e

Working in a Workshared Project - MEP

Practice Objectives

- Work in pairs to simulate a worksharing environment.
- Update an existing central model for use in the practice.
- Create a local file of the central model from each copy of the software.

In this practice, you will need to work in pairs to simulate a worksharing environment. On your individual machines, User1 and User2 will each create a local file and select specific worksets to open in each project, as shown in Figure 6–86. One user within the pair will create the central model.

*A video called **Intro to Worksharing.mp4** (Architectural) is located in the practice files Videos folder.*

- Instructors: You will need to create a shared network folder for students to work in pairs to simulate the work environment.
- Students: If this is self-paced training and you are not able to work in pairs or save a central model to a shared network location, Architectural videos are available in the practice files *Videos* folder for each of the tasks for Practice 6d for your reference.

"User1" and "User2" are referenced throughout the practice but you will see your unique Revit username instead.

Worksets

Active workset:

| HVAC | Gray Inactive Workset Graphics |

Name	Editable	Owner	Borrowers	Opened	Visible in all views
Data and Security	No			No	☑
Electrical	No			No	☑
Fire Safety	No			Yes	☑
HVAC	Yes	User1		No	☑
Lighting	No			No	☑
Linked Architectural	No			Yes	☑
Plumbing	No			No	☑
Shared Levels and Grids	No			Yes	☑

Figure 6–86

This practice uses a project that has been subdivided into worksets. To simulate a worksharing environment, work in groups of two. To keep the practices simple, the terms "User1" and "User2" will be used to indicate which user is to do certain tasks.

- **User1** updates the central model and focuses on the HVAC portion of the project.

- **User2** focuses on the lighting portion of the project.

Task 1 - Update the central model.

A video called
Task1.mp4
(Architectural) is located in the practice files Videos folder.

1. **User1**, in the Quick Access Toolbar, click (Open). In the practice files folder, open **Elementary-School-MEP.rvt**.

2. Alert boxes about a Copied Central Model and Cannot find Central Model display. Read and then close the alert boxes.

3. In the *File* tab, expand (Save As) and click (Project).

4. In the Save As dialog box, click **Options...**.

A central model needs to be repathed if it has been relocated. You will typically not have to do this in a work environment, but will need to do it for this practice to work.

5. In the File Save Options dialog box, select **Make this a Central Model after save** and then click **OK**.

6. Verify that the name is still set to **Elementary-School-MEP.rvt** and then click **Save**.

7. When the Workset File Already Exists dialog box displays, click **Yes** to replace the existing file.

8. Close the project.

Task 2 - Create the local file for User1.

A video called
Task2.mp4
(Architectural) is located in the practice files Videos folder.

1. **User1**, in the Quick Access Toolbar, click (Open). In the practice files folder, open **Elementary-School-MEP.rvt**.

   - Do not select central models from the startup screen as it opens the central model directly. Instead, use the **Open** command and create a new local file.

2. Verify that **Create New Local** is selected and click **Open**.

3. In the *Collaborate* tab>Manage Collaboration panel or in the Status Bar, click (Worksets).

4. In the Worksets dialog box, make **HVAC** the Active workset. Set *Editable* to **Yes** and select **Visible in all views** for this workset.

5. Select all the other worksets except **Linked Architectural** and **Shared Levels and Grids**. Click **Close** so that the worksets are not open in this session, as shown in Figure 6–87.

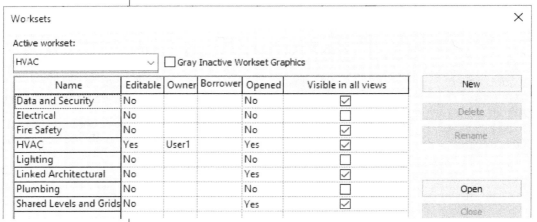

Figure 6–87

6. Click **OK** to finish.

7. In the Quick Access Toolbar, click 💾 (Save) to save the local file.

8. Keep the file open.

Task 3 - Create the local file for User2.

A video called
Task3.mp4
*(Architectural) is located
in the practice files
Videos folder.*

1. **User2**, in the Quick Access Toolbar, click 🗁 (Open) and
   select the file **Elementary-School-MEP.rvt**. Verify that
   Create New Local is selected, click the arrow next to **Open**,
   and select **Specify...** in the drop-down list, as shown in
   Figure 6–88.

Figure 6–88

2. Click **Open** to open the project.

3. In the Opening Worksets dialog box, select the **Data and
   Security**, **Fire Safety**, **HVAC**, and **Plumbing** worksets and
   click **Close** so that these worksets are not opened in this
   session, as shown in Figure 6–89.

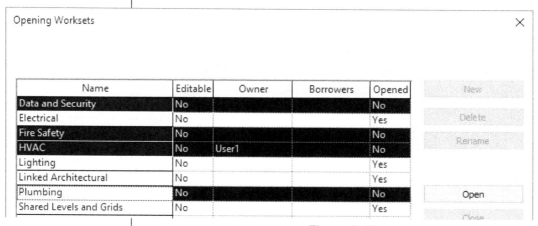

Figure 6–89

4. Click **OK** to finish.

5. Save the local file and keep it opened.

Task 4 - Add and modify elements in worksets.

1. **User1**, in your local file for **Elementary-School-MEP**, open the Coordination>MEP>**Ceiling Plans:01 RCP** view.

2. Zoom in on the lower left classroom. You should see elements related to HVAC. (If you do not, open the Worksets dialog box and ensure that the HVAC workset is opened.)

3. Move the second row of air terminals one ceiling grid to the left, similar to that shown in Figure 6–90. Reattach the flex duct, if required.

Figure 6–90

4. Open the Worksets dialog box and select the Lighting workset. Open it and make it visible in all views. Click **OK**. Now the air terminals are on top of the lights.

5. Select one of the lighting fixtures. It has an icon connected to it, as shown in Figure 6–91, indicating that it belongs to another workset. Click the icon to make the element editable.

Figure 6–91

6. Move the lighting fixture so it does not conflict with the air terminal.

7. Open the Worksets dialog box. **User1** is noted as the *Owner* of the **HVAC** workset and a *Borrower* of the **Lighting** workset, as shown in Figure 6–92.

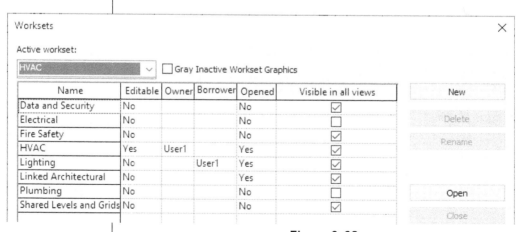

Name	Editable	Owner	Borrower	Opened	Visible in all views	
Data and Security	No			No	☑	New
Electrical	No			No	☐	Delete
Fire Safety	No			No	☑	
HVAC	Yes	User1		Yes	☑	Rename
Lighting	No		User1	Yes	☑	
Linked Architectural	No			Yes	☑	
Plumbing	No			No	☐	Open
Shared Levels and Grids	No			No	☑	Close

Figure 6–92

8. Click **OK** to close the dialog box.

9. In the *Collaborate* tab>Synchronize panel or the Quick Access Toolbar, click ⌨ (Synchronize and Modify Settings) to open the Synchronize with Central dialog box, as shown in Figure 6–93. The **Borrowed Elements** option should be selected. Add a comment about moving the air terminals and light fixtures and select **Save Local File before and after synchronizing with central**. Click **OK**.

Synchronize with Central	✕

Central Model Location:

:\Revit Collaboration Tools Practice Files\Elementary-School-MEP.rvt	Browse...

☐ Compact Central Model (slow)

After synchronizing, relinquish the following worksets and elements:

☐ Project Standard Worksets   ☐ View Worksets
☐ Family Worksets   ☐ User-created Worksets
☑ Borrowed Elements

Comment:

Moved air terminals and light fixtures|

☑ Save Local File before and after synchronizing with central

OK   Cancel   Help

Figure 6–93

Task 5 - Check out a workset.

*A video called **Task5.mp4** (Architectural) is located in the practice files Videos folder.*

1. **User2**, open the Coordination>MEP>**Ceiling Plans: 01 RCP** view in your local file. Neither the HVAC elements nor the changes show in the local file.

2. In the *Collaborate* tab>Synchronize panel, click ⌨ (Reload Latest or type **RL**. The light fixture location changes but you do not see the air terminals because that workset is not open.

3. Click ⌨ (Worksets) to open the dialog box and open the HVAC workset. Verify that it is **Visible in all views**.

4. Select **Lighting** in the *Active workset* drop-down list and make it editable (select **Yes** in the *Editable* column). The *Owner* should display as **User2**, as shown in Figure 6–94.

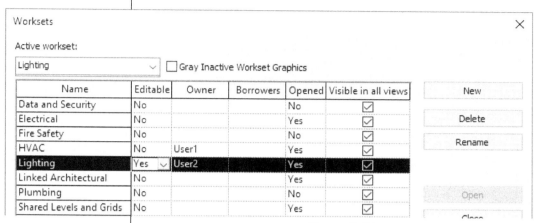

Figure 6–94

5. Click **OK** to close the dialog box.

6. Add another lighting fixture in the room.

7. In the Quick Access Toolbar, click 🖫 (Save) to save the local file.

8. **User1**, type **RL** (Reload Latest). There are no new changes to load, as shown in Figure 6–95, because User2 has not saved back to the central model. Close the dialog box.

Figure 6–95

9. **User2** will click ⟳ (Synchronize Now). This saves the changes to the central model without relinquishing the Lighting workset.

A video called
Task6.mp4
*(Architectural) is located
in the practice files
Videos folder.*

Task 6 - Request permission to edit.

1. **User1**, type **RL** (Reload Latest) again. This time, the new lighting fixture displays because it was saved to the central model.

2. Try to move one of the lighting fixtures. This time, an error message displays that cannot be ignored, as shown in Figure 6–96. **User2** has made the Lighting workset editable. Therefore, no one else can edit elements in it without permission.

Figure 6–96

3. Click **Place Request**. The Editing Request Placed dialog box opens. Leave it open.

4. **User2** now gets an alert box display, as shown in Figure 6–97.

Figure 6–97

5. Hover the cursor over the **Show** button to highlight the lighting fixture. (Move the dialog box out of the way if needed to see the modified lighting fixture.)

6. Click **Grant** to give **User1** permission to modify the placement of this lighting fixture. By doing so, you enable the other user to have full control over this element in the workset.

7. **User1** will get an Editing Request Granted dialog box, as shown in Figure 6–98.

Figure 6–98

8. Close the Editing Request Granted dialog box. Because your request was granted, the lighting fixture moves.

9. Move the lighting fixture again to exactly where you want it. This time, you are not prompted to ask to move the element because you are still borrowing it.

10. Try to move another lighting fixture. You do not have permission to move this or any others. Click **Cancel** rather than place the request. The lighting fixture returns to its original location.

A video called
Task7.mp4
(Architectural) is located in the practice files Videos folder.

Task 7 - View information about the worksets.

1. In the View Control Bar, expand the Worksharing Display and click (Owners). Different colors highlight the elements and their respective owners. Hover the cursor over one of the elements to display the information about the owner, as shown in Figure 6–99.

Owners

Lighting : Lighting Fixtures : Troffer Light - 2x4 Parabolic : 2'x4'(2 Lamp) - 120V
Current Owner: User2
Created by: User2
Last Update in central by: User2
Requested by: (None)

Figure 6–99

- The color on your display might be different.

2. Click ⬡ (Synchronize and Modify Settings) and relinquish **User-created Worksets** and **Borrowed Elements.**

3. Toggle the Worksharing Display off and zoom out to see the full building.

4. Save the local file.

5. **User2**, click ⬡ (Synchronize Now). The lighting fixture moves to the location where **User1** moved it. When you save to the central model, it also reloads the latest changes.

6. Close the project. When the Editable Elements dialog box opens, as shown in Figure 6–100, click **Relinquish elements and worksets**.

Figure 6–100

7. Close the project.

Practice 6f

Working in a Workshared Project - Structural

Practice Objectives

- Work in pairs to simulate a worksharing environment.
- Update an existing central model for use in the practice.
- Create a local file of the central model from each copy of the software.

In this practice, you will need to work in pairs to simulate a worksharing environment. On your individual machines, User1 and User2 will each create a local file and select specific worksets to open in each project, as shown in Figure 6–101. One user within the pair will create the central model.

*A video called **Intro to Worksharing.mp4** (Architectural) is located in the practice files Videos folder.*

- Instructors: You will need to create a shared network folder for students to work in pairs to simulate the work environment.
- Students: If this is self-paced training and you are not able to work in pairs or save a central model to a shared network location, Architectural videos are available in the practice files *Videos* folder for each of the tasks for Practice 6d for your reference.

"User1" and "User2" are referenced throughout the practice but you will see your unique Revit username instead.

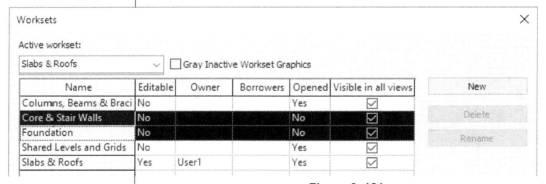

Figure 6–101

This practice uses a project that has been subdivided into worksets. To simulate a worksharing environment, work in groups of two.To keep the practices simple, the terms "User1" and "User2" will be used to indicate which user is to do certain tasks.

- **User1** updates the central model and focuses on the floor slabs.
- **User2** focuses on the core and stair walls.

Task 1 - Update the central model.

*A video called **Task1.mp4** (Architectural) is located in the practice files Videos folder.*

1. **User1**, in the Quick Access Toolbar, click ⬚ (Open). In the practice files folder, open **Syracuse-Suites-S.rvt**.

2. Alert boxes about a Copied Central Model and Cannot find Central Model display. Read and then close the alert boxes.

3. In the *File* tab, expand ⬚ (Save As) and click ⬚ (Project).

4. In the Save As dialog box, click **Options...**.

5. In the File Save Options dialog box, select **Make this a Central Model after save** and then click **OK**.

A central model needs to be repathed if it has been relocated. You will typically not have to do this in a work environment, but will need to do it for this practice to work.

6. Verify that the name is still set to **Syracuse-Suites-S.rvt** and then click **Save**.

   - If the Workset File Already Exists dialog box displays, click **Yes** to replace the existing file.

7. Close the project.

Task 2 - Create the local file for User1.

*A video called **Task2.mp4** (Architectural) is located in the practice files Videos folder.*

1. **User1** continues working within Revit.

2. In the Quick Access Toolbar, click ⬚ (Open). In the practice files folder, open **Syracuse-Suites-S.rvt**.

   - Do not select central models from the startup screen as it opens the central model directly. Instead, use the **Open** command and create a new local file.

3. Verify that **Create New Local** is selected and click **Open**. A file with the name **Syracuse-Suites-S_User1.rvt** is opened.

   - Note what the file name is at the top of your Revit user interface. It should have the file name with your unique username at the end.

4. In the *Collaborate* tab>Manage Collaboration panel or in the Status Bar, click ⬚ (Worksets).

5. In the Worksets dialog box, make **Slabs & Roofs** the Active worverset. Set *Editable* to **Yes** and select **Visible in all views** for this workset. Select the **Core & Stair Walls** and **Foundation** worksets. Click **Close** so the worksets are not open in this session, as shown in Figure 6–102.

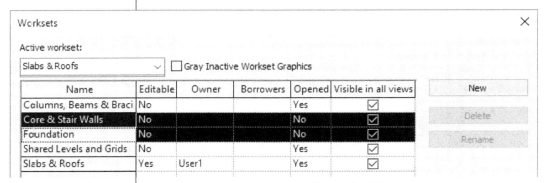

Figure 6–102

6. Click **OK** to finish.

7. In the Quick Access Toolbar, click 💾 (Save) to save the local file.

Task 3 - Create the local file for User2.

A video called **Task3.mp4** *(Architectural) is located in the practice files Videos folder.*

1. **User2**, in the Quick Access Toolbar, click 📂 (Open) and select the file **Syracuse-Suites-S.rvt**. Verify that **Create New Local** is selected, click the arrow next to **Open**, and select **Specify...** in the drop-down list, as shown in Figure 6–103.

Figure 6–103

2. Click **Open** to open the project.

3. In the Opening Worksets dialog box, select the **Columns, Beams & Bracing** and **Slabs & Roofs** worksets and click **Close** so these worksets are not opened in this session, as shown in Figure 6–104.

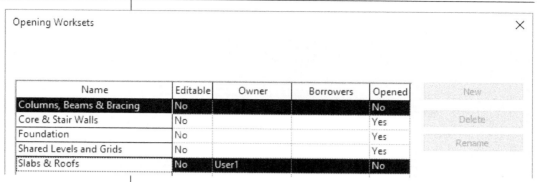

Figure 6–104

4. Click **OK** to finish.

- Note what the file name is at the top of your Revit user interface. It should have the file name with your unique username at the end.

5. Save the local file.

Task 4 - Add and modify elements in worksets.

A video called
Task4.mp4
(Architectural) is located in the practice files Videos folder.

1. **User1**, in your local file for **Syracuse-Suites-S**, open the **Structural Plans: 1ST FLOOR** view.

2. Zoom in on the beam system between grids 6 and 7 and C and D. Stay far enough out so that you can see the edge of the building, as shown in Figure 6–105. Do not select the beam system.

Figure 6–105

3. Select the second beam from the top and type **UP** to unpin it from the beam system. Move it up so that the distance between the beams is larger, as shown in Figure 6–106.

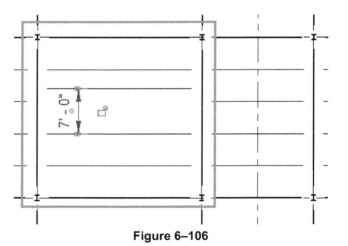

Figure 6–106

4. Hover the cursor over the edge of the building and press <Tab> until the floor is highlighted. Select the floor.

5. In the *Modify | Floors* tab>Mode panel, click ⬚ (Edit Boundary).

6. In the Draw panel, click ⌐ (Boundary Line) and draw a rectangle, as shown in Figure 6–107, to add a new opening in the floor. Move the opening inside the framing system between two beams, as shown in Figure 6–107. An exact location is not required for this practice.

Figure 6–107

7. Click ✓ (Finish Edit Mode).

8. In the *Collaborate* tab>Manage Collaboration panel, in the Active Workset drop-down list, select the **Columns, Beams & Bracing** workset to make it the active workset. It should be listed as **(Not Editable)**.

9. In the *Structure* tab>Structure panel, click 🪵 (Beam).

10. In the Type Selector, verify that the selected beam is **W-Wide Flange: W12x26**. In the Options Bar, set the *Structural Usage* to **Joist** and clear the **Chain** option, as shown in Figure 6–108.

Figure 6–108

11. Add two beams to frame the new opening on the unsupported sides, as shown in Figure 6–109.

Figure 6–109

12. Click 🔧 (Modify) to end the Beam command.

13. In the *Collaborate* tab>Manage Collaboration panel or in the Status Bar, click 🗂 (Worksets).

14. In the Worksets dialog box, **User1** is noted as the *Owner* of the **Slabs & Roofs** workset and as a *Borrower* of **Columns, Beams & Bracing**, as shown in Figure 6–110.

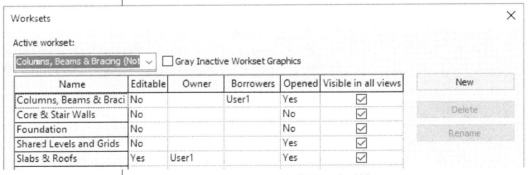

Figure 6–110

15. Close the dialog box.

16. In the Quick Access Toolbar, click 🗂 (Synchronize and Modify Settings).

17. In the Synchronize with Central dialog box, the **Borrowed Elements** option should be selected. Add a comment about adding an opening to the first floor slab and select the **Save Local File before and after synchronizing with central** option, as shown in Figure 6–111.

Figure 6–111

18. Click **OK** to finish synchronizing.

Task 5 - Check out a workset.

A video called **Task5.mp4** *(Architectural) is located in the practice files Videos folder.*

1. **User2**, in the local Syracuse-Suites-S file, open the **Structural Plans: 1ST FLOOR** view if it is not already open. None of the changes display in the local file yet.

2. In the Status Bar, click 🗇 (Worksets).

3. In the Worksets dialog box, open the **Columns, Beams & Bracing** and **Slabs & Roofs** worksets by setting the *Opened* column to **Yes**, as shown in Figure 6–112. Click **OK**.

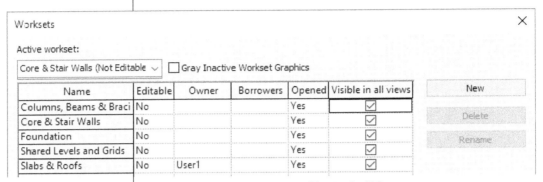

Figure 6–112

4. In the **Structural Plans: 1ST FLOOR** view, you can now see the beams and other elements, but the changes are still not displayed.

5. In the *Collaborate* tab>Synchronize panel, click 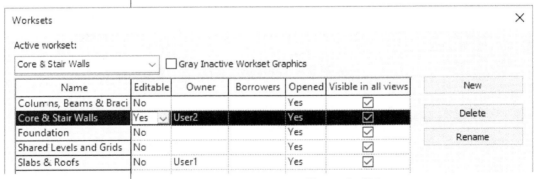 (Reload Latest) or type **RL**. The new opening and joists display.

6. Open the Worksets dialog box.

7. In the Worksets dialog box, select **Core & Stair Walls** in the list of worksets and make it **Editable**. The *Owner* should change to **User2**, as shown in Figure 6–113.

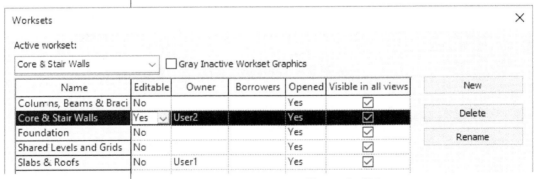

Figure 6–113

8. Click **OK**.

9. Zoom in on the elevator in the upper right of the building.

10. Move the core's north wall approximately **1'-0"** up.

11. In the Quick Access Toolbar, click 🖫 (Save) to save the local file.

12. **User1**, type **RL** (**Reload Latest**). There are no new changes to load because User2 has not saved back to the central model.

13. **User2** will click 📷 (Synchronize Now). This saves the changes to the central model without relinquishing the Core & Stair Walls workset.

Task 6 - Request permission to edit.

A video called
Task6.mp4
(Architectural) is located
in the practice files
Videos folder.

1. **User1**, open the Worksets dialog box.

2. Select **Core & Stair Walls** in the list of worksets and click **Open**. Click **OK** to exit the dialog box.

3. Type **RL** (**Reload Latest**) again. This time, the core wall moves in response to the change made by **User2**.

4. Try to move the core wall back to its previous position. An error message opens that cannot be ignored. **User2** has made the Core & Stair Walls workset editable. Therefore, no one else can edit elements in it without permission, as shown in Figure 6–114.

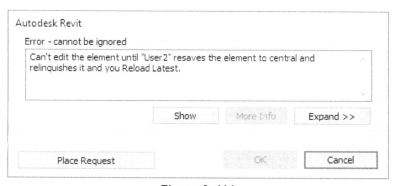

Figure 6–114

5. Click **Place Request**. The Editing Request Placed dialog box opens. Leave it open.

6. **User2** now has an alert box displayed, as shown in Figure 6–115.

Figure 6–115

7. Hover the cursor over the **Show** button to highlight the wall. (Move the box out of the way as required to display the modified wall.)

8. Click **Grant** to give **User1** permission to modify the placement of this core wall. By doing so, you enable the other user to have full control over this one element in the workset.

9. **User1** will get an Editing Request Granted dialog box.

10. Close the Editing Request Granted dialog box. Because your request was granted, the core wall moves.

11. Move the core wall again. This time, you are not prompted to ask permission to move the core wall because you are still borrowing it.

12. Try to move another core wall. You do not have permission to move this wall. Click **Cancel** rather than place the request. The core wall returns to its original location.

Task 7 - View information about the worksets.

*A video called **Task7.mp4** (Architectural) is located in the practice files Videos folder.*

1. **User1**, in the Status Bar, expand the Worksharing Display, and select **Owners**, as shown in Figure 6–116.

Figure 6–116

2. The view displays in color showing the two owners. Different colors highlight the elements and their respective owners, as shown in Figure 6–117. Hover the cursor over one of the walls to display information about the owner.

Figure 6–117

3. Open the Worksets dialog box. The owner of Core & Stair Walls is listed as **User2**, but **User1** is also listed as a borrower. Click **Cancel**.

4. Toggle the Worksharing Display off and zcom out to see the full building.

5. In the *Collaborate* tab>Manage Collaboration panel, click

   (Gray Inactive Worksets) to gray out the elements that you cannot modify without requesting permission. This also grays out the core walls, although you have a right to edit the wall that you borrowed.

6. Click (Synchronize and Modify Settings) and verify that all of the worksets will be relinquished before clicking **OK**.

7. Close the project.

8. **User2**, click (Synchronize Now). The core wall moves to the location selected by **User1**. When you sync with the central model, it also reloads the latest changes.

9. Close the project. When the Editable Elements dialog box opens, select **Relinquish elements and worksets**.

6.9 Best Practices for Worksharing

Working with Company Policies

There are different practices regarding the frequency of synchronizing with the central model. Some companies ask users to synchronize before lunch and at the end of the day. Other companies require users to synchronize every 30 to 60 minutes. As the file size gets larger, synchronizing more often prevents the loss of data and also makes the synchronization finish quicker than if there are several hours worth of work to synchronize. However, there can be many reasons to change this frequency or to do additional synchronizations at specific points in time. They are:

- Major or critical changes to the project, such as moving an elevator core, reorienting the building on the site, etc.

- Users working in close proximity inside the model, to reduce permission issues.

When users need to leave their work for an hour or more (for lunch or a meeting or at the end of the day), it is best to synchronize and relinquish all. Then, upon returning, they should create a new local file (with a new name if you want the previous file saved as a backup). This ensures their file is up to date and eliminates the update time.

Tips for Using Worksets

Working with the Local File

- Be selective about which worksets you open. Avoid opening worksets that are not required for the work you are doing in the project. Limiting the number of worksets that will be opened with the file speeds up the process of opening and saving the file.

- Close unused views on a regular basis.

- Use a Starting View that is a drafting view, 2D plan, or elevation view. The Autodesk Revit software only loads into memory what it displays, so this saves memory the next time the file is opened. This can also be used before plotting to increase the amount of available RAM.

- If you have been away from an active project for some time, it is better to create a new local file rather than depend on the **Reload Latest** command to update your current local file for you.

- If you are not sure what workset to put certain elements in, you can use *Workset1* or a specific temporary workset to put them in until the decision can be finalized.

- Restart the software before performing memory-intensive operations, such as printing an entire document set.

Saving to the Central Model

- Stagger syncing to the central model among users so that they are not saving concurrently.

- Type **RL** (Reload Latest) to update your copy of the project without changing the central model. This saves time by eliminating the need to reload as part of the **Synchronize and Modify Settings** command.

- Periodically synchronize with the central model using the **Compact File** option. This takes longer to save, but frees up more memory.

- If you get an error, such as *Unable to Save* or *File not found*, you might have run out of memory. Close the major worksets and view so that the Autodesk Revit software releases some of the virtual memory that can be used to then save the file.

Requesting Edits

- Enable elements, not worksets, whenever possible. The Autodesk Revit software automatically borrows the unowned elements without user intervention. This saves time by not having to request an edit in the first place.

- Communicate with the team members working on a project to avoid working on the same elements at the same time.

Tips for Creating Worksets

Worksets and the Team

- Assign one person to enable worksharing and create worksets and the central model.

- Create your project team structure to correspond with the new way of working with the building model. For example, architects and engineers do much of the work directly without needing an intern or drafter to create working drawings until the later parts of a project.

- Divide worksets according to components of a building rather than drawing types (such as plans, elevations, and sections), as these are created automatically.

- Key considerations when determining how to divide a project into worksets include the ability to load only those worksets that are required at the time and the ability to control visibility by worksets.

- As the project progresses, more worksets can be added.

- Using worksets does not negate the need for good team communication. You still need to have scheduling and planning meetings.

- Be sure that everyone knows which part of the model they are responsible for.

- File sharing should be a tool that is used in the workflow of the project; it should not be something that is disruptive.

Creating Worksets

- A multi-floor building does not need to have a workset for each floor until you are working on the floor-specific layouts.

- If you have a project with a large floor plate that needs to be divided by match lines to fit on sheets, you should divide the various parts of the building into separate worksets.

- If you have imported files into a project, each import should be in a separate workset that is not visible by default. They should also be closed when not in use.

- Every linked file should be in a separate workset not visible by default. They should also be closed when not in use.

- Worksets cannot be included in templates.

Default Workset Visibility

- As you create worksets, you should set the visibility. For example, the exterior and core of a building should be visible in all views, but furniture layouts or tenant partitions only need to be visible in specific views.

- Set up a standard for typical workset visibility designations. There are always exceptions, but working with the standard first is simpler.

Ending the Day

IMPORTANT: When you have finished working on the project for the day, you need to save, synchronize to central, and relinquish all borrowed and user-created worksets. If you are working on a project with other people, you need to relinquish all your worksets when closing a project so they can edit them if needed.

- When you close a project, if you did not relinquish elements and all worksets when you saved to the central model, the alert shown in Figure 6–118 will display.

Figure 6–118

- To relinquish worksets without saving to the central model, in the *Collaborate* tab>Synchronize panel, click 🖼 (Relinquish All Mine).

Do not delete any files in these directories.

- The backup directory for central models and local files, as shown in Figure 6–119, holds information about the editability of worksets, borrowed elements, and workset/element ownership. If required, you can restore the backup directory. In the *Collaboration* tab>Synchronize panel, click 🖼 (Restore Backup).

Figure 6–119

Chapter Review Questions

1. When setting up a project to be workshared, which of the following is performed first?

   a. Use Save As and, in Options, select **Make this a Central Model** after save.

   b. Start the project using a Central Model template.

   c. Use the Collaborate tool to enable worksharing, then use the **Worksets** command and add worksets.

   d. All of the grids and levels need to be in place.

2. Where should a central model be located?

   a. On your computer.

   b. On the company server.

   c. On each of the computers used by the team.

3. When you want to update the work that you have done and receive any changes others have made, but you do not want to change anything else, which command do you use?

   a. (Synchronize and Modify Settings)

   b. (Synchronize Now)

   c. (Relinquish All Mine)

   d. (Reload Latest)

4. Where should a local file be located?

   a. On the project manager's computer.

   b. On the company server.

   c. On each team member's computer.

5. What do you need to do so that any new elements you add are placed in a particular workset?

   a. Gray out inactive worksets so you know not to work in them.

   b. Make the workset editable.

   c. Set the workset as active.

   d. Create a new workset.

6. When selecting an element to edit, the icon shown in Figure 6–120 displays. What do you need to do?

Figure 6–120

   a. You can either edit the element without checking it out if it is not owned by someone else or place a request to edit it if it is owned by someone else.

   b. Click the icon and an error dialog box displays indicating that you cannot edit the element.

   c. Click the icon and an error dialog box displays indicating that you cannot edit the element, but you can request permission to edit it.

   d. Click the icon and a dialog box displays granting you permission to edit the element.

7. You have the most recent updates from the central model but some elements in a workset are not displaying, as shown in Figure 6–121. Which of the following should you do? (Select all that apply.)

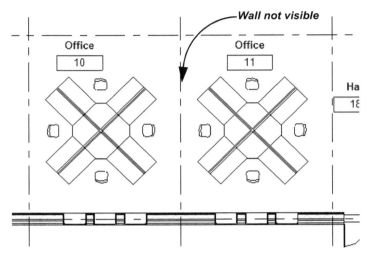

Figure 6–121

a. In the Visibility/Graphic Overrides dialog box, change the Visibility Setting of the workset to **Visible**.

b. In the Worksets dialog box, request permission to edit.

c. Set the workset as active.

d. In the Status Bar, change the Worksharing Display.

e. In the Worksets dialog box, verify if the workset is open.

Command Summary

Button	Command	Location
	Collaborate	• **Ribbon**: *Collaborate* tab>Manage Collaboration panel
	Editing Requests	• **Ribbon**: *Collaborate* tab> Synchronize panel
		• **Status Bar**
	Gray Inactive Worksets	• **Ribbon**: *Collaborate* tab>Manage Collaboration panel
	Owners (Display)	• **Status Bar**: expand Worksharing Display Off
	Relinquish All Mine	• **Ribbon**: *Collaborate* tab> Synchronize panel
	Reload Latest	• **Ribbon**: *Collaborate* tab> Synchronize panel
		• **Shortcut**: RL
	Restore Backup	• **Ribbon**: *Collaborate* tab> Synchronize panel
	Show History	• **Ribbon**: *Collaborate* tab> Synchronize panel
	Synchronize and Modify Settings	• **Quick Access Toolbar**
		• **Ribbon**: *Collaborate* tab> Synchronize panel>expand Synchronize with Central
	Synchronize Now	• **Quick Access Toolbar**
		• **Ribbon**: *Collaborate* tab> Synchronize panel>expand Synchronize with Central
	Worksets	• **Ribbon**: *Collaborate* tab>Manage Collaboration panel>Worksets
		• **Status Bar**
	Worksets (Display)	• **Status Bar**: expand Worksharing Display Off
	Worksharing Display Off	• **Status Bar**

Annotation Tools and Creating Details

Creating details is a critical part of the design process, as it is the step where you specify the exact information that is required to build a construction project. The elements that you can add to a model include detail components, detail lines, text, keynotes, tags, symbols, and filled regions for patterning. Details can be created from views in the model, but you can also draw 2D details in separate views.

Learning Objectives in This Chapter

- Create drafting views where you can draw 2D details.
- Add detail components that indicate the typical elements in a detail.
- Annotate details using detail lines, text, tags, symbols, and patterns that define materials.

A.1 Working with Dimensions

You can create permanent dimensions using aligned, linear, angular, radial, diameter, and arc length dimensions. These can be individual or a string of dimensions, as shown in Figure A–1. With aligned dimensions, you can also dimension entire walls with openings, grid lines, and/or intersecting walls.

Figure A–1

- Dimensions referencing model elements must be added to the model in a view. You can dimension on sheets, but only to items added directly on the sheets.

- Dimensions are available in the *Annotate* tab>Dimension panel, shown in Figure A–2, and the *Modify* tab>Measure panel.

(Aligned) is also located in the Quick Access Toolbar.

Figure A–2

How To: Add Aligned Dimensions with Options

1. Start the ✎ (Aligned) command or type **DI**.
2. In the Type Selector, select a dimension style.

3. In the Options Bar, select the location line of the wall to dimension from, as shown in Figure A–3.

  • This option can be changed as you add dimensions.

Figure A–3

4. In the Options Bar, select your preference from the *Pick* drop-down list:

  • **Individual References**: Select the elements in order (as shown in Figure A–4) and then click in an empty space in the view to position the dimension string.

Figure A–4

  • **Entire Walls**: Select the wall you want to dimension and then click the cursor to position the dimension string, as shown in Figure A–5.

Figure A–5

- When dimensioning entire walls you can specify how you want *Openings*, *Intersecting Walls*, and *Intersecting Grids* to be treated by the dimension string. In the Options Bar, click **Options**. In the Auto Dimension Options dialog box, shown in Figure A–6, select the references you want to have automatically dimensioned.

*If the **Entire Wall** option is selected without additional options, it places an overall wall dimension.*

Figure A–6

How To: Add Other Types of Dimensions

*When the **Dimension** command is active, the dimension methods are also accessible in the Modify | Place Dimensions*

1. In the *Annotate* tab>Dimension panel, select a dimension method.

	Aligned	Most commonly used dimension type. Select individual elements or entire walls to dimension.
	Linear	Used when you need to specify certain points on elements.
	Angular	Used to dimension the angle between two elements.
	Radial	Used to dimension the radius of circular elements.
	Diameter	Used to dimension the diameter of circular elements.
	Arc Length	Used to dimension the length of the arc of circular elements.

2. In the Type Selector, select the dimension type.
3. Follow the prompts for the selected method.

Modifying Dimensions

When you move elements that are dimensioned, the dimensions automatically update. You can also modify dimensions by selecting a dimension or dimension string and making changes, as shown in Figure A–7.

Toggle dimension equality

Click to edit dimension text

Move (dimension line)

Drag text

Lock/Unlock

Move witness line

Set gap between witness line and reference

Figure A–7

- To move the dimension text, select the **Drag text** control under the text and drag it to a new location. It automatically creates a leader from the dimension line if you drag it away. The style of the leader (arc or line) depends on the dimension style.

- To move the dimension line (the line parallel to the element being dimensioned) simply drag the line to a new location or select the dimension and drag the ⁺‡⁺ (Drag to new position) control.

- To change the gap between the witness line and the element being dimensioned, drag the control at the end of the witness line.

- To move the witness line (the line perpendicular to the element being dimensioned) to a different element or face of a wall, use the **Move Witness Line** control in the middle of the witness line. While moving the witness line, you can hover your cursor over a element or component and press <Tab> repeatedly to cycle through the various options. You can also drag this control to move the witness line to a different element, or right-click on the control and select **Move Witness Line**.

Adding and Deleting Dimensions in a String

- To add a witness line to a string of dimensions, select the dimension and, in the *Modify | Dimensions* tab>Witness Lines panel, click ⊢⊣ (Edit Witness Lines). Select the element(s) you want to add to the dimension. Click in an empty space in the view to finish.

- To delete a witness line, drag the **Move Witness Line** control to a nearby witness lines element. Alternatively, you can hover the cursor over the control, right-click, and select **Delete Witness Line**.

- To delete one dimension in a string and break the string into two separate dimensions, select the string, hover your cursor over the dimension that you want to delete, and press <Tab>. When it highlights (as shown on top in Figure A–8), pick it and press <Delete>. The selected dimension is deleted and the dimension string is separated into two elements as shown on the bottom in Figure A–8.

Figure A–8

Modifying the Dimension Text

Because the Autodesk® Revit® software is parametric, changing the dimension text without changing the elements dimensioned would cause problems throughout the project. These issues could cause problems beyond the model if you use the project model to estimate materials or work with other disciplines.

You can append the text with prefixes and suffixes (as shown in Figure A–9), which can help you in renovation projects.

Figure A–9

Double-click on the dimension text to open the Dimension Text dialog box, as shown in Figure A–10, and make modifications as needed.

Figure A–10

Setting Constraints

The three types of constraints that work with dimensions are locks and equal settings, as shown in Figure A–11, as well as labels.

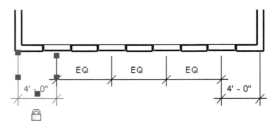

Figure A–11

Locking Dimensions

When you lock a dimension, the value is set and you cannot make a change between it and the referenced elements. If it is unlocked, you can move it and change its value.

Note that when you use this and move an element, any elements that are locked to the dimension also move.

Setting Dimensions Equal

For a string of dimensions, select the **EQ** symbol to constrain the elements to be at an equal distance apart. This actually moves the elements that are dimensioned.

- The equality text display can be changed in Properties, as shown in Figure A–12. The style for each of the display types is set in the dimension type.

Figure A–12

Labeling Dimensions

If you have a distance that needs to be repeated multiple times, such as the *Wall to Window* label shown in Figure A–13, or one where you want to use a formula based on another dimension, you can create and apply a global parameter, also called a label, to the dimension.

Figure A–13

- To apply an existing label to a dimension, select the dimension and in the *Modify | Dimension* tab>Label Dimension panel, select the label in the drop-down list, as shown in Figure A–14.

Figure A–14

How To: Create a Label

1. Select a dimension.
2. In the *Modify | Dimension* tab>Label Dimension panel, click
   📑 (Create Parameter)
3. In the Global Parameter Properties dialog box type in a *Name* as shown in Figure A–15 and click **OK**.

Figure A–15

4. The label is applied to the dimension.

How To: Edit the Label Information

1. Select a labeled dimension.

2. Click ✎ (Global Parameters), as shown in Figure A–16.

Figure A–16

3. In the Global Parameters dialog box, in the *Value* column, type the new distance, as shown in Figure A–17.

Figure A–17

4. Click **OK**. The selected dimension and any other dimensions using the same label are updated.

- You can also edit, create, and delete Global Parameters in this dialog box.

Working with Constraints

To find out which elements have constraints applied to them, in the View Control Bar, click ⊢⊟ (Reveal Constraints). Constraints display as shown in Figure A–18.

Figure A–18

- If you try to move the element beyond the appropriate constrains, a warning dialog box displays, as shown in Figure A–19.

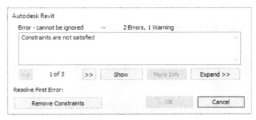

Figure A–19

- If you delete dimensions that are constrained, a warning dialog box displays, as shown in Figure A–20. Click **OK** to retain the constraint or **Unconstrain** to remove the constraint.

Figure A–20

A.2 Working with Text

The **Text** command enables you to add notes to views or sheets, such as the detail shown in Figure A–21. The same command is used to create text with or without leaders.

Figure A–21

The text height is automatically set by the text type in conjunction with the scale of the view (as shown in Figure A–22, using the same size text type at two different scales). Text types display at the specified height, both in the views and on the sheet.

Scale: 1/8"=1'-0" *Scale: 1/4"=1'-0"*

Figure A–22

How To: Add Text

1. In the Quick Access Toolbar or *Annotate* tab>Text panel, click A (Text).

The text type sets the font and height of the text.

2. In the Type Selector, set the text type.
3. In the *Modify | Place Text* tab>Leader panel, select the method you want to use: A (No Leader), ←A (One Segment), ↙A (Two Segments), or ⌐A (Curved).
4. In the Alignment panel, set the overall justification for the text and leader, as shown in Figure A–23.

Figure A–23

Use alignment lines to help you align the text with other text elements.

5. Select the location for the leader and text.
   - If **No leader** is selected, select the start point for the text and begin typing.
   - If using a leader, the first point places the arrow and you then select points for the leader. The text starts at the last leader point.
   - To set a word wrapping distance, click and drag the circle grip controls to set the start and end points of the text.
6. Type the needed text. In the *Edit Text* tab, specify additional options for the font and paragraph, as shown in Figure A–24.

Figure A–24

7. In the Edit Text tab>Edit Text panel, click ☒ (Close) or click outside the text box to complete the text element.
   - Pressing <Enter> after a line of text starts a new line of text in the same text window.

How To: Add Text Symbols

1. Start the **Text** command and click to place the text.
2. As you are typing text and need to insert a symbol, right-click and select **Symbols** from the shortcut menu. Select from the list of commonly used symbols, as shown in Figure A–25.

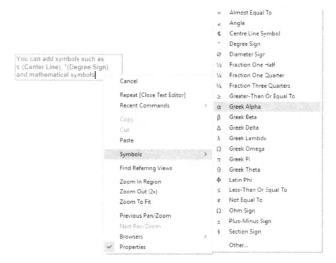

Figure A–25

3. If the symbol you need is not listed, click **Other**.
4. In the Character Map dialog box, click on a symbol and click **Select**, as shown in Figure A–26.

Figure A–26

5. Click **Copy** to copy the character to the clipboard and paste it into the text box.

•   The Font in the Character Map should match the font used by the text type. You do not want to use a different font for symbols.

Editing Text

Editing text notes takes place at two levels:

- Modifying the text note, which includes the **Leader** and **Paragraph** styles.

- Editing the text, which includes changes to individual letters, word, and paragraphs in the text note.

Modifying the Text Note

Click once on the text note to modify the text box and leaders using controls, as shown in Figure A–27, or using the tools in the *Modify | Text Notes* tab.

Figure A–27

How To: Add a Leader to Text Notes

1. Select the text note.
2. In the *Modify | Text Notes* tab>Leader panel, select the direction and justification for the new leader, as shown in Figure A–28.
3. The leader is applied, as shown in Figure A–29. Use the drag controls to place the arrow as needed.

Figure A–28

Figure A–29

- You can remove leaders by clicking ⁻A (Remove Last Leader).

Editing the Text

The *Edit Text* tab enables you to make various customizations. These include modifying the font of selected words as well as creating bulleted and numbered lists, as shown in Figure A–30.

General Notes
1. Notify designer of intention to start construction at least 10 days prior to start of site work.
2. Installer shall provide the following:
   - 24-hour notice of start of construction
   - Inspection of bottom of bed or covering required by state inspector
   - All environmental management inspection sheets must be emailed to designer's office within 24 hours of inspection.

Figure A–30

- You can **Cut**, **Copy**, and **Paste** text using the clipboard. For example, you can copy text from a document and then paste it into the text editor in Revit.

- To help you see the text better as you are modifying it, in the *Edit Text* tab, expand the Edit Text panel, and select one or both of the options, as shown in Figure A–31.

Figure A–31

How To: Modify the Font

1. Select Individual letters or words.
2. Click on the font modification you want to include:

B (Bold)	X_2 (Subscript)
I (Italic)	X^2 (Superscript)
U (Underline)	ªÂ (All Caps)

- When pasting text from a document outside of Autodesk Revit, font modifications (e.g, Bold, Italic, etc.) are retained.

How To: Create Lists

1. In Edit Text mode, place the cursor in the line where you want to add to a list.
2. In the *Edit Text* tab>Paragraph panel, click the type of list you want to create:

≡ (Bullets)	≡ (Uppercase Letters)
≡ (Numbers)	≡ (Lowercase Letters)

3. As you type, press <Enter> and the next line in the list is incremented.
4. To include sub-lists, at the beginning of the next line, click ≡ (Increase Indent). This indents the line and applies the next level of lists, as shown in Figure A–32.

The indent distance is set up by the Text Type Tab Size.

> 4. The applicant shall be responsible:
>   A. First Indent
>   a. Second Indent
>   • Third Indent

Figure A–32

- You can change the type of list after you have applied the first increment. For example, you might want to use a list of bullets instead of letters, as shown in Figure A–33.

5. Click ≡ (Decrease Indent) to return to the previous list style.

- Press <Shift>+<Enter> to create a blank line in a numbered list.

- To create columns or other separate text boxes that build on a numbering system (as shown in Figure A–33), create the second text box and list. Then, place the cursor on one of the lines and in the Paragraph panel, click (Increment List Value) until the list matches the next number in the sequence.

General Notes
1. Notify designer of intention to start construction at least 10 days prior to start of site work.
2. Installer shall provide the following:
   - 24-hour notice of start of construction
   - Inspection of bottom of bed or covering required by state inspector
   - All environmental management inspection sheets must be emailed to designer's office within 24 hours of inspection.
3. Site layout and required inspections to be made by designer:
   - Foundations and OWTS location and elevation
   - Inspection of OWTS bottom of trench
4. The applicant shall be responsible for:
   - New Application for redesign.
   - As-built location plans

General Notes (cont.)
5. The installer/applicant shall provide the designer with materials sheets for all construction materiasl prior to designer issuing certificate of construction.
6. The applicant shall furnish the original application to the installer prior to start of constuction

List Incremented

Figure A–33

6. Click (Decrement List Value) to move back a number.

Hint: Model Text

Model text is different from annotation text. It is designed to create full-size text on the model itself. For example, you would use model text to create a sign on a door, as shown in Figure A–34. One model text type is included with the default template. You can create other types as needed.

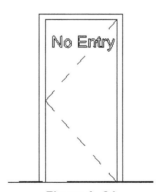

Figure A–34

- Model text can be viewed in all views.
- Model text is added from the *Architecture* tab>Model panel, by clicking (Model Text).

Spell Checking

The Spelling dialog box displays any misspelled words in context and provides several options for changing them, as shown in Figure A–35.

Figure A–35

- To spell check all text in a view, in the *Annotate* tab>Text panel, click ^{ABC} (Spelling) or press <F7>. As with other spell checkers, you can **Ignore**, **Add**, or **Change** the word.

- You can also check the spelling in selected text. With text selected, in the *Modify | Text Notes* tab>Tools panel, click ^{ABC} (Check Spelling).

Creating Text Types

If you need new text types with a different text size or font (such as for a title or hand-lettering), you can create new ones, as shown in Figure A–36. It is recommended that you create these in a project template so they are available in future projects.

General Notes

1. This project consists of
   furnishing and installing...

Figure A–36

- You can copy and paste text types from one project to another or use **Transfer Project Standards**.

How To: Create Text Types

1. In the *Annotate* tab>Text panel, click ⌄ (Text Types).
2. In the Type Properties dialog box, click **Duplicate**.
3. In the Name dialog box, type a new name and click **OK**.
4. Modify the text parameters, as needed. The parameters are shown in Figure A–37.

Parameter	Value
Graphics	⊼
Color	■ Black
Line Weight	1
Background	Opaque
Show Border	☐
Leader/Border Offset	5/64"
Leader Arrowhead	Arrow 30 Degree
Text	⊼
Text Font	Arial
Text Size	1/4"
Tab Size	1/2"
Bold	☐
Italic	☐
Underline	☐
Width Factor	1.000000

Figure A–37

- The **Background** parameter can be set to **Opaque** or **Transparent**. An opaque background includes a masking region that hides lines or elements behind the text.

- In the *Text* area, the **Width Factor** parameter controls the width of the lettering, but does not affect the height. A width factor greater than **1** spreads the text out and a width factor less than **1** compresses it.

- The **Show Border** parameter, when selected, includes a rectangle around the text.

5. Click **OK** to close the Type Properties dialog box.

A.3 Adding Detail Lines and Symbols

While annotating views for construction documents, you might need to add detail lines and symbols to clarify the design intent or show information, such as the life safety plan exit information, as shown in Figure A–38.

Symbol

Detail line

Figure A–38

- Detail lines and symbols are view-specific, which means that they only display in the view in which they were created.

How To: Draw a Detail Line

1. In the *Annotation* tab>Detail panel, click 🔲 (Detail Line).
2. In the *Modify | Place Detail Lines* tab>Line Style panel, select the type of line you want to use, as shown in Figure A–39.

Figure A–39

3. Use the tools in the Draw panel to create the detail line.

Using Symbols

Symbols are 2D elements that only display in one view, while components can be in 3D and display in many views.

Many of the annotations used in working drawings are frequently repeated. Several of them have been saved as symbols in the Autodesk Revit software, such as the North Arrow, Center Line, and Graphic Scale annotations as shown in Figure A–40.

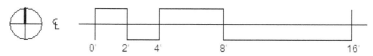

Figure A–40

- You can also create or load custom annotation symbols.

How To: Place a Symbol

1. In the *Annotate* tab>Symbol panel, click ⊕ (Symbol).
2. In the Type Selector, select the symbol you want to use.
3. In the *Modify | Place Symbol* tab>Mode panel, click

   (Load Family) if you want to load other symbols.
4. In the Options Bar, as shown in Figure A–41, set the *Number of Leaders* and select **Rotate after placement** if you want to rotate the symbol as you insert it.

Figure A–41

5. Place the symbol in the view. Rotate it if you selected the **Rotate after placement** option. If you specified leaders, use the controls to move them into place.

- In the *Annotate* tab>Symbol panel, click ▦ (Stair Path) to label the slope direction and walk line of a stair, as shown in Figure A–42.

Figure A–42

A.4 Setting Up Detail Views

Most of the work you do in the Autodesk® Revit® software is exclusively with *smart* elements that interconnect and work together in the model. However, the software does not automatically display how elements should be built to fit together. For this, you need to create detail drawings, as shown in Figure A–43.

Details are created either in 2D drafting views, or in callouts from plan, elevation, or section views.

Figure A–43

How To: Create a Drafting View

1. In the *View* tab>Create panel, click (Drafting View).
2. In the New Drafting View dialog box, enter a *Name* and set a *Scale*, as shown in Figure A–44.

Drafting views are listed in their own section in the Project Browser.

Figure A–44

3. Click **OK**. A blank view is created with space in which you can sketch the detail.

How To: Create a Detail View from Model Elements

1. Start the **Section** or **Callout** command.
2. In the Type Selector, select the **Detail View: Detail** type.
   - The marker indicates that it is a detail, as shown for a section in Figure A–45.

Callouts also have a Detail View Type that can be used in the same way.

Figure A–45

3. Place the section or a callout of the area you want to use for the detail.
4. Open the new detail.

- Change the detail level to see more or less of the element materials.

- Use the Detail Line tool to sketch on top of or add to the building elements.

- Because you are working with smart elements, a detail of the model is a true representation. When the building elements change, the detail changes as well, as shown in Figure A–46.

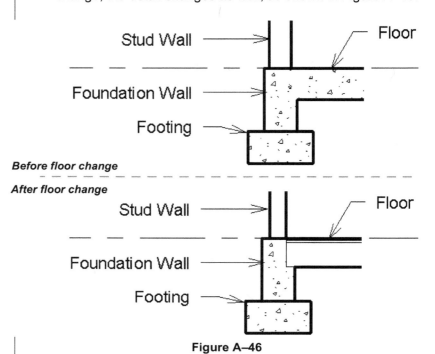

Before floor change

After floor change

Figure A–46

- You can create detail elements on top of the model and then toggle the model off so that it does not show in the detail view. In Properties, in the *Graphics* area, change *Display Model* to **Do not display**. You can also set the model to **Halftone**, as shown in Figure A–47.

Figure A–47

Referencing a Drafting View

Once you have created a drafting view, you can reference it in another view (such as a callout, elevation, or section view), as shown in Figure A–48. For example, in a section view, you might want to reference an existing roof detail. You can reference drafting views, sections, elevations, and callouts.

Figure A–48

- You can use the search feature to limit the information displayed.

How To: Reference a Drafting View

1. Open the view in which you want to place the reference.
2. Start the **Section, Callout,** or **Elevation** command.
3. In the *Modify | <contextual>* tab>Reference panel select **Reference Other View**.
4. In the drop-down list, select **<New Drafting View>** or an existing drafting view.
5. Place the view marker.

6. When you place the associated drafting view on a sheet, the marker in this view updates with the appropriate information.

- If you select **<New Drafting View>** from the drop-down list, a new view is created in the *Drafting Views (Detail)* area in the Project Browser. You can rename it as needed. The new view does not include any model elements.

- When you create a detail based on a section, elevation, or callout, you do not need to link it to a drafting view.

- You can change a referenced view to a different view. Select the view marker and in the ribbon, select the new view from the list.

Saving Drafting Views

To create a library of standard details, save the non-model specific drafting views to your server. They can then be imported into a project and modified to suit. They are saved as .RVT files.

Drafting views can be saved in two ways:

- Save an individual drafting view to a new file.
- Save all of the drafting views as a group in one new file.

How To: Save One Drafting View to a File

1. In the Project Browser, right-click on the drafting view you want to save and select **Save to New File...**, as shown in Figure A–49.

Figure A–49

2. In the Save As dialog box, specify a name and location for the file and click **Save**.

How To: Save a Group of Drafting Views to a File

You can save sheets, drafting views, model views (floor plans), schedules, and reports.

1. In the *File* tab, expand ⬛ (Save As), expand ⬛ (Library) and then click ⬛ (View).
2. In the Save Views dialog box, in the *Views:* pane, expand the list and select **Show drafting views only**.
3. Select the drafting views that you want to save, as shown in Figure A–50.

Figure A–50

4. Click **OK**.
5. In the Save As dialog box, specify a name and location for the file and click **Save**.

How To: Use a Saved Drafting View in Another Project

1. Open the project to which you want to add the drafting view.

2. In the *Insert* tab>Load from Library panel, expand (Insert from File) and click (Insert Views from File).

3. In the Open dialog box, select the project in which you saved the detail and click **Open**.

4. In the Insert Views dialog box, limit the types of views to **Show drafting views only**, as shown in Figure A–51.

Figure A–51

5. Select the view(s) that you want to insert and click **OK**.

Hint: Importing Details from Other CAD Software

You might already have a set of standard details created in a different CAD program, such as the AutoCAD® software. You can reuse the details in the Autodesk Revit software by importing them into a temporary project. Once you have imported the detail, it helps to clean it up and save it as a view before bringing it into your active project.

1. In a new project, create a drafting view and make it active.
2. In the *Insert* tab>Import panel, click ⬚ (Import CAD).
3. In the Import CAD dialog box, select the file to import. Most of the default values are what you need. You might want to change the *Layer/Level colors* to **Black and White**.
4. Click **Open**.

- If you want to modify the detail, select the imported data. In the *Modify | [filename]* tab>Import Instance panel, expand ⬚ (Explode) and click ⬚ (Partial Explode) or ⬚ (Full Explode). Click ⬚ (Delete Layers) before you explode the detail. A full explode greatly increases the file size.

- Modify the detail using tools in the Modify panel. Change all the text and line styles to Autodesk Revit specific elements.

A.5 Adding Detail Components

Autodesk Revit elements, such as the casework section shown in Figure A–52, typically require additional information to ensure that they are constructed correctly. To create details such as the one shown in Figure A–53, you add detail components, detail lines, and various annotation elements.

Section
Figure A–52

Detail built on section
Figure A–53

- Detail elements are not directly connected to the model, even if model elements display in the view.

- If you want to draw detail lines in 3D, use the Model Line tool. Detail Line is grayed out when you are in a 3D view or perspective view.

Detail Components

Detail components are families made of 2D and annotation elements. Over 500 detail components organized by CSI format are found in the *Detail Items* folder of the library, as shown in Figure A–54.

Figure A–54

How To: Add a Detail Component

1. In the *Annotate* tab>Detail panel, expand ⊡ (Component) and click ⊡ (Detail Component).
2. In the Type Selector, select the detail component type. You can load additional types from the Library.
3. Many detail components can be rotated as you insert them by pressing <Spacebar>. Alternatively, select **Rotate after placement** in the Options Bar, as shown in Figure A–55.

☐ Rotate after placement

Figure A–55

4. Place the component in the view.

Adding Break Lines

The Break Line is a detail component found in the *Detail Items\ Div 01-General* folder. It consists of a rectangular area (shown highlighted in Figure A–56) which is used to block out elements behind it. You can modify the size of the area that is covered and change the size of the cut line using the controls.

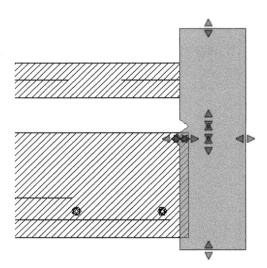

Figure A–56

Hint: Working with the Draw Order of Details

When you select detail elements in a view, you can change the draw order of the elements in the *Modify | Detail Items* tab> Arrange panel. You can bring elements in front of other elements or place them behind elements, as shown in Figure A–57.

Draw order: front   *Draw order: back*

Figure A–57

- ⬜ **(Bring to Front):** Places element in front of all other elements.

- ⬜ **(Send to Back):** Places element behind all other elements.

- ⬜ **(Bring Forward):** Moves element one step to the front.

- ⬜ **(Send Backward):** Moves element one step to the back.

- You can select multiple detail elements and change the draw order of all of them in one step. They keep the relative order of the original selection.

Repeating Details

Instead of having to insert a component multiple times (such as brick or concrete block), you can use ⬚ (Repeating Detail Component) and create a string of components, as shown in Figure A–58.

Figure A–58

How To: Insert a Repeating Detail Component

1. In the *Annotate* tab>Detail panel, expand ⊡ (Component) and click ⊟ (Repeating Detail Component).
2. In the Type Selector, select the detail you want to use.
3. In the Draw panel, click ╱ (Line) or ⬩ (Pick Lines).
4. In the Options Bar, type a value for the *Offset*, if needed.
5. The components repeat to fit the length of the sketched or selected line, as shown in Figure A–59. You can lock the components to the line.

Existing line —   — Repeating detail

Figure A–59

Hint: ⊗ (Insulation)

Adding batt insulation is similar to adding a repeating detail component, but instead of a series of bricks or other elements, it creates the linear batting pattern, shown in Figure A–60.

Figure A–60

Before you place the insulation in the view, specify the *Width* and other options in the Options Bar, as shown in Figure A–61.

Modify | Place Insulation   Width 0' 3 1/2   ☐ Chain   Offset: 0' 0"   to center ▾

Figure A–61

A.6 Annotating Details

After you have added components and sketched detail lines, you need to add annotations to the detail view. You can place text notes and dimensions as shown in Figure A–62, as well as symbols and tags. Filled regions are used to add hatching.

Figure A–62

Creating Filled Regions

Many elements include material information that displays in plan and section views, while other elements need more details to be added. For example, the concrete wall shown in Figure A–63 includes material information, while the earth to the left of the wall needs to be added using the **Filled Region** command.

Figure A–63

The patterns used in details are *drafting patterns*. They are scaled to the view scale and update if you modify it. You can also add full-size *model patterns*, such as a Flemish Bond brick pattern, to the surface of some elements.

How To: Add a Filled Region

1. In the *Annotate* tab>Detail panel, expand ⬚ (Region) and click ⬚ (Filled Region).
2. Create a closed boundary using the Draw tools.
3. In the Line Style panel, select the line style for the outside edge of the boundary. If you do not want the boundary to display, select the <Invisible lines> style.
4. In the Type Selector, select the fill type, as shown in Figure A–64.

Figure A–64

5. Click ✓ (Finish Edit Mode).

- You can modify a region by changing the fill type in the Type Selector or by editing the sketch.

- Double-click on the edge of the filled region to edit the sketch.

  If you have the Selection option set to ⬚ (Select elements by face) you can select the pattern.

Hint: Creating a Filled Region Pattern Type

You can create a custom pattern by duplicating and editing an existing pattern type.

1. Select an existing region or create a boundary.
2. In Properties, click (Edit Type).
3. In the Type Properties dialog box, click **Duplicate** and name the new pattern.
4. Select the *Foreground/ Background Fill Pattern* and *Color* and specify the *Line Weight* and *Masking*, as shown in Figure A–65.

Graphics	≳
Foreground Fill Pattern	Wood 3 [Drafting]
Foreground Pattern Color	■ Black
Background Fill Pattern	
Background Pattern Color	■ Black
Line Weight	1
Masking	☑

Figure A–65

5. Click **OK**.

• You can select from two types of Fill Patterns: **Drafting**, as shown in Figure A–66, and **Model**. Drafting fill patterns scale to the view scale factor. Model fill patterns display full scale on the model.

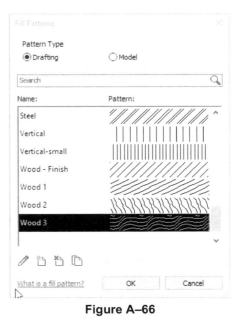

Figure A–66

Adding Detail Tags

Besides adding text to a detail, you can tag detail components using (Tag By Category). The tag name is set in the Type Parameters for that component, as shown in Figure A–67. This means that if you have more than one copy of the component in your project, you do not have to rename it each time you place its tag.

*The **Detail Item Tag.rfa** tag is located in the Annotations folder in the Library.*

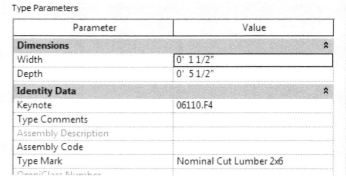

Figure A–67

Hint: Multiple Dimension Options

If you are creating details that show one element with multiple dimension values, as shown in Figure A–68, you can easily modify the dimension text.

Figure A–68

Select the dimension and then the dimension text. The Dimension Text dialog box opens. You can replace the text, as shown in Figure A–69, or add text fields above or below, as well as a prefix or suffix.

Figure A–69

- This also works with Equality Text Labels.

Practice A1

Create Details - Architectural

Practice Objectives

- Create a detail based on a section.
- Add filled regions, detail components, and annotations.

In this practice, you will create a detail based on a callout of a wall section. You will add repeating detail components, break lines, and detail lines, and add annotation to complete the detail, as shown in Figure A–70.

Figure A–70

Task 1 - Create a callout of a wall section.

1. Open the file **Modern-Hotel-Detailing.rvt** from the practice files folder.

2. Open the **Floor Plans: Floor 1** view.

3. Double-click on the wall section head shown in Figure A–71. This guarantees that you open the right section.

Figure A–71

4. Zoom in to the top of the wall showing the parapet and the roof.

5. In the *View* tab>Create panel, click ⌀ (Callout).

6. In the Type Selector, select **Detail View: Detail**.

7. Create a callout as shown in Figure A–72.

Figure A–72

8. Double-click on the callout bubble to open the callout view.

9. In the View Control Bar, set the following parameters:
   - *Scale*: **1"=1'-0"**
   - *Detail Level*: ▨ (Fine)

10. Hide the levels, grids, and section markers (if displayed).

11. Toggle off the Crop Region.

12. In the Project Browser, in the *Detail Views (Detail)* node, rename the view to **Parapet Detail**.

13. Save the project.

Task 2 - Add repeating detail components and break lines.

---

1. In the *Annotate* tab>Detail panel, expand 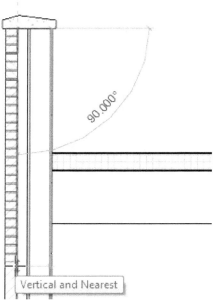 (Component) and click (Repeating Detail Component).

2. In the Type Selector, set the type to **Repeating Detail: Brick**.

3. Draw the brick line from the top of the parapet cap down, as shown in Figure A–73.

Drawing from the top down insures that "mortar" is between the cap and the brick. This is how the detail elements were created.

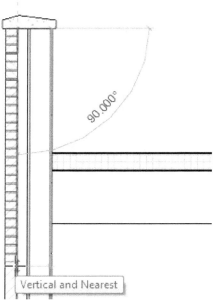

Figure A–73

4. In the Type Selector, select **Repeating Detail: CMU**. Draw over the other side of the wall, as shown in Figure A–74.

Figure A–74

The Autodesk Revit software lists the last tool you used at the top of the drop-down list.

5. In the *Annotate* tab>Detail panel, expand [icon] (Repeating Detail Component) and click [icon] (Detail Component).

6. In the *Modify | Place Detail Component* tab>Mode panel, click [icon] (Load Family).

7. In the Load Family dialog box, navigate to the *Detail Items> Div 01-General* folder, select **Break Line.rfa**, and then click **Open**.

8. Add break lines to the bottom and right side of the detail. Press <Spacebar> to rotate the Break Line as needed and use the controls to modify the size and depth, as shown in Figure A–75.

    •   If you added the break line going in the wrong direction, select the break line in the view and press <Spacebar> until it is rotated correctly.

Figure A–75

9. Save the project.

Task 3 - Draw flashing using detail lines.

1. In the *Annotate* tab>Detail panel, click ⌐ (Detail Line).

2. In the *Modify | Place Detail Lines* tab>Line Style panel, verify that **Wide Lines** is selected and, from the Option Bar, that **Chain** is selected.

3. Draw flashing similar to that shown in Figure A–76.

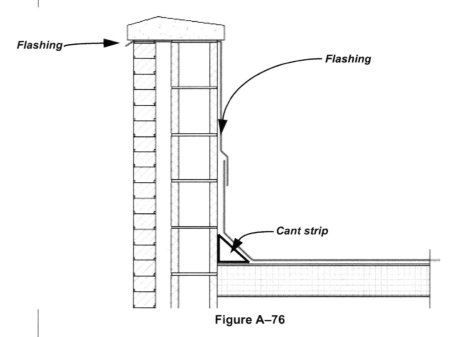

Flashing

Flashing

Cant strip

Figure A–76

4. Using Detail Line, add a cant strip under the flashing.

5. Save the project

Task 4 - Annotate the detail.

1. In the Quick Access Toolbar or on the *Annotate* tab>Text panel, click **A** (Text).

2. In the *Modify | Place Text* tab>Format panel, select ⌐**A** (Two-Segments).

3. Add the text and leaders shown in Figure A–77. Use Alignments to place the leader points and text.

Figure A–77

4. Save and keep the project opened.

At this point, you have a hybrid between detail items and model items. You can continue to add detail items to replace the roofing. You can also add structural elements if you have time.

Practice A2 | Create Details - MEP

Practice Objectives

- Create a drafting view.
- Add filled regions, detail components, and annotations.

In this practice, you will create a drafting view. In the new view you will add detail lines of different weights, insulation, and filled regions. You will also add detail components, including Break Lines and text notes. Finally, you will place the detail view on a sheet (as shown in Figure A–78) and place a reference section.

WALL CONSTRUCTION,
SEE ARCHITECTURAL
DWGS

EXPANSION GAP TO BE
FILLED WITH MINERAL WOOL

SUPPORT ANGLE (TYP)

ACCORDION FOLD
FIRE DAMPER

DUCT

① Fire Damper Detail
1 1/2" = 1'-0"

Figure A–78

Task 1 - Create a drafting view.

1. In the practice files folder, open **Detailing-School-MEP.rvt**.

2. In the *View* tab>Create panel, click ⌸ (Drafting View).

3. In the New Drafting View dialog box, set the name and scale as follows:
   - *Name*: **Fire Damper Detail**
   - *Scale*: **1-1/2"=1'-0"**

4. In the Project Browser, expand the **Coordination** node until you can see the new detail view. Select the view, as shown in Figure A–79.

Figure A–79

5. In Properties, change *Discipline* to **Mechanical** and *Sub-Discipline* to **HVAC**. The new view moves to that node in the Project Browser.

Task 2 - Draw detail lines.

1. In the *Annotate* tab>Detail panel, click ⌐ (Detail Line).

2. In the *Modify | Place Detail Lines* tab, set the *Line Style* to **Thin Lines** and make sure **Chain** is unchecked. Draw the two vertical lines shown in Figure A–80.

3. Change the *Line Style* to **Wide Lines** and draw the two horizontal lines shown in Figure A–80. These become the primary duct and wall lines.

   • If the difference in the line weights does not display clearly, zoom in and, in the Quick Access Toolbar, toggle off ⌐ (Thin Lines).

The dimensions are for information only.

Figure A–80

4. Continue adding and modifying detail lines to create the elements shown in Figure A–81. Use modify commands (such as **Split** and **Offset**) and the draw tools.

Figure A–81

5. Save the project.

Task 3 - Add detail components.

1. In the *Annotate* tab>Detail panel, expand ⬚ (Component) and select ⬚ (Detail Component).

2. In the Type Selector, select **AISC Angle Shapes - Section L3X2X1/4**.

3. Place the angle on the top left, as shown in Figure A–82.

   • Press <Spacebar> to rotate the angle before placing it.

4. Change the type **to AISC Angle Shapes - Section L2X2X1/4** and place the angle on the bottom of the duct, as shown in Figure A–82.

5. Select the two angle components and mirror them to the other side, as shown in Figure A–82.

1. Place L3X2X1/4

3. Mirror both angles

2. Place L2X2X1/4

Figure A–82

6. Add four break line components. Rotate and use the controls to modify the size until all of your excess lines are covered, as shown in Figure A–83

The exact location and size of your break lines might vary.

Figure A–83

7. Save the project.

Task 4 - Add insulation and filled regions.

1. In the *Annotate* tab>Detail panel, click ⊠ (Insulation).

2. In the Options Bar, set the *Width* to **1"**.

3. Draw the insulation lines in the two expansion gaps, as shown in Figure A–84.

4. In the *Annotate* tab>Detail panel, expand Region and click ⬚ (Filled Region).

5. In the Type Selector, select **Filled region: Diagonal Down**.

6. Draw rectangles around the wall areas as shown in Figure A–84.

7. Click ✓ (Finish). The filled regions display.

The filled region pattern does not display until you finish the process.

Figure A–84

8. Save the project.

Task 5 - Add text notes.

1. In the *Annotate* tab>Text panel, click A (Text).

2. In the *Modify | Place Text* tab>Leader panel, select A (Two Segments) as the leader style.

3. In the Type Selector, select **Text: 3/32" Arial**.

4. Add text notes, as shown in Figure A–85.

WALL CONSTRUCTION,
SEE ARCHITECTURAL
DWGS

EXPANSION GAP TO BE
FILLED WITH MINERAL WOOL

SUPPORT ANGLE (TYP)

ACCORDION FOLD
FIRE DAMPER

DUCT

Figure A–85

5. Save the project.

Task 6 - Place the detail on a sheet and reference it in the project.

1. In the Project Browser, open the sheet **M601 - HVAC Details**.

2. In the Project Browser, drag the **Fire Damper Detail** view to the sheet.

3. Open the Mechanical>HVAC>**1 - Mech** view.

4. Zoom in on one of the duct systems.

5. In the *View* tab>Create panel, click (Callout).

6. In the *Modify | Callout* tab>Reference panel, select **Reference Other View**.

7. Expand the drop-down list and select the new **Fire Damper Detail**, as shown in Figure A–86.

8. Place the callout at the intersection of a duct and the wall, as shown in Figure A–86. The information is filled out based on the location of the detail view on the sheet.

Figure A–86

9. Save the project.

Practice A3

Create Details - Structural

Practice Objectives

- Create a detail based on a section.
- Add filled regions, detail components, and annotations.

In this practice, you will create an enlarged detail based on a section, modify line weights, create filled regions, and add detail components, and annotation as shown in Figure A–87.

3" LW Concrete on 2" Metal Deck

Finish Floor: See Architectural Drawings

W 14x30

TOS-1ST FLOOR
14' - 7"

2-L3x3x1/4"

L 3x3x1/4"

W 10x33

W 14x30

CMU: where indicated in plan

Figure A–87

Task 1 - Create an enlarged detail.

1. Open **Detailing-Syracuse-Suites.rvt** from the practice files folder.

2. Open the **Sections (Building Section): North-South Section** view.

3. Zoom in on the intersection of the **TOS-1ST FLOOR** level and **Grid B** (on the left). Adjust the crop region.

4. In the *View* tab>Create panel, click ⌀ (Callout).

5. Create a callout as shown in Figure A–88 and double click on the callout head to open it.

Figure A–88

Set the Detail Level to *(Fine) if required.*

6. In the View Control Bar, set the *Scale* to **3/4"=1'-0"**.

7. Select the **TOS-1ST FLOOR** level datum and use the **Hide Bubble** control to hide the bubble on the right.

8. Hide the linked .RVT file in this view.

9. Zoom in close to the intersection to display the line thicknesses. The slab and beam section cut lines are too heavy.

10. Select the slab. Right-click and select **Override Graphics in View> By Element...**

11. In the View-Specific Element Graphics dialog box, change the *Cut Lines Weight* to **2** as shown in Figure A–89.

Figure A–89

12. Click **OK**.

13. Select the beam that is cut in section and change the *Cut Lines Weight* to **3**.

14. Save the project.

Task 2 - Create filled regions to display an architectural floor.

---

1. In the *Annotate* tab>Detail panel, click (Filled Region).

2. In the Type Selector, select **Filled Region: Solid Black.**

3. Click (Edit Type).

4. In the Type Properties dialog box, click **Duplicate...** and create a new type named **Solid Gray**.

5. In the Type Parameters, change the *Color* to a light gray.

6. Click **OK** to return to the sketch.

7. In the *Modify | Create Filled Region Boundary* tab>Draw panel, use the drawing tools to create a **1"** thick boundary above the floor slab, as shown in Figure A–90.

Figure A–90

8. Click ✓ (Finish Edit Mode) in the Mode panel. The region representing an architectural floor, displays as shown in Figure A–91.

Architectural floor

Figure A–91

Task 3 - Add detail components.

1. In the *Annotate* tab>Detail panel, click ⬚ (Detail Component).

2. In the *Modify | Place Detail Component* tab>Mode panel, click ⬚ (Load Family).

3. Browse to the practice files *Custom Library>050500-Common Work Results for Metals>050523-Metal Fastenings* folder. Press <Ctrl> to select both **L-Angle-Bolted Connection-Elevation.rfa** and **L-Angle-Bolted Connection-Section.rfa**, then click **Open**.

4. In the Type Selector, select **L-Angle-Bolted Connection-Elevation: L3x3x1/4"**.

5. Click ⬚ (Edit Type).

6. In the Type Properties dialog box, change the *Number Of Bolts* to **3**. Click **OK**.

7. Place the component at the intersection of the midpoint on the beam in elevation and the column it frames into as shown in Figure A–92.

Figure A–92

8. Repeat the procedure. This time place the **L-Angle-Bolted Connection-Section** on the sectioned beam. After it is placed, select it and stretch the grips ◀ ▶ to be tight around the member as shown in Figure A–93.

Figure A–93

9. Save the project.

To make it easier to see, toggle on 🗔 *(Thin Lines) in the Quick Access Toolbar.*

Task 4 - Add repeating detail components.

1. In the *Annotate* tab>Detail panel, expand Component, and
   click ⊟ (Repeating Detail Component).

2. In the Type Selector, select **Repeating Detail: CMU**.

3. In the Options Bar, set the *Offset* to **0'-3-13/16"**
   (or **=7-5/8" / 2**). (Hint: You can type formulas wherever a
   number can be added.)

4. Select the bottom midpoint of the **W14x30** section and draw a
   line down to display at least 2 CMU blocks, as shown in
   Figure A–94.

Figure A–94

5. Select the new CMU wall, and in the *Modify | Detail Items>*
   Arrange tab, click ⬚ (Send to Back).

6. Click ✛ (Move) to move the entire CMU wall down **1"** to
   create space for a bearing plate for the beam.

7. Save the project.

Task 5 - Annotate the detail.

1. In the *Annotate* tab>Detail panel, click (Detail Component). Click (Load Family) to add a break line.

2. Browse to the *Detail Items>Div 01-General* folder and open the file **Break Line.rfa**.

3. Add break lines to the top, bottom, and right side of the detail as shown in Figure A–95. Press <Spacebar> to rotate the Break Line as required.

Figure A–95

Modify the crop region so that excess elements do not display on the outside of the break lines.

4. Leave plenty of room for annotation by making the annotation crop region larger.

5. In the *Annotate* tab>Text panel, click A (Text).

6. Add notes to complete the detail as shown in Figure A–96.

Figure A–96

7. In the View Control Bar, click ![Hide Crop Region icon] (Hide Crop Region).

8. Save and close the project.

Chapter Review Questions

1. Which of the following are ways in which you can create a detail? (Select all that apply.)

   a. Make a callout of a section and sketch over it.

   b. Draw all of the elements from scratch.

   c. Import a CAD detail and modify or sketch over it.

   d. Insert an existing drafting view from another file.

2. In which type of view (access shown in Figure A–97) can you NOT add detail lines?

Figure A–97

   a. Plans

   b. Elevations

   c. 3D views

   d. Legends

3. How are detail components different from building components?

   a. There is no difference.

   b. Detail components are made of 2D lines and annotation only.

   c. Detail components are made of building elements, but only display in detail views.

   d. Detail components are made of 2D and 3D elements.

4. What is a true statement about detail lines?

   a. Always the same width.

   b. Vary in width according to the view.

   c. Display in all views associated with the detail.

   d. Display only in the view in which they were created.

5. When a wall is moved (as shown in Figure A–98), how do you update the dimension?

Figure A–98

a. Edit the dimension and move it over.

b. Select the dimension and then click **Update** in the Options Bar.

c. The dimension automatically updates.

d. Delete the existing dimension and add a new one.

6. When you edit text, how many leaders can be added using the leader tools shown in Figure A–99?

Figure A–99

a. One

b. One on each end of the text.

c. As many as you want at each end of the text.

7. Which command do you use to add a pattern (such as concrete or earth, as shown in Figure A–100) to part of a detail?

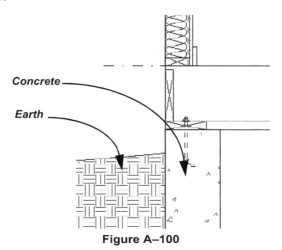

Concrete

Earth

Figure A–100

a. Region

b. Filled Region

c. Masking Region

d. Pattern Region

Command Summary

Button	Command	Location
Detail Tools		
	Aligned (Dimension)	• **Ribbon:** *Annotate* tab>Dimension panel or *Modify* tab>Measure panel, expanded drop-down list • **Quick Access Toolbar** • **Shortcut:** DI
	Detail Component	• **Ribbon:** *Annotate* tab>Detail panel> expand Component
	Detail Line	• **Ribbon:** *Annotate* tab>Detail panel
	Filled Region	• **Ribbon:** *Annotate* tab>Detail panel
	Insulation	• **Ribbon:** *Annotate* tab>Detail panel
	Repeating Detail Component	• **Ribbon:** *Annotate* tab>Detail panel> expand Component
A	Text	• **Ribbon:** *Annotate* tab>Text panel • **Shortcut:** TX
View Tools		
	Bring Forward	• **Ribbon:** *Modify	Detail Items* tab> Arrange panel
	Bring to Front	• **Ribbon:** *Modify	Detail Items* tab> Arrange panel
	Drafting View	• **Ribbon:** *View* tab>Create panel
	Insert from File: Insert Views from File	• **Ribbon:** *Insert* tab>Load from Library panel>expand Insert from File
	Send Backward	• **Ribbon:** *Modify	Detail Items* tab> Arrange panel
	Send to Back	• **Ribbon:** *Modify	Detail Items* tab> Arrange panel
CAD Import Tools		
	Delete Layers	• **Ribbon:** *Modify	<imported filename>* tab>Import Instance panel
	Full Explode	• **Ribbon:** *Modify	<imported filename>* tab>Import Instance panel> expand Explode

	Import CAD	• **Ribbon:** *Insert* tab>Import panel
	Partial Explode	• **Ribbon:** *Modify	<imported filename>* tab>Import Instance panel> expand Explode

Index